**SANITATION STRATEGY
FOR A LAKEFRONT
METROPOLIS**

Sanitation Strategy for a Lakefront Metropolis

The Case of Chicago

Louis P. Cain

NORTHERN ILLINOIS UNIVERSITY PRESS

Publication of this book was made possible by a grant from Loyola
University of Chicago.

Cain, Louis P.
   Sanitation strategy for a lakefront metropolis.

   Bibliography: p.
   Includes index.
   1. Chicago—Water-supply. 2. Chicago—Sewerage. 3. Sewage dispos-
al—Illinois—Chicago. I. Title.
TD225.C5C22   363.6   76-14711
ISBN 0-87580-064-5

CONTENTS

PREFACE

This book is an examination of the problem of sanitation in Chicago by an economic historian. It focuses on the economic and technological decisions affecting the utilization and conservation of Lake Michigan, the city's principal water resource. Cities located on freshwater lakes, such as Chicago, typically have drawn their water supply and discharged their wastes into the lake. Water pollution and a high incidence of water-borne disease are the predictable results of this approach. Thus, lakefront cities have been forced to invest in water and/or sewage treatment works to improve conditions for their citizenry. Questions concerning the quality of life, in general, and of urban life, in particular, consume a great deal of the scholarly energies of a wide range of disciplines, from social scientists to natural scientists, from humanists to engineers. Each discipline brings its own unique elements to bear on these complex questions; each has its own comparative advantage. Such is the nature of multidisciplinary questions. One problem faced by all these studies is that the answers presented by each discipline are likely to be simultaneously rewarding and frustrating to other disciplines. Such studies can be rewarding, because they give instruction and insight; but they can be frustrating, because they don't follow each thread of the narrative to what others would consider a logical conclusion. I hope this book will prove interesting both to those who share the methodology of the economic historian and to those who do not.

It is difficult to know how much information one must develop within such a study, and how much can be taken as given. Several excellent histories of Chicago are listed in the bibliography; most notable among these are the multivolume works of Andreas, Condit, and Pierce. Chicago was a dynamic city in the years covered by this study. Some idea of the city's population growth can be seen in the first table of the introductory chapter. I have tried to suggest something of the city's underlying industrial growth, especially the changing pattern of land use within the drainage area. An explicit treatment of this topic can be found in Homer Hoyt's excellent book, *One Hundred Years of Land Values in Chicago.* I also have tried to relate something of the rapid underlying technical changes in the field of sewage treatment. There are several references to early sanitation texts in the footnotes and bibliography. When they are read sequentially, they give some idea of the basic changes.

There are many people to thank for their help on what has been a long project. First on the list are my good friends Hal Williamson and John Hughes, who were my dissertation advisers at Northwestern University. Next are all those friends and colleagues who have given me the benefit of their wisdom, or at least their opinions. Notable among these are Bob Aduddell, Bob Allen, Ron Ehrenberg, Eric Jones, George Harmon, Jon Laing, Dave Mirza, Joel Mokyr, Leon Moses, Don Paterson, Tony Scott, Fran Topping, Tom Weiss, and Jim Wilen. Bits and pieces of this work have appeared as two articles in *Technology and Culture,* and I would be remiss not to acknowledge Melvin Kranzberg and the anonymous referees of that excellent journal. Of the numerous librarians who added their expertise, none was more helpful than Joanell Breen and Margaret Nophiesen of the Sanitary District. In fact, I received complete cooperation from the district, and I especially wish to acknowledge Gus. G. Sciaqua, the clerk, for making records available. Various drafts of the manuscript were typed by Julia Morrill and Lee Brigagliano. My parents and my wife's parents lent their support in an active way. Finally, there is my wife herself. We started dating at the start of my research on this book, married when the basic research was completed, and experienced the rest together. This book is dedicated to her.

Louis P. Cain

Vancouver, British Columbia

INTRODUCTION

Originally, the site of the city of Chicago was a swamp-like area, and the problems that needed to be solved if the city were to experience urban growth were the problems of water supply, sewage disposal, and drainage. This book will study the evolution of Chicago's sanitation strategy as it emerged through solutions to these problems. The ultimate strategy required an integrated approach that had its roots in Chicago's location and history. The site where the Chicago River emptied into Lake Michigan was visited by Indians and Europeans traveling between the Great Lakes and the Mississippi River and its tributaries. A few miles southwest of Chicago, these two great water systems were separated by an extremely low divide. In dry seasons it was necessary to portage over this divide, but in wet seasons a small lake was formed which created a through water route. The idea of building a canal across this divide between the Great Lakes and the Mississippi River drainage systems was one that had a long history. Construction on the Illinois and Michigan Canal (1822–1848) triggered Chicago's initial growth; later the canal itself became the crucial link in the city's sewage disposal scheme. Yet Chicago's site was low-lying and given to flooding, an inauspicious beginning for a giant metropolis. The growth of Chicago from mud to metropolis cannot be understood fully without an understanding of the city's solution to the interrelated urban problems of water supply, sewage disposal, and drainage.

The growth of Chicago entailed increases in the demand for water and waste removal. Table 1 displays the population tributary to Chicago's waterworks and the works' daily average per capita pumpage. The table shows that the daily average per capita pumpage from Lake Michigan initially increased as the tributary population increased. When the population growth rate decreased around the turn of the century, the pumpage figure continued to increase. This was the result of the area's industrial growth. These increases in the daily average per capita pumpage placed significant pressure on the city's waterworks. City engineers continually faced the near-capacity operation of the existing works; consequently they were continually faced with the need to enlarge the capacity of their operations. It was not until 1930 that the daily average per capita pumpage began to decrease. By that time Chicago's waterworks were pumping over one billion gallons of Lake Michigan water on the average day.

Table 2 displays the expenditures on sewage disposal and appurtenances such as sewers and pumping stations for those cities with a 1930 population greater than 500,000.[1] The table clearly illustrates the magnitude of the sewage disposal problems of freshwater cities, in general, and of Chicago, in particular. Chicago, Milwaukee, and Baltimore were the only freshwater lake cities treating some part of their sewage completely; complete treatment was defined to include the removal of settling solids and oxidation. Chicago and Cleveland were the only cities utilizing any form of tank treatment. Detroit, which looked to the Detroit River for both water supply and sewage disposal, was the only other freshwater city proposing a substantial future expenditure. The important aspect of table 2 is that Chicago's expenditures to January 1928 were unparalleled in absolute terms, and only Milwaukee was close in per capita terms. Chicago's proposed future expenditures were rivaled only by those of Detroit and Philadelphia,

Table 1. *Population and Pumpage of Chicago Waterworks*

Year	Tributary Population	Daily Average Per Capita Pumpage	Year	Tributary Population	Daily Average Per Capita Pumpage
1854	65,000	9.1	1898	1,627,000	167.7
1855	80,000	29.9	1899	1,667,000	180.2
1856	90,000	44.4	1900	1,727,000	186.6
1857	90,000	39.5	1901	1,776,000	193.0
1858	90,000	33.2	1902	1,825,000	196.3
1859	100,000	38.8	1903	1,874,000	200.7
1860	109,000	43.2	1904	1,922,000	207.6
1861	120,000	40.4	1905	1,971,000	208.5
1862	136,000	44.7	1906	2,020,000	216.4
1863	150,000	42.7	1907	2,068,000	220.1
1864	161,000	42.9	1908	2,117,000	221.7
1865	178,000	42.8	1909	2,165,000	222.1
1866	200,000	43.4	1910	2,214,000	234.2
1867	230,000	50.3	1911	2,263,000	224.2
1868	256,000	57.7	1912	2,345,000	235.1
1869	281,000	66.3	1913	2,372,000	243.6
1870	307,000	70.9	1914	2,393,000	256.3
1871	332,000	70.7	1915	2,447,000	247.9
1872	357,000	77.2	1916	2,493,000	252.0
1873	382,000	84.1	1917	2,572,000	249.4
1874	395,000	96.4	1918	2,680,000	249.2
1875	408,000	97.7	1919	2,788,000	256.3
1876	421,000	99.6	1920	2,906,000	266.0
1877	441,000	118.3	1921	2,979,000	264.5
1878	461,000	116.3	1922	3,054,000	262.1
1879	482,000	116.8	1923	3,129,000	257.6
1880	503,000	114.1	1924	3,225,000	261.0
1881	538,000	118.8	1925	3,311,000	268.0
1882	561,000	117.9	1926	3,390,000	226.0
1883	601,000	121.9	1927	3,470,000	272.0
1884	641,000	124.8	1928	3,571,000	282.9
1885	681,000	134.6	1929	3,655,000	287.5
1886	721,000	135.6	1930	3,684,000	287.6
1887	762,000	133.8	1931	3,688,000	280.2
1888	803,000	129.9	1932	3,709,000	272.2
1889	850,000	130.5	1933	3,714,000	279.4
1890	1,170,000	130.2	1934	3,718,000	279.1
1891	1,235,000	141.0	1935	3,722,000	265.1
1892	1,360,000	142.7	1936	3,731,000	283.3
1893	1,485,000	159.2	1937	3,736,000	274.3
1894	1,505,000	158.5	1938	3,741,000	261.6
1895	1,525,000	165.0	1939	3,746,000	257.5
1896	1,555,000	163.3	1940	3,761,000	256.2
1897	1,590,000	166.8			

Source: *A Statistical Supplement to the Annual Report of the Department of Water and Sewers*, City of Chicago.

and then only in per capita terms. In total, Chicago's expenditures were greater than the sum of those of the other twelve enumerated cities, and almost twice those of its closest rival, Milwaukee, relative to per capita expenditures. The reason behind these large expenditures was the sanitation strategy that Chicago developed.

Table 2. *Expenditures for Sewage Disposal and Appurtenances—Cities above 500,000 Population, 1930*

City	1930 Population	Expended to Jan. 1928 (per capita)	Proposed Future Expenditures (per capita)	Total (per capita)
New York	6,930,446	$ 5,559,000 ($0.80)	$ 37,000,000 ($5.34)	$ 42,599,000 ($6.14)
Philadelphia	1,950,961	3,500,000 (1.79)	52,500,000 (26.91)	56,000,000 (28.70)
Detroit	1,568,662	3,748,000 (2.39)	42,497,000 (27.09)	46,245,000 (29.48)
Los Angeles	1,238,048	29,538,000 (23.86)	—	29,538,000 (23.86)
Cleveland	900,429	10,194,000 (11.32)	6,606,000 (7.34)	16,800,000 (18.66)
St. Louis	821,960	—	1,500,000 (1.82)	1,500,000 (1.82)
Boston (met. dist.)	2,307,897	26,900,000 (11.66)	—	26,900,000 (11.66)
Baltimore	804,874	11,794,000 (14.65)	1,706,000 (2.12)	13,500,000 (16.77)
Pittsburgh	669,817	38,000* (0.06)	—	38,000* (0.06)
San Francisco	634,394	7,000,000 (10.34)	4,000,000 (6.31)	11,000,000 (16.65)
Milwaukee	578,249	23,905,858 (41.34)	—	23,905,858 (41.34)
Buffalo	573,076	225,000 (0.39)	—	225,000 (0.39)
Combined Totals	18,978,813	122,401,858 (6.45)	145,809,000 (7.68)	268,210,858 (14.13)
Sanitary District of Chicago	3,901,569	182,169,000 (46.69)	120,000,000 (30.76)	302,169,000 (77.45)

*Expenditures for investigations.

Source: Sanitary District of Chicago, *Formal Opening Program: The North Side Sewage Treatment Project*, 3 October 1928, p. 18.

This book studies the evolution of Chicago's sanitation strategy through sequential decisions made with respect to water supply, sewage disposal, and drainage. It investigates how that sanitation strategy worked to solve a particular economic problem: the allocation of a natural resource, Lake Michigan, between two production processes, water supply and waste removal (which includes both sewage disposal and drainage), in a situation where the two processes are interdependent. Chicago was fortunate in having a large freshwater supply on its front doorstep, but conventional wisdom suggested that the lake be used simultaneously as water supplier and waste depository. Chicago, like other freshwater lake cities, faced the danger of polluting its own water supply if it adopted conventional techniques. Thus, there was a trade-off in the lake's ability to produce these two services. This, however, is not the only interdependency in the system. Pollution can be combated by some form of treatment, and there is a trade-off between water and sewage treatment.

Chicago's sanitation strategy had to make difficult choices between complex and interdependent alternatives. History afforded few guidelines for Chicago to follow. Most early nineteenth-century cities were located on salt water or on rivers, and they had not developed systems applicable to Chicago's needs. In fact, cities located on salt water were faced with the opposite of Chicago's circumstances; they could dispose of their sewage into the adjoining water but often had to seek a freshwater supply many miles inland. River cities withdrew their water upstream and discharged their sewage downstream, perhaps polluting the water supply of a downstream city, but not their own. In these two cases the interdependent relationships were minimized, and a city could consider water supply and waste removal as separate problems.[2] It is only in freshwater lake cities that the sanitation strategy must confront these interdependencies, and that is what makes the study of Chicago especially interesting. At this time Chicago has the largest water and sewage treatment plants in the world, and its waste removal system has been cited as "one of seven wonders of United States Civil Engineering."[3]

The question raised by Chicago's sanitation strategy is whether it makes sense economically, as well as technologically. To an economist this raises questions of economic efficiency. There is a considerable body of literature that discusses the efficiency of alternative institutions and methods; several of the best sources that explicitly develop these ecological and environmental questions are referenced below.[4]

Ideally, one should attempt to analyze the efficiency of Chicago's institutions and methods in a dynamic setting, to examine the costs and benefits of alternative schemes over time. There are two problems facing this ideal approach. First, economic theory has not developed sufficiently to permit a truly dynamic analysis of this question. The closest approximations to dynamic processes are sequential decisions made at discrete time intervals, and, as noted, that is the approach used in this book. It begins with the first collective decisions made by Chicagoans and ends with the adoption of sewage treatment as the primary technique of sewage disposal in the 1930s. By that time, Chicago's sanitation strategy had become almost identical to that in use today—close enough that the subsequent changes are of greater interest to engineers and political scientists than they are to economic historians.

Second, the usual idea of cost-benefit analysis is confronted by special difficulties in this study; many of the benefits are nonquantifiable, and the cost figures are suspect. Over time there was a growing awareness of the cost of pollution, of the benefits to Chicagoans from a relatively unpolluted Lake Michigan. The value of part of this benefit can be calculated from statistics on the decline in cholera and dysentery, for example. Many other benefits, however, are not as simple to quantify. Throughout most of the nineteenth century the lake was not used as a recreational resource; a bathing beach was just what the name implied. In the early years of the twentieth century, industrial development was steered away from the lakeshore, and the city enjoyed the amenities generated by the parks that grace the shoreline.[5]

Furthermore, the reported cost data are probably in excess of what was needed to acquire and operate the required capital. The Sanitary District of Chicago, the major institution affecting the ultimate strategy, has been the scene of political corruption, real estate speculation, and several investigations into even greater undesirable practices. The data from the Water and Sewer departments are subject to similar doubts. The appendixes in this book attempt to answer the questions of who ultimately paid for the works and whether good financial (as opposed to economic) management was the rule. These appendixes do not attempt to answer the question of whether the reported costs were excessive.

The approach used in this book concentrates on the decisions that were made and examines the motivation of the decision-makers. There exists a relatively complete record of how Chicago made major decisions concerning water supply, sewage disposal, and drainage. Beginning in 1855, when Chicago made the first major decision, one can investigate the alternatives and their costs that Chicago's decision-makers considered, their reasons for acceptance or rejection, and the controversy that some of these decisions evoked. By and large, the various engineering departments were free of scandal. Neither the engineers nor the politicians included the potential for graft in their decision process; the politicians accepted the recommendations of the engineers. Graft was a cost over and above that estimated by the engineers; it was a transfer from taxpayers to corrupt public officials. It is assumed that corruption played no role in the evolution of Chicago's sanitation strategy other than to increase the total cost of the alternative the engineers recommended.[6]

Each decision was constrained by two factors: the existing capital equipment and the specified benefits. Eventually the interdependence of solutions to the water supply and sewage disposal problems was recognized as an additional constraint. Given these constraints, the alternative selected was that which minimized cost, as the engineers estimated it. This book examines five major decisions made with respect to water supply, sewage disposal, and drainage. The conclusion that emerges is that Chicago's solution to these interdependent problems evolved rationally, as determined by the city's location and history.

NOTES

1. The public works expenditures of the New Deal changed this picture dramatically.

2. See Louis P. Cain, "The Economic History of Urban Location and Sanitation," *Research in Economic History,* vol. 2 (1977), pp. 337–89. See also p. 165.

3. This honorific title was bestowed upon the Metropolitan Sanitary District of Greater Chicago in 1955 by the American Society of Civil Engineers.

4. The classic source on the economics of water use, broadly defined, is J. Hirshleifer, J. C. DeHaven, and J. Milliman, *Water Supply: Economics, Technology and Policy* (Chicago: University of Chicago Press, 1960). The classic source on water quality maintenance is A. V. Kneese and B. T. Bower, *Managing Water Quality: Economics, Technology, Institution* (Baltimore: Johns Hopkins University Press, 1968). Other major works concerned with project evaluation and water basin development include: A. Maass et al., *Design of Water-Resource Systems* (Cambridge: Harvard University Press, 1962); Otto Eckstein, *Water Resource Development, the Economics of Project Evaluation* (Cambridge: Harvard University Press, 1958); and Roland McKean, *Efficiency in Government with Emphasis on Water Resources Development* (New York: John Wiley and Sons, 1958). Sources dealing with sewage disposal, in particular, include Paul B. Downing, *The Economics of Urban Sewage Disposal* (New York: Praeger Publishers, 1969), and the same author's "Extension of Sewer Service at the Urban-Rural Fringe," *Land Economics* (February 1969).

5. See, for example, Daniel Burnham's 1908 plan for the development of Chicago's lakefront.

6. A test of this hypothesis is beyond the scope of the present work.

SANITATION STRATEGY
FOR A LAKEFRONT
METROPOLIS

1

Early Chicago and the Illinois and Michigan Canal

THE PHYSICAL GEOGRAPHY

The continental glaciers of the Ice Age dominate Chicago's earliest history and are largely responsible for the Great Lakes and the area's rich soil.[1] The Ice Age was not one period of continuous cold; the ice advanced and withdrew perhaps a half-dozen times before its final retreat to Greenland. The last great advance, the Wisconsin sheet, is the one most responsible for Chicago's physiography.

Billions of tons of ice and rock slowly grinding down from Wisconsin leveled hills and plugged valleys as far south as the Ohio River. The ice carried granite blocks from the "crystalline lands" of Canada and used them "like sand grains in a great sheet of sandpaper," albeit a sheet which only "sanded" in one direction.[2] The ice, when it finally melted, smoothed the surface over which it passed and covered it with the rich soils collected on the southbound course. It is interesting to note that when the ice advanced, it was split by the Keweenaw peninsula, which acted like a giant wedge in the southern flank of Lake Superior. In its lee the ice thinned and melted, leaving a large unglaciated section in southwestern Wisconsin. This thin-soiled region was typical of the glaciated area before the ice sheet smoothed it and deposited new soil. Prices per acre in the unglaciated section normally are significantly less than those in the contiguous glaciated sections.

The glacial scour easily removed sandstone and shale, leaving the basins of the upper Great Lakes. As the ice receded, however, a new drainage system was imposed on the uncovered ground. Lake Chicago was formed at the southern end of the present basin of Lake Michigan, discharging to the southwest through the Illinois River. Lake Chicago is the dark area at the base of Lake Michigan in map 1; three of its various stages are depicted in map 2. When Lake Chicago was at its fullest, during the Glenwood stage, the present site of Chicago was entirely underwater. The Illinois River of that time was, perhaps, as wide as the present Mississippi River at the Missouri-Iowa border. Many years later, when the ice had receded down the St. Lawrence Valley beyond Lake Ontario, a river developed which took the drainage of the Great Lakes basin eastward. This river traveled by way of the Mohawk Pass to the Hudson River estuary at Troy, New York. The river smoothed a trench in the Appalachian highland, which was to become the route of the Erie Canal and the New York Central Railroad.

The area originally covered by Lake Chicago is included in a zone that geographers call the Lake Plain.[3] The dominant feature of the Lake Plain is its flatness; few large cities have been as free of a grad-

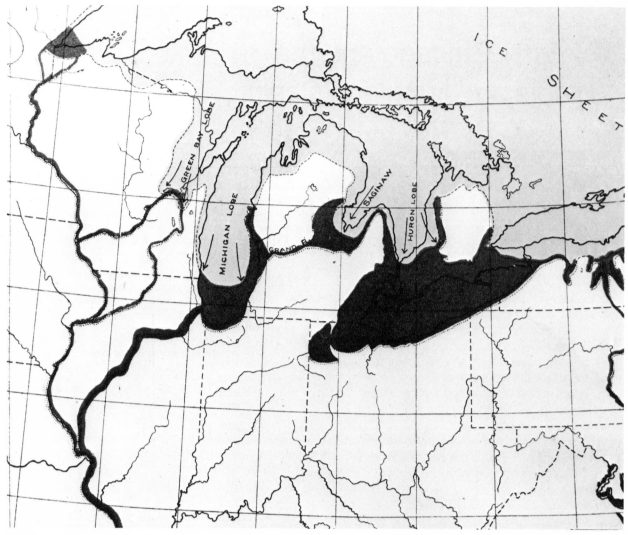

Map 1.   The glacial drainage pattern past Chicago when the waters of Lake Chicago (the southern appendage of today's Lake Michigan) were at their highest. At this time, the ice had begun to recede northward, the present site of Chicago was underwater, and Lake Chicago drained to the southwest through an enlarged Illinois River. Chicago Historical Society.

ing problem as has Chicago. The flatness, however, introduced a drainage problem; much of the Lake Plain was originally swamp-like and had to be drained before significant habitation could proceed.

The most important streams within the Lake Plain are the Chicago, Calumet, and Des Plaines rivers (see maps 2 and 3). The Chicago River's two branches provide the only natural drainage in the northern part of the Lake Plain. The North Branch rose four miles west of Highland Park and flowed southeast until it met the South Branch, which rose northeast of Summit and flowed to the northeast. The combined streams flowed eastward through the city, discharging into Lake Michigan. The Calumet River, formed by the confluence of its two parallel branches, the Grand and Little Calumet rivers, drained the southern

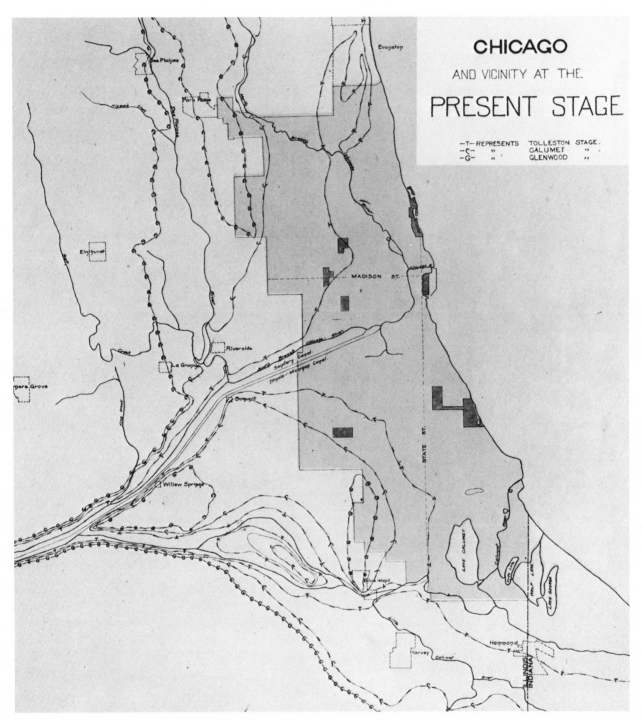

The extent of the Chicago area covered by Lake Chicago at the three glacial stages.
Chicago Historical Society.

Map 2.

part of the Lake Plain. Like the Chicago River, the Calumet had a low
gradient, which led to a sluggish current and the possibility of overflow.
It also discharged into Lake Michigan.

3

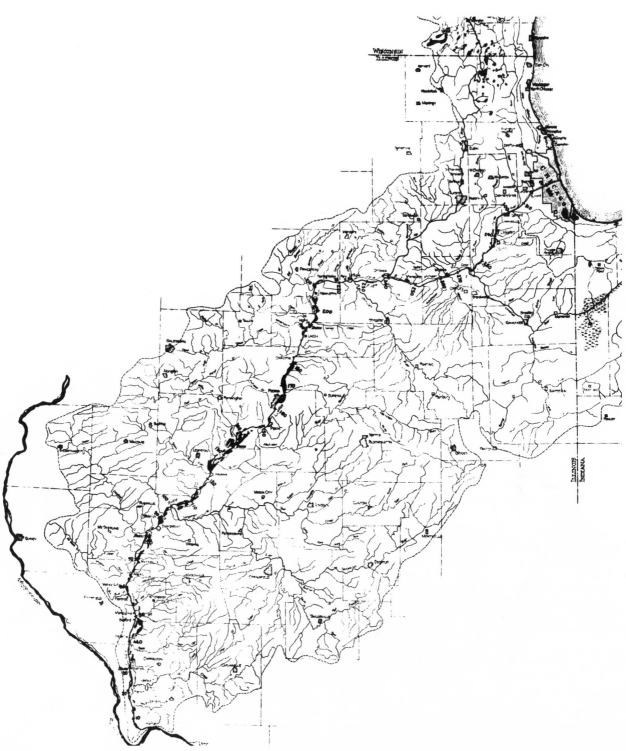

Map 3.

The watershed of the Illinois River indicating the drainage areas of main stream and principal tributaries. From Bulletin no. 23, *The Disposal of the Sewage of the Sanitary District of Chicago: A Report to the District Engineer.* Chicago: U.S. Engineer Office, 1927.

The Des Plaines River rightly belongs to the Chicago Outlet, the name given to the Mississippi Valley pass that leaves the Lake Plain in a southwestward direction. As such, the Chicago Outlet encompasses the lower part of the Des Plaines River and the upper part of the Illinois River (formed by the confluence of the Des Plaines and Kankakee rivers). The Des Plaines enters the Lake Plain north of Maywood and seems to have had a free choice of emptying into either the Mississippi or the St. Lawrence drainage areas. The plain is so flat that its westward movement appears to be little more than accidental.[4] A well-defined slough, called Mud Lake, moved eastward to a junction with the South Branch and was a line of escape used extensively by the Des Plaines River in spring flooding. Mud Lake was the famed Chicago portage where, during spring freshets and autumn rains, one could paddle a canoe from Lake Michigan to the headwaters of the Illinois River. The Illinois is the master stream of the Chicago region; all the important rivers drain into it, save for the few that drain eastward into Lake Michigan.

The Chicago Outlet is of crucial importance to the city. This channel, carved by the river that drained Lake Chicago, is one of the great natural passes. The continental divide in this valley is only fifteen feet above Lake Michigan; the next lowest point on the divide, near Fort Wayne, Indiana, is 190 feet above the lake. The outlet's flatness virtually eliminated grading problems for land- and water-based transportation. It is little wonder that suggestions for an artificial channel across the divide date from an early time.

The explorer Joliet suggested the feasibility of a canal to Father Dablon, superior of Jesuit missions in Canada, in the fall of 1673. Joliet and Marquette journeyed to the mouth of the Mississippi, via the Fox and Wisconsin rivers, and progressed far enough south to convince them that the Mississippi River flowed into the Gulf of Mexico. On the return trip north they reached the Illinois River, ascended it, and made the portage to reach Lake Michigan. Joliet's papers were lost during the return to Montreal, and, consequently, the report to his superior was verbal. Father Dablon reported his conversations with Joliet about a year after the latter's return. He quoted Joliet as having said:

> . . . we can quite easily go to Florida in boats, and by a very good navigation. There would be only one canal to make by cutting only half a league of prairie, to pass from the lake of Illinois [Lake Michigan] into the St. Louis River [the Des Plaines and Illinois rivers].[5]

Chicago enjoys the advantage of both the Mississippi and the St. Lawrence drainage systems, and profits by improvements in either. As Condit explains,

> The geographical location, at the farthest interior penetration of the Great Lakes-St. Lawrence system, placed the city in the agricultural heartland of North America and at the same time gave it immediate access to the greatest body of interconnected inland waterways in the world. . . . The level prairie setting meant that the city could expand radially in all directions except east, but this expansion was hampered in the early years of the pioneer community by the need to drain and fill the

low marshy tracts that lay between the moraines and near the lake. It was the advantageous natural factors, however, that determined the location of the original settlement and hence of the central business district of the mature city.[6]

Chicago's economic location was largely influenced by these natural factors. The economic opportunities presented by the geographical location were apparent; future technological changes augmented them.[7] The constraints imposed by the location were principally related to drainage. Early Chicagoans believed that the opportunities outweighed the constraints. Chicago's economic success has been due, in large part, to its ability to utilize its geographical assets, but an important element in that success has been its ability to overcome the geographical constraints.

THE FORTS DEARBORN

The Treaty of Greenville, signed in 1795, brought an end to the struggle between the British and Americans for ownership of the Northwest Territory. A part of this treaty was a cession by the Indians of a "piece of land six miles square, emptying into the southwest end of Lake Michigan, where a fort formerly stood."[8] No trace of any such fort was ever found.[9] The treaty also gave the United States free use of the Chicago-Des Plaines-Illinois River waterway, plus land at Peoria and the mouth of the Illinois, as well as at Chicago, upon which forts might be erected to safeguard the waterway.[10] Ownership, however, was quite a different thing from control. The British-dominated Canadian economy was dependent on the fur trade, much of which was centered in the Great Lakes basin.[11]

In 1803, the desire to secure the western frontier and to sever British control of the Indian trade brought about orders to build a permanent garrison at Chicago. The Louisiana Purchase of the same year gave added importance to the Chicago portage. Fort Dearborn, named after General Henry Dearborn, Thomas Jefferson's secretary of war, became a link in a chain of American fortresses that stretched from Mackinac Island in the north to the Gulf of Mexico in the south.

The story is told that commissioners from Washington had selected a site at the mouth of the St. Joseph River, the present city of St. Joseph, Michigan, for the proposed Lake Michigan fort. The Indians would not consent to a fort at this location, and so the commissioners decided in favor of the Chicago River site as an alternative. A writer in the *Michigan Pioneer Collection of Historical Publications* wrote: "We conclude that had the fort been built at St. Joseph there would have been no Chicago." Another writer, referring to the above, wryly observed that

> This matter of a fort seems to have been peculiarly disastrous to the St. Joseph country. When it had one it constantly invited capture, and caused the inhabitants to spend more or less of their lives as prisoners of war, and when it did not have one it thereby lost the opportunity of becoming the commercial metropolis of the Northwest. I know of no such tract of land in all this section which has been so singularly unfortunate as the St. Joseph Region.[12]

The coming of the War of 1812 posed a great threat to isolated frontier posts, such as Fort Dearborn. Hostile relations with the Indians were brought to a head by the Indian chief Tecumseh. His defeat at the Battle of Tippecanoe, in 1811, brought a temporary feeling of peace, but the agitation of British agents along the Canadian border renewed Indian hostility toward the United States. The attacks on American settlers by British-agitated Indians were one of the causes President Madison cited in his message to Congress prior to the 1812 declaration of war.[13] When war was apparent, the Indians sided against the United States; they felt their interests were better served by the British.

When the British captured the fort at Mackinac, the U.S. Army headquarters at Detroit ordered Fort Dearborn's evacuation. The first Fort Dearborn was destroyed on 15 August 1812, as the Indians attacked the evacuating residents. As soon as peace was established in 1815, it was inevitable that an attempt would be made to reassert U.S. power in the area of the first Fort Dearborn. To this end, ground was broken during the Fourth of July celebration, 1816, for the erection of the second Fort Dearborn.[14]

By 1818, in addition to the fort, there was a village of about one dozen log huts, which Major Long characterized as "low, filthy, and disgusting."[15] These huts were occupied by about sixty fur-trading half-breeds, and this group, plus those at the fort, constituted Chicago's population for the next twelve years. The Chicago area was far removed from the course of western migration, which prior to 1830 had utilized the Cumberland Gap or the Ohio River to southern Illinois.[16] In 1825 and 1826, Chicago had fourteen taxpayers, thirty-five voters, and the great bulk of some $8,000 in taxable property belonging to the American Fur Company's agents, who had obtained a monopoly of the area's trade.[17]

EARLY CHICAGO

By 1835, Chicago was growing more populous every day. The newcomers were part of the great western migration of the 1830s that followed the Erie Canal's opening in 1825. The decade of the 1830s saw the population of the Mississippi River valley increase from one-fourth to one-third of the total U.S. population. The Erie Canal provided a continuous water highway from the Atlantic seaboard to the Great Lakes during seven months of the year, before the upper lakes became clogged with ice. The canal redirected and stimulated New England migration toward the Great Lakes region, and, more importantly, it accelerated the rise of steam navigation, which lessened the time involved in traveling between Chicago and the East.

The most significant factor in Chicago's rising urban growth rate was the proposed Illinois and Michigan Canal.[18] This canal (see map 3) was similar to the one first projected by Joliet and would connect Lake Michigan and the Chicago River with the Illinois River. Such a canal would complete the through-water route from the Great Lakes to the Mississippi River. The 1820s witnessed a growing national interest in the canal project, which was sharpened by an insistent local realization of a need for better contact with the East. Two canal commissions and a company chartered for the purpose of building the canal yielded no tangible results in the late 1820s and early 1830s; yet the promise was still there. Much of the difficulty was the inability to attract eastern capital; however, land grants had been obtained by the state from the federal government.

The full effect of these land grants was not realized until after the Black Hawk War ended in 1832. The enthusiasm of returning soldiers for the Chicago area's excellent farmland created a demand for the "canal lands," which, in turn, generated great excitement over the canal's construction. Emigrants and speculators came to Chicago, which, because of its location at the head of the proposed canal, would be the key to opening the new region. This new constituency was active in voicing its hope that canal construction, or even railroad construction, would begin immediately. For the remainder of the 1830s the canal and the trade in canal lots provided a focus for the belief that a man could realize a high return on an investment in Chicago.

In 1830 there was no harbor on Lake Michigan south of the Manitou Islands, off the northwestern coast of Michigan's lower peninsula. At Chicago, it was customary for ships to anchor at a distance of not less than a half-mile from the shore. Consequently, concomitant with the agitation for the canal was the realization that harbor improvements had to be made. In 1832 the federal government began to construct a lighthouse at Chicago, and, in 1833, an appropriation of $25,000 was made for harbor improvements, most of which was expended on dredging the sandbars that blocked the Chicago River's mouth.[19] This work began in 1832 and was sustained by continued appropriations as a result of local agitation, favorable engineering reports, and the harbor's growing commercial importance. These efforts barely lasted into the next decade, as new sandbars developed to block access to the harbor. Consequently, the river was dredged again. Once the initial channel was cut through the sandbar, shelter and harbor facilities were available to lake-going vessels. Within a year after the dredging began in the 1840s, a ship with a capacity of 100 tons was able to enter the harbor. Chicago became the leading western port, the logical end of the line for lake-going vessels from the East.

Chicago's growth, from a swamp-like village at the mouth of the Chicago River to a large metropolitan node, can be described by economic factors which led to commercial and industrial agglomerations.[20] The geological phenomena that created the Chicago area placed it in a strategic position on a water route between the Great Lakes and the Mississippi River. Although the French and British evidently failed to construct garrisons in the Chicago area, they were accustomed to using the Chicago portage. The Americans did construct a fort at the Chicago River's mouth for the dual purpose of securing the portage and the area's fur trade.

The Chicago River, and its connection to the Mississippi River through the Des Plaines and Illinois rivers, was the key to Chicago's growth. The river was the decisive factor in locating the city, and the

Illinois and Michigan Canal, eventually built across the Chicago portage, was largely responsible for securing the potential for a commercial and an industrial agglomeration. The node at Chicago, with its accessibility to the backcountry, attracted the railroads next, and they, in turn, accelerated Chicago's development as a major metropolitan node.

Economic location theory suggests that a metropolitan node is most likely to develop at a break-in transport.[21] With the lake, river, and, later, the canal, Chicago had such a break. The coming of the railroad accentuated this break, as Chicago was either a western terminus for eastern roads or an eastern terminus for western roads. Chicago had the theoretical potential for growth, and it did grow.

EARLY CANAL CONSIDERATION

From the time of the first white men to visit the area, the possibility of a canal across the Chicago portage had been discussed. The reasons given for such a waterway were primarily to aid the military and to facilitate traffic from north to south. As time passed, the military consideration decreased in importance relative to the commercial possibilities.

When the United States began to expand westward, the canal idea began to spread in legislative bodies and in the press. President James Madison acknowledged the importance of such a canal in his 1814 inaugural address, four years after Representative Porter of New York State brought the matter before Congress. The Niles, Michigan, *Register* of 6 August 1814 remarked:

> By the Illinois River it is probable that Buffalo, in New York, may be united with New Orleans by inland navigation, through Lakes Erie, Huron and Michigan, and down that river to the Mississippi. What a route! How stupendous the idea! How dwindles the importance of the artificial canals of Europe compared to *this* water communication. If it should ever take place—and it is said the opening may be easily made—the Territory [of Illinois] will become the seat of an immense commerce, and a market for the commodities of all regions.[22]

The first steps toward the construction of the Illinois and Michigan Canal were taken on 24 August 1816, when the Potawatomi relinquished their title to a strip of land extending twenty miles between Chicago and Ottawa, the navigable water route across the Chicago portage.(see map 3).

In the autumn of 1816, Major S. H. Long, U.S.E., passed through the portage from the south to Lake Michigan. When his party reached Chicago it noted that the river discharged into Lake Michigan over a sandbar. The river at this point was a stream ten to fifteen yards wide and a few inches deep. The little Calumet River, fifteen miles to the south (see map 2), also discharged into the lake, but was effectively dammed by a high sandbar. The Long party arrived in the area during the dry season. In spring, water would flow over the bar at the little Calumet, but it was not of sufficient depth to cause difficulties.

In June 1823 Major Long was again in the Chicago area. He recorded in his writings a visit to the portage site. The purpose was to observe the divide west of Chicago. Since it was June, the portage was much less navigable than it would have been a few weeks earlier. Long noted that progress through the swamp was quite difficult due to the high grass and weeds. He then observed:

> When we consider the facts . . . we are irresistibly led to the conclusion that an elevation of the lakes of a few feet (not exceeding ten or twelve) above their present level would cause them to discharge their waters, partly, at least, into the Gulf of Mexico; . . . and . . . an expenditure, trifling in comparison with the importance of this object, would again render Lake Michigan a tributary to the Mexican Gulf. Impressed with the importance of this object, the Legislature of Illinois has already caused some observations to be made upon the possibility of establishing this communication; . . . we have been informed that they [the canal commissions] had considered the elevation of the *petit lac* [Mud Lake, or the swampiest part of the Chicago portage] above Chicago to be somewhat greater than we had estimated it. It is the opinion of those best acquainted with the nature of the country, that the easiest communication would be between the little Calamick [Calumet] and some point of the Des Plaines, probably below the portage road; between these two points, there is in wet seasons, we understand, a water communication of ten or twelve miles. Of the practicability of the work, and of the sufficiency of a supply of water no doubt can exist. The only difficulty will, we apprehend, be in keeping the communication open after it is once made, as the soil is swampy, and probably will require particular care to oppose the return of the soft mud into the excavations.[23]

THE FIRST ATTEMPT

When Illinois became a state in 1818, one of the first proposals discussed was for a regular preliminary survey of the land obtained from the Indians. Chicago's inclusion within the state boundary brought the canal project entirely under Illinois' control, thus increasing interest and facilitating action.[24] On 30 March 1822, Congress gave Illinois permission to cut a canal through public lands, donated a strip of land for the canal and an additional ninety feet on each bank, and appropriated $10,000 for the surveys. Early in the 1822–1823 state legislative session resolutions were adopted by the House authorizing the Internal Improvements Committee to inquire into the practicability of a canal.[25] This empowered the governor to employ engineers to examine the Chicago portage for the purpose of estimating the construction cost of a canal connecting Lake Michigan with the Des Plaines and/or Illinois River. A bill was passed on 14 February 1823, which provided that commissioners should be appointed to survey the canal route, prepare cost estimates, and report to the next legislature.

Five possible routes were surveyed by the commission, and a cost estimate was made for each. The construction plan was on the order of the Erie Canal, then under construction. In January 1825 the commissioners made their report to the legislature, and a few days later, on 17 January 1825, the Illinois and Michigan Canal Company was incorporated, with a capital stock of $1 million. This group was unable to dispose of its stock. Consequently, the Legislature of 1826 annulled the act of the preceding year. This was not done to end the canal project but to enable any future management to begin its work unencumbered by the mistakes of former managements.

THE SECOND ATTEMPT

In January 1826 a memorial was sent to the U.S. Congress requesting a further grant of land, because fluctuating conditions in the money market prohibited a long-term loan. On 2 March 1827, Congress donated alternate sections in strips five miles wide on either bank; the remaining land was held by the federal government. A. T. Andreas was unreserved in assessing the significance of this event:

> The obtaining of this magnificent land grant made the building of the canal a certainty, and in after time was the means of lifting the State from the slough of financial despair. It made possible and necessary the survey of Chicago Town, and flourishing villages were eventually born along the route of the proposed improvements.[26]

In 1828 another bill was passed which provided for the sale of lots and lands, for the appointment of new canal commissioners, and for the commencement of work, but all that ever transpired under this law was the sale of some land and a new survey and cost estimate. In 1829 a second state commission was appointed and empowered to raise funds by selling land, obtaining a loan, or other means.

The new survey established that the highest elevation along the proposed canal route between the Chicago and Des Plaines rivers was fourteen feet above the surface of Lake Michigan; the average height, ten feet. Thirty-four miles downstream the level of the Des Plaines River was identical with the level of Lake Michigan. The plan was to connect the lake and this point in the river by means of a deep-cut channel. Downstream, however, the rock was so near the surface that it became evident that the cost would be much higher than originally thought. Nevertheless, all reports suggested that the expected benefits would be greater than the estimated expenses. Such cost considerations led the Illinois legislature to appoint additional commissioners, in February 1831, to ascertain whether the Calumet River could be used as a feeder. These commissioners were also to determine whether a railroad would be preferable to the canal. Putnam contended that in the end the commission members became convinced a railroad was preferable, but the Illinois legislature decided to build neither railroad nor canal at that time, and, in March 1833, repealed its acts of 1829 and 1831.[27] In 1833 the legislature discovered that the latest estimated construction costs had increased considerably from earlier estimates. Since the state had little money and less credit, all public improvements remained in abeyance.[28]

THE THIRD ATTEMPT

On 10 February 1835, the Illinois legislature authorized a third attempt at constructing the proposed Illinois and Michigan Canal. This bill empowered the governor, who had been elected on a platform of staunch canal support, to negotiate a $500,000 loan for construction costs, to cause stock to be issued, and to appoint a new board of canal commissioners. The work was to be deep cut; the depth was to be such as to allow boats with four feet draughts an unimpeded passage. The proposed canal was to be forty-five feet wide at the surface and thirty feet at the bottom. A direct supply of water would be drawn from Lake Michigan through the South Branch.[29]

After initial difficulties, an eastern loan was finally obtained.[30] The news of the loan, which insured the beginning of canal construction, gave "new life to everything" in Chicago. Property values, which were considered high already, advanced rapidly. The opening of Great Lakes navigation in 1836 brought large numbers of visitors who were anxious to engage in land speculation. The effects of readily available credit and a plentiful currency were augmented when the federal treasury distributed its surplus among the states. This distribution led many states to adopt ambitious schemes for internal improvements.[31]

The new canal commission encouraged an early start to the project, believing that this would facilitate the financing of it; however, it became apparent that the project's magnitude had been underestimated. The cost estimate of over $4 million for a lake-fed canal, originally thought to be excessive, was found to be inadequate to build a canal of the desired dimensions. Consequently, since the initial costs would be larger, no matter what size canal was constructed, the commissioners decided to build a larger canal. This new plan proposed a lake-fed canal sixty feet wide at the water level, thirty-six feet wide at the bottom, and a minimum of six feet deep. The commissioners argued that the increased utility of the larger canal would counterbalance the increased construction costs, and that it was preferable, and probably cheaper, to build a canal adequate to meet future demands than to enlarge existing facilities when they became inadequate.[32]

THE BEGINNING OF CONSTRUCTION

The commissioners expected that actual construction would begin in the spring of 1837, but they were disappointed. A labor scarcity continued into the summer, until many immigrants arrived from the eastern United States and Canada.

Further, the canal's construction plan was being investigated, and work was not available to match the incoming labor supply. The original construction plan was attacked by the Illinois House Committee on Internal Improvements, who considered it as being beyond the state's financial capabilities. They claimed the engineering estimates were not trustworthy because they had entirely omitted several important expense items and severely underestimated others. The House Committee's canal construction cost estimate of $13.25 million was over $4.5 million more than the commissioners' revised estimate. It was proposed, therefore, that the deep-cut plan be supplanted by a shallow-cut plan.

Finally, the financial situation tended to further embarrass the commission's activities and inhibit the work's progress. Under the conditions of the 9 January 1836 Act, the canal bonds were marketable securities. The governor had easily negotiated the $500,000 loan, and, by an act of 2 March 1837, the governor was authorized to make a second $500,000 loan. The prospect of the canal's early completion gave an already active real estate market firm support. With the first installments from a September 1836 land sale (the second installments due a year later), and the proceeds of the loans which the governor had negotiated, it was expected that there would be sufficient funds to support the work through the year. Under these conditions, the commissioners sold 375 Chicago canal lots at $1,355,755, in June 1836, and 78 Ottawa canal lots at $21,358, in September 1836. This was approximately 10 percent above the appraised value. In accordance with the act providing for these land sales, one-fourth of the proceeds and the interest on the remaining three-fourths were placed into the canal fund.[33]

In 1837 the Internal Improvement Act was passed by the Illinois General Assembly. The act incorporated "plans for a system of railroads and river improvements which, together with the canal, would give her [Illinois] an unsurpassed system of transportation and communication."[34] The railroad system, which was to become the Illinois Central, was given the task of supplying a thinly settled western state with rail services sufficient to meet the needs of the populous East. Additionally, the act authorized a $4 million loan for further work on the canal. The expectations which this act manifested were completely unrealistic under the most optimistic interpretation of the state's finances. As a matter of convenience, the act kept the canal loan separate from the internal improvement funds, but they failed together when the state temporarily lost its credit during the Panic of 1837. Subsequently, the act was repealed.

By the autumn of 1837, the pace of canal work reached the commissioners' anticipations. In spite of an increased financial burden on the contractors, caused by the increased population and the resulting demand for materials and provisions in an undeveloped Chicago, the work progressed to such an extent that, by the end of 1838, all but twenty-three miles of the canal were under contract. Several sections were completed, and others were near completion. In the first years following the Panic of 1837 the canal construction continued, and the commissioners' payments to the construction companies furnished temporary support to Chicago's business interests. This support lasted until an agricultural surplus from the interior appeared to furnish a firmer foundation for economic growth.

THE WORK CESSATION

In spite of all their efforts to remain liquid, the canal commissioners, on 1 March 1840, were forced to issue checks bearing 6 percent interest and payable when the necessary funds became available—the canal treasury was depleted. An effort was made to replenish the treasury by further bond and canal land sales. It was hoped that these sales would generate sufficient funds to meet the interest payments on the check issue; however, sales were small, and payment was principally received in canal scrip.[35] Thus, finding it impossible to continue land sales at the existing price, the canal commissioners abandoned them because they felt a low price would prejudice the state's interest. Recognizing the implications of a work cessation, the contractors offered to take $1 million of the authorized bonds at par and to bear the discount at which they could have been sold. The commissioners accepted this offer, and this move prolonged construction for several months, albeit with a diminished labor force.

In March 1841 the canal treasury was empty, once again. The contractors continued the construction and made preparations for the future, hopeful that the state legislature could resolve the financial problems. The legislature devoted itself to this task throughout the winter of 1840–1841, but failed to find a solution. The large state bond sales of the 1830s (including Illinois) depressed the market for that type of security.

The General Assembly's failure to provide any financing was generally interpreted as leaving the canal to its fate. Contractors who could abandon their work without excessive financial loss did so. All means of payment to the contractors failed, and, by late November 1841, construction was suspended, save for the very few contractors who bore their own burdens and awaited a better day for their pay. In February 1842 the Illinois State Bank failed, and the financial affairs of the state seemed hopeless.

Desperate financial measures paid the interest on the state debt and the canal debt through 1841, but the estimated canal expenditures for 1842 could not be met, and, in March 1843, the Illinois and Michigan Canal project was virtually abandoned after an outlay of over $5 million. When the construction ceased in March 1843, over $4.6 million had been expended, and large amounts were still outstanding in the form of superintendents' and contractors' claims (see table 3).

Table 3. *Illinois and Michigan Canal Expenses*

Year	Amount
1836	$ 39,260.58
1837	350,649.90
1938	911,902.40
1839	1,479,907.58
1840	1,117,702.30
1841	644,675.94
1842	155,193.33
Superintendents	210,000.00
Contractors' damage	230,000.00
Total	$5,139,492.03

Source: A. T. Andreas, *History of Chicago from the Earliest Period to the Present Time*, vol. 1, p. 169.

The completion of the canal appeared to be the only hope in this crisis. The completed canal would benefit the state's finances both directly and indirectly. It would give direct benefit to the state by yielding a toll-based revenue that could be used partially to offset the interest charges the state could not meet. It would indirectly benefit the state by increasing the tax base in two ways:

. . . first, through the raising of property values by the capitalization of the dimunition in transportation charges; and secondly, by making the state a more attractive place for settlement and investment through this provision for lightening its financial burdens, which would tend to draw the population and capital that naturally shun a debt-ridden community with its exorbitant taxes.[36]

In addition, sufficiently increased property values meant that canal land sales could be utilized to diminish the debt burden.

In short, the difference between a completed and an uncompleted canal appeared to be the difference between a solvent and an insolvent Illinois. Although this was a widely held view, there was lack of official enthusiasm for completing the canal. What was needed was an additional $3 million, but the state's insolvent condition made it clear to all that raising such a sum would be impossible.

THE WORK RESUMPTION

Of all the internal improvements projects that Illinois conceived, the canal was the only one near completion. Furthermore, the canal commission possessed 230,476 acres of land and 3,491 town lots in its own right, assets that had not been sold or mortgaged during the panic's aftermath.[37] Fortunately for both Chicago and the canal, three groups formed a coalition to complete the canal.

These were, first, the citizens of Chicago, who fondly expected that the canal would make the city a great emporium; second, the bondholders, who had already sunk their money into the enterprise and who by putting in a little more might recover their entire investment; and, third, the state, which by opening up a profitable market for the products of the Illinois River Valley would enable farmers to pay the taxes that would enable the state to meet its obligations.[38]

It was in this situation that the shallow-cut plan came to be reconsidered. It was estimated that only $1.5 million would be required to complete the canal on the shallow-cut plan, one-half the $3 million required to complete the canal on the deep-cut plan. The principal bondholders, the state legislature, and the canal commissioners all deemed it possible to raise this smaller sum on a pledge of the canal lands and revenues, and the canal itself. An act of February 1843 authorized the governor to negotiate a new loan for $1.5 million and to secure payment by a deed of trust. American creditors subscribed their portion of the new loan, but foreign creditors were hesitant.

The commissioners agreed to a complete report of the canal's financial condition during the winter of 1843–1844. This report, prepared by a committee from Baring Brothers, a London investment house, representing the European bondholders, recommended the acceptance of the loan as a "safe financial proposition."[39] The Baring Brothers report showed the total canal debt as of 1 January 1844 to be $5,400,000; the net debt, $4,850,000. The assets included, in addition to the the canal, 230,476 acres of canal land worth an estimated $10 an acre at the canal's completion, and 3,491 city lots in Chicago, Lockport, Ottawa, and LaSalle worth $1,900,000. Additionally, waterpower rentals would gross $75,000 to $100,000 per year, and tolls for the canal's second year of operation were estimated in excess of $360,000. Consequently, the European creditors subscribed their portion of the new loan. The first installment was due 20 September 1845.

Necessary preparation for the work resumption took place in the summer of 1845. Sections that had been preempted by former contractors were reassigned to them. New contracts were let on the remaining sections to the "lowest responsible bidder." After the 1843 cessation and the resulting deterioration of the existing structures, time was needed to restore the completed canal sections for the resumption of construction. The February 1843 act required that the canal be completed within three years after it was turned over to the canal trustees, who received it in 1845. Flood delays and excessive labor absence due to sickness slowed progress, but the work was completed in the alloted time, and the canal was opened for navigation in April 1848.

The change from the deep-cut to the shallow-cut plan necessitated several additions. A series of locks was necessary to overcome the elevation of the low divide. Three feeders became necessary because the shallow-cut plan, by itself, could not generate a sufficient flow during the dry seasons.[40] One of these feeders, from the Calumet River through the "Sag," played a crucial role in much of Chicago's later sanitary history.

There seems to have been no shortage of reports as to whether a sufficient quantity of water could be obtained to operate the canal at the higher level required by the shallow-cut plan. Later, experience proved that it could not. During the dry seasons the waters from the Des Plaines River and Mud Lake would have been inadequate to meet navigational demands, even if the deep-cut plan had been used. This problem was discussed by the engineers at the Chicago Mechanics' Institute.[41] In the autumn of 1843 an Institute committee recommended a plan whereby sufficient water would be supplied to the canal, above its summit level, by a set of steel pumps. These pumps were designed to lift the water above the level of the Des Plaines River.

In 1845, with the work resumption close at hand, the water supply problem for the shallow-cut canal was still an undecided issue. The canal commissioners had determined that it was necessary to obtain a flow of about 6,000 cubic feet per minute, more than could be provided by the Des Plaines and Calumet feeders at low water. The Institute plan was one alternative; the other was the construction of a thirty-mile Fox River feeder line. The pumping plan was adopted on the basis of its being both more effective and less expensive, and this proved to be a significant decision, because these pumps also played a crucial role in Chicago's sanitary history.

It is interesting to note that during 1845–1846, when the Illinois and Michigan Canal was conceded to be the foundation of Chicago's prosperity, the stabilization of the canal project was one of the principal arguments against annexing the northern tier of counties in Illinois to the territory of Wisconsin, as the tentative boundary was drawn in the Land Ordinance of 1787. That ordinance authorized the organization of "three states south of a line drawn due east and west from the most southerly bend of Lake Michigan to the Mississippi River, and two states north of such a line . . ." John Wentworth's reminiscences noted that many settlements north of this line, yet within Illinois, were unanimously in favor of belonging to Wisconsin. Illinois' two congressmen, including John Wentworth, resided in this area. Many area residents made promise after promise if the Illinois congressmen would support annexation. Mr. Wentworth recalled the following:

> The disputed tract had two Congressmen, the Hon. Joseph P. Hoye, of Galena, . . . and myself. And Wisconsin offered to make us the first two Senators, and also offered to give the disputed tract the first Governor. It was proposed to enact a law submitting the binding forces of the ordinance of 1787 to the Supreme Court of the United States. Our Chicago people were much divided upon the question, and I really believe serious consequences would have grown out of it but for the embarrassments that would be caused by having the Illinois and Michigan Canal owned by two states. As an original question, all the fine states being out of the Union, there is no doubt but Congress would have enforced the provisions of the ordinance, and Illinois been cut off from the lakes, and her Legislature saved from the annoyance of Chicago lobbyists. But might made right. Wisconsin being out of the Union she could only come into it with boundaries prescribed by a majority of the states in it, and I lost the honor of being a Wisconsin United States Senator.[42]

By 1857, the shallow-cut Illinois and Michigan Canal was in full operation. While the trustees were inclined to enlarge the canal to the dimensions prescribed by the original deep-cut plan, Illinois' limited financial resources prevented it.

SUMMARY

The Illinois and Michigan Canal provided the necessary break-in transport which developed a commercial agglomeration at Chicago. The city's commercial potentialities, with the completed canal, were sufficient to draw a significant population, prior to the canal's completion. Once canal operations began, Chicago immediately became involved in handling the commerce of its agriculturally rich hinterland. This necessitated additions to the city's commercial population and to the city's service population. The expansion of rail facilities only served to accelerate the trends which the canal established.

Ironically, it was the railroads that were given credit for establishing Chicago's nodal superiority—ironic because it was only a few short months after the canal's opening that the city's first railroad, the Galena and Chicago Union Railroad, made its maiden journey. It was, however, several years before the railroad superseded the canal. Competition between the canal and the railroad resulted in lower freight rates for the Illinois River valley than for other middle western routes. Even when the canal's importance became secondary, it expedited the economic development of both the valley and the city.

The canal's importance in directing attention to Chicago and in spurring a land boom cannot be overemphasized. The Erie Canal experience was crucial. Both the success of the Erie Canal and the rapid rise in land values along the canal route led to similar expectations for the Illinois and Michigan Canal. Population moved into Chicago seeing not the squalid village of log huts on the Chicago River's banks but the large city that was expected to rise when the canal was completed.

The *Chicago Tribune* of 13 May 1900 summarized the Illinois and Michigan Canal's importance to Chicago in an editorial entitled "The Canal Made Chicago."

Chicago was then [pre-1830] only a military post with an Indian agency attached to it. It didn't have enough taxable property to support a bridge tender, much less build a canal. When the preliminaries to the building of the canal did come about, Chicago immediately leaped into existence as a village. The first plot of Chicago was made by the Canal Commissioners; the first sale of lots was made by the Canal Commissioners. Chicago was made by the canal as clearly and as positively as Western towns have been made in recent years and are still being made by the advent of railroads. Chicago was a canal town.[43]

NOTES

1. See Jack L. Hough, *Geology of the Great Lakes* (Urbana: University of Illinois Press, 1958).
2. Ibid., chap. 5.
3. F. M. Fryxell, *The Physiography of the Region of Chicago* (Chicago: University of Chicago Press, 1927), p. 1.
4. Ibid., p. 18.
5. From " 'Relations' of Father Dablon," *Historical Magazine,* p. 237, quoted in A. T. Andreas, *History of Chicago from the Earliest Time to the Present,* vol. 1 (Chicago: A. T. Andreas, 1884), p. 165.
6. Carl W. Condit, *Chicago, 1910–1929* (Chicago: University of Chicago Press, 1973), p. 6.
7. Ibid., pp. 3–4.
8. Bessie Louise Pierce, *A History of Chicago,* vol. 1 (New York: Alfred A. Knopf, 1937), p. 14.
9. J. Seymour Currey, *The Story of Old Fort Dearborn* (Chicago: A. C. McClurg and Co., 1912), p. 19.
10. Milo M. Quaife, *Chicago's Highways: Old and New* (Chicago: D. F. Keller and Co., 1923), p. 15.
11. See W. T. Easterbrook and H. G. J. Aitken, *Canadian Economic History* (Toronto: Macmillan Company of Canada, 1956).
12. Edward G. Mason, quoted in Currey, *Old Fort Dearborn,* p. 21.
13. Currey, *Old Fort Dearborn,* p. 98.
14. Pierce, *A History of Chicago,* 1:25.
15. Quoted in Milo M. Quaife, *Chicago and the Old Northwest* (Chicago: University of Chicago Press, 1913), p. 281.
16. Homer Hoyt, *One Hundred Years of Land Values in Chicago* (Chicago: University of Chicago Press, 1933), p. 10.
17. Pierce, *A History of Chicago,* 1:31.
18. The interested reader is referred to almost any basic text on American economic history for a description of the western migration and the internal improvements mania of the 1820s and 1830s.
19. John Wentworth, *Early Chicago: Fort Dearborn,* Fergus Historical Series, no. 16 (Chicago: Fergus Printing Co., 1881), p. 80.
20. See Louis P. Cain, "The Sanitary District of Chicago: A Case Study of Water Use and Conservation" (Ph.D. diss., Northwestern University, 1969).
21. C. H. Cooley, "The Theory of Transportation," *American Economic Review* (1894), pp. 223–371, is the original source.
22. Quoted in Andreas, *History of Chicago,* 1:166.
23. From *Major Long's Expedition,* pp. 165, 167, quoted in Andreas, *History of Chicago,* 1:166, 167.
24. Originally, the Northwest Territory was divided into five potential states, with the line between Illinois and Wisconsin drawn at the bottom of Lake Michigan.

25. Andreas, *History of Chicago,* 1:166.

26. Ibid., p. 167.

27. James William Putnam, *The Illinois and Michigan Canal,* (Chicago: University of Chicago Press, 1918), p. 21. This is the most authoritative history of the canal. Putnam's book is strongly recommended to readers interested in a detailed account of the canal and its economic influence on Chicago.

28. "Report of the Illinois and Michigan Canal Commissioners," 1844. See also Andreas, *History of Chicago,* 1:168.

29. Pierce, *A History of Chicago,* 1:31. See also Andreas, *History of Chicago,* 1:168.

30. Putnam, *The Illinois and Michigan Canal,* p. 31ff.

31. Pierce, *A History of Chicago,* 1:80.

32. Putnam, *The Illinois and Michigan Canal,* p. 35.

33. Ibid., p. 42.

34. Pierce, *A History of Chicago,* 1:61.

35. On 11 April 1839 the canal commissioners decided to issue a large amount of ninety-day scrip, based on the canal fund, which was to be used to pay contractors. The total amount of the May 1839 issue was $266,237; the August 1839 issue, $128,317. See Andreas, *History of Chicago,* 1:168.

36. Putnam, *The Illinois and Michigan Canal,* p. 55.

37. Ibid., p. 58.

38. Hoyt, *Land Values in Chicago,* p. 45.

39. Putnam, *The Illinois and Michigan Canal,* p. 58.

40. Ibid., p. 66. Three feeders were constructed: (1) from the Fox River at Dayton to Ottawa; (2) from the Kankakee River to the Dresden level; and (3) from the Calumet River through the "Sag" to the Summit level.

41. Andreas, *History of Chicago,* 1:170.

42. Quoted in Andreas, *History of Chicago,* 1:171.

43. *Chicago Tribune,* editorial page, 13 May 1900. Quoted in Hoyt, *Land Values in Chicago,* p. 13.

2
The
Sewerage
Decision
of 1855

Chicago was so nearly level that rainwater could not run off; it either had to evaporate or be absorbed. A short distance below ground level, clay and loam commingled until the mixture eventually became solid. Consequently, while the ground was suitable for building, in rainy seasons it became swamp-like and muddy. A drainage system was a necessity, and a successful system could solve two further urban problems: waste disposal and road building.

THE BACKGROUND

Chicago's city fathers failed twice to find a solution to the drainage problem. First, they attempted to construct crude sluices to drain surface water, and later they attempted to dig sewers. Both the sluices and the sewers were constructed so that they emptied into the Chicago River.[1] In those days the Chicago River was a little stream, not much larger than a creek. Only during times of heavy rain or melting snow did the river come to life and discharge large volumes of water into Lake Michigan. Its banks were only two feet above the water, yet the Chicago River was the master stream, the conduit which drained early Chicago into Lake Michigan (see maps 3 and 4).

The first attempt to improve Chicago's drainage was undertaken in 1834. The town borrowed sixty dollars to dig a drainage ditch down State Street to the river.[2] Initially, this ditch became swampy and had to be bridged. A more serious problem was that instead of draining, it did the opposite. When heavy rains caused the river to rise, the ditch provided a channel by which the water could back up and flood the town. In 1837, Chicago became a city under a charter granted by the state legislature. The city's need for passable thoroughfares was recognized from the beginning, as was the dependence of this need on a solution to the drainage problem. In the years that followed, numerous ordinances were presented to improve the streets, but they were all ineffective. According to Pierce,

> Visitors to the city unfailingly noted the impassability of the streets, frequently the haunt of wandering beasts as well as the highway of man; often seas of mud or beds of thick dust, sometimes leading into a deep, impeding slough.[3]

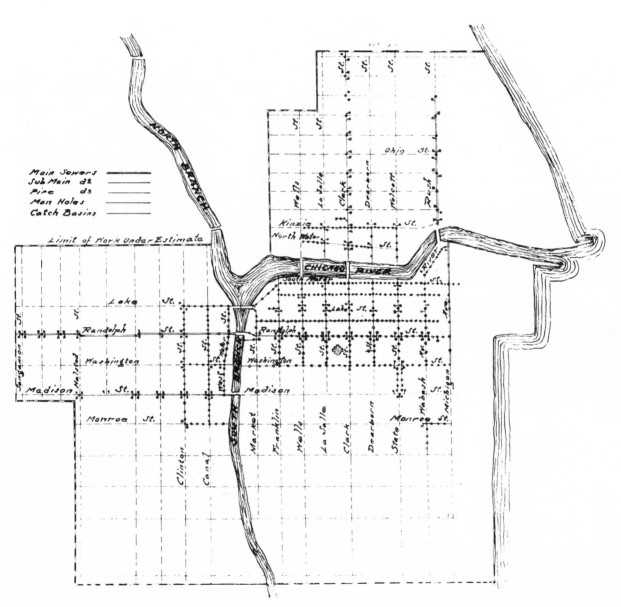

Chesbrough's sewerage system indicating the sewers laid to the end of 1857. Chicago Historical Society.

Map 4.

In 1847 the state legislature gave the Chicago City Council the power to plank any street which it saw fit. It was felt that planking might partially remove the difficulties that the mud created. The planks, however, did not prevent horses from breaking through and going to parts unknown. Often the timbers would rot, and the planked roadway would become so uneven that riders would not risk horses over the planks for fear of injury to the horse and carriage. They would detour through the mud to avoid the "bumpy ride and to avoid the risk of breaking a wheel. Mud and Chicago became synonymous terms."

By 1848, Chicago was a city of nearly 30,000. Roadside ditches were the main drainage medium.[4] There was no sewer system, and garbage was simply dumped in the ditches so that the next rain could flush it to the Chicago River. Animals, particularly hogs, prowled the streets and rooted the garbage.[5] In February 1847 the Illinois legislature, in an act supplementing the city's charter, gave the Chicago City Council the power to construct and repair sewers. Additionally, sewers and main drains so constructed and repaired belonged to the city, and owners of property drained by the city's sewers were required to pay a City-Council-determined share of the total sewerage and drainage costs.[6]

In 1850, Chicago constructed sewers down the centers of Clark, LaSalle, and Wells streets, from Randolph Street to the Chicago River. A total of $2,871.90 was spent on main and side sewers; and the contiguous property was assessed the full amount.[7] The sewers were typically triangular in shape, constructed of heavy oak plank, and laid five to eight feet deep. While these early sewers were considered satisfactory, the entire drainage scheme was still very experimental, and those sewers which had been laid were only of temporary construction.[8]

The last major attempt to drain a large area, without the benefit of an overall drainage plan, began under an Illinois legislative act of June 1852.[9] This act created commissioners who were authorized to

> . . . locate, construct, and maintain ditches, embankments, culverts, bridges, and roads, on any lands lying in Townships 37, 38, 39, and 40, in Ranges 12, 13, and 14, Cook County; and to take land and materials, necessary for these purposes, and to assess the cost of such improvements upon the lands they might deem to be benefitted thereby.[10]

While prosecuting their work, the commissioners discovered that 150,000 acres within their limits, theretofore considered worthless, could be rendered useful with proper drainage. These lands lay four to twelve feet above the level of Lake Michigan.

When the commission had been newly formed, objections were raised that its powers were too broadly conceived. The fear was that the commission's reforms would lead to land speculation resembling that of 1837. Subsequent events diminished these fears. By 1854, the commission had spent $100,000 in state money on authorized improvements. Large tracts were drained by ditches, most of which were dug along section lines to either the Chicago or Calumet rivers. These lands extended four miles north, five miles west, and ten miles south of the city, and people inhabited land that previously had been considered uninhabitable.[11]

All of these attempted improvements could have been termed progress by contemporaries, but there were many who recognized that a more adventurous program was necessary. The *Gem of the Prairie* provided an outlet for these ideas:

> To any intelligent person going about our city, who understands the physical conditions of health, and causes which, with mathematical certainty generate disease, the wonder is not that we have had cholera in our midst for two seasons in succession, and that the common diseases of the country are fatally prevalent during the summer months, but that a worse plague does not take up a permanent residence with us. Many of the populous localities are noisome quagmires, the gutters running with filth at which the very swine turn up their noses in supreme disgust. Even some portions of the planked streets . . . are scarcely in better sanitary condition than those which are not planked. The gutters at the crossings are clogged up, leaving standing pools of an undescribable liquid, there to salute the noses of passers by. There being no chance to drain them properly, the water accumulates underneath the planking, into which flows all manner of filth, and during the hot weather of the last few weeks, the whole reeking mass of abominations has steamed up through every opening, and the miasma thus elaborated has been wafted into the neighboring shops and dwellings, to poison their inmates. Such being the state of facts, the people naturally expect the corporation will do something to abate the universal nuisance, or at least make the attempt to do so.[12]

It was later estimated that 5.5 percent of the population in the Chicago area died as a result of the 1854 cholera and typhoid epidemics.

In the early 1850s these random waste disposal methods led to a succession of cholera and dysentery epidemics, as disposed sewage reached the intake of the city's Lake Michigan water supply. (The early history of Chicago's water supply is developed in the following chapter.) In 1850 the water supply intake was within a block or so of the mouth of the Chicago River. In 1853 the intake was moved a half-mile north, but even that was insufficient to keep it out of the reach of the sewage pollution. While there was reason to suspect the interdependency of water supply and waste disposal solutions, Chicago, at this time, attempted to solve them on an individual basis. Thus, the Illinois legislature created the Board of Sewerage Commissioners, on 14 February 1855, to combat what was generally conceded to be an intolerable situation. The board was empowered to (1) supervise the then present drainage and sewage disposal of Chicago's three natural divisions; (2) plan a coordinated system for the future; and (3) issue loans, purchase lots, and erect buildings implementing their plan. The board's actions were subject to the approval of Chicago's city council. The commissioners sought "the most competent engineer of the time who was available for the position of chief engineer." Their selection, Ellis Sylvester Chesbrough, resigned his position as Boston's city engineer to come to Chicago.[13]

THE RESEARCH

Immediately after accepting the position, Chesbrough submitted a report in which he outlined his plan for a sewerage system designed to solve Chicago's drainage and water disposal problem. Chesbrough's task was to construct a sewerage system whose main objective was to

Ellis Sylvester Chesbrough, engineer responsible for Chicago's first large sanitation systems. Chicago Historical Society.

"improve and preserve" the city's health. In his opinion, the existing privy vaults and drainage sluices were "abominations that should be swept away as speedily as possible," and that "to construct the vaults as they should be, and maintain them even in a comparatively inoffensive condition, would be more expensive than to construct an entire system of sewerage for no other purpose. . . ."[14]

Chesbrough's 1855 report considered four alternative drainage schemes: (1) drainage directly into the Chicago River, and then into Lake Michigan; (2) drainage directly into Lake Michigan; (3) drainage into artificial reservoirs to be pumped and used as fertilizer (sewage farming); or (4) drainage directly into the Chicago River, and then by a proposed steamboat canal into the Des Plaines River. The first plan was recommended because it involved "the fewest uncertainties and took the best and most economical advantage of the opportunities of the site."[15] This is not to say that Chesbrough failed to realize that his preferred method was a potential health hazard, particularly during the warmer months, or that this method might obstruct river navigation by making the waterways shallower. He proposed to lessen the health hazard by flushing the North and South branches with Lake Michigan water. He also proposed to

. . . supply the main sewers with a constant current of fresh water by pumping from the lake to a height of 8 to 10 feet, and in the west district, by draining directly from the Illinois and Michigan Canal at Bridgeport to keep water in the South Branch fresh, especially during the warm months of the year, and to construct a canal 20 feet wide and 6 feet deep at low water between the lake and the South Branch (along the line of Sixteenth Street).[16]

Chesbrough discussed the objections to his recommended alternative thus:

It is proposed to remove the first [health hazard] by pouring into the river from the lake a sufficient body of pure water to prevent offensive or injurious exhalations . . . The latter objection [obstruction of navigation] is believed to be groundless, because the substances to be conveyed through the sewers to the river could in no case be heavier than the soil of this vicinity, but would generally be much lighter. While these substances might, to some extent, be deposited there when there is little or no current, they would, during the seasons of rain and flood, be swept on by the same force that has hitherto preserved the depth of the river.[17]

Apparently, the potential effects of drainage directly into the Chicago River on the Lake Michigan water supply were not considered.

Chesbrough had three objections to the second alternative, drainage directly into Lake Michigan. First, it would require a greater sewer length and, consequently, would incur greater cost. Second, he supposed that this alternative would seriously affect the water supply, if any sewer outlets were located near the pumping station. At that time, the water supply intake was located a short distance offshore at the Chicago Avenue lakefront, approximately one-half mile north of the Chicago River's mouth. His report, however, did not elaborate on this objection. Third, Chesbrough felt that direct lake drainage would create difficulties in preventing sewer outlet injury during stormy weather or during snow and ice obstruction in the winter.[18]

The third alternative, sewage farming, was rejected in part because of the uncertainty whether future fertilizer demand would be sufficient to cover distribution costs. Further, Chesbrough was uncertain as to both the needed reservoir capacity and the expense of building ample-sized reservoirs. Finally, the report accepted the contemporary assumption that airborne diseases were a greater potential danger than waterborne diseases, and, therefore, rejected the idea on the basis that such a farm would be a great health hazard created by foul odors emanating from sewage spread over a wide surface.[19]

The fourth alternative, using a steamboat canal, not yet constructed, to flush the sewage into the Des Plaines River was termed "too remote." What was really under discussion was a deep-cut Illinois and Michigan Canal. Although Chesbrough was aware of the "evils" that would result when raw sewage passed into Lake Michigan, he felt it impossible to create an outlet to the southwest. Brown claims, however, that "he appears to have believed that this would be the ultimate solution of the sewerage problem."[20] Certainly, the recommended plan was readily adaptable to such a scheme. Chesbrough reported:

> With regard to the fourth plan, or draining into the proposed steamboat canal, which would divert a large and constantly flowing stream from Lake Michigan into the Illinois River, it is too remote a contingency to be relied upon for present purposes; besides, the cost of it, or any other similar channel in that direction, sufficient to drain off the sewage of the city, would be not only far more than the present sewerage law provides for, but more than would be necessary to construct the sewers for five times the present population. Should the proposed steamboat canal ever be made for commercial purposes the plan now recommended would be about as well adapted to such a state of things, as it is to the present, making it necessary to abandon only the proposed method of supplying the South Branch with fresh water from the lake, and to pump up from the West district, instead of obtaining it from the present canal [the Illinois and Michigan Canal] at Bridgeport.[21]

In sum, four alternatives had been considered. Drainage directly into the lake was rejected on the basis of its greater cost, and, in addition, there was some concern that it would prove a health hazard. Sewage farming was rejected on both cost and health grounds. The idea of diverting the sewage through a proposed steamboat canal to the southwest was considered "too remote." Although this alternative was not rejected on a cost basis, it is clear that it would have involved substantially greater cost. Thus, drainage into the Chicago River was accepted as the least costly and, simultaneously, the least health hazard of the three feasible alternatives. Since the potential effects of this alternative on the water supply were not considered, one can argue that cost was the more important consideration.

THE ADOPTED APPROACH

In December 1855 Chesbrough submitted his plan for Chicago's sewage disposal and drainage to the Board of Sewerage Commissioners. In spite of considerable opposition predicated on the novelty and cost of Chesbrough's recommended plan, it was adopted. Cost estimates were prepared only for the recommended alternative. They did not cover sewers for the entire territory considered, but only for that part of the territory deemed necessary for 1855 purposes. These estimates were as follows: South district, $157,893; West, $188,831; North, $156,522.[22] Under this plan (see map 4) all the West division's sewage, all the North division's sewage except the lake-front area, and about one-half of the South division's sewage was deposited in the Chicago River, from which it passed into Lake Michigan. The dividing line in the South division was State Street; the residential area east of

State Street drained directly into the lake. Chicago's business district, primarily west of State Street, deposited its sewage in the river. This district included the majority of Chicago's packinghouses, distilleries, and hotels. Thus, the river would receive large quantities of pollutants daily. Systematic sewage disposal was unknown in this country, and Chicago was in a position to become the first important U.S. city to build a comprehensive sewer system.[23]

As previously noted, Chicago's topography was unfavorable to sewer construction. The Chicago River's banks were only two feet above the water. Properly graded sewers, laid underground, would discharge below the river's level, increasing the probability that the sewers would reverse and flood streets and cellars. The task of constructing underground sewers was, in reality, also the task of raising street grades.[24] From the first, Chesbrough insisted that a high grade was necessary for proper drainage and dry streets. Chicago lacked this grade. The grade which the Chicago City Council adopted was lower than Chesbrough advocated, but it was high enough to permit the construction of seven- to eight-foot cellars. The council's decision was to raise the grade to ten feet on streets adjacent to the river; Chesbrough's twelve-foot grade was rejected on the grounds that sufficient fill would be difficult to locate.[25] While this decision helped to reduce the total cost of implementing the plan, it increased the risk that the sewers would reverse. Apparently the incremental increase in risk was small, because Chesbrough did not strenuously object to this change.

The plan called for an intercepting sewer system which emptied into the Chicago River. The sewers were constructed on the combined system; that is, they would receive water from both homes and the streets. This was consistent with the best contemporary thinking and practice, based principally on English experience. The main sewers were to be three to six feet in diameter, running along alternate streets. These sewers would be intersected by sewers two feet in diameter, running along streets perpendicular to the main sewers (see map 4). As constructed, the sewer system was capable of handling, at capacity, a one-inch-per-hour rainfall.[26]

Chesbrough's brick sewers were laid above the ground, down the center of a street. As sewer construction progressed away from the river, the sewers were raised to preserve the slope, and, consequently, the streets had to be raised. After the sewers were laid, earth was filled in around them, entirely covering them. The packed-down fill provided roadbeds for new, higher streets. These streets were rounded in the center, with gutter apertures leading to the sewer. Such streets would stay dry and could be paved, as contrasted to the mud which plagued the city.

A second facet of Chesbrough's sewerage plan involved dredging the Chicago River. The river had been dredged previously. The federal government straightened the bend where Fort Dearborn had stood in 1833, when, as part of the Illinois and Michigan Canal project, Chicago was made a federal harbor. Nevertheless, the Chicago River was still too small to handle the anticipated sewage load. The river was to be

The north side of Lake Street between Clark and LaSalle streets. This 1857 view shows the two levels of the city. Chicago Historical Society.

widened, deepened, and straightened. The dredged soil was to be utilized as fill for the sewer. Thus, the report recommended that the Chicago River be committed to the life of an open sewer.

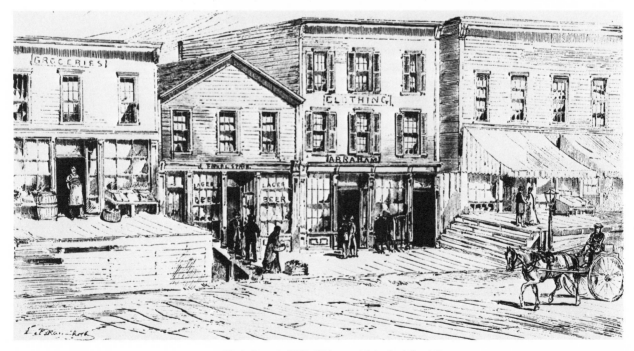

Clark Street, 1857. Chicago Historical Society.

Chesbrough's sewer system was not considered to be a threat to the city's water supply. The decision was made without consideration of the potential effects of this approach on the pollution of the water supply. Nevertheless, soon after the new sewers became operative the Chicago River became polluted and, consequently, so did Lake Michigan. In time, the pollution increased and reached the water supply intake, forcing another decision. That is the subject of the following chapter.

It is interesting to digress on the consequences of raising the city. Where vacant lots existed, they were filled to the new level. A few old frame buildings were torn down, and the lots filled. It proved relatively easy to raise frame buildings to the new level, if the owners could afford it. The city's newer buildings were brick and stone, however, and they were constructed on the old level. These newer buildings would not be torn down, and many of Chicago's homes and offices were left "in the hole." When new buildings and sidewalks were constructed on the new level, Chicago increasingly became a city built on two levels, a fact which caused some inconvenience. Additionally, for many years some sewers lay wholly above the ground, at the same level as or higher than adjoining buildings.[27] Legal attempts to maintain the lower level were uniformly settled in favor of the city and its new level.[28]

Raising brick buildings proved to be a difficult proposition. George Pullman, who later became famous for his "Palace cars," devised and instituted a method to raise brick buildings.[29] Pullman first used his

Raising the Briggs House, a hotel at the corner of Randolph and Wells, 1857. Chicago Historical Society.

Women working on Damen Avenue in 1910, showing the city on two levels. Chicago Historical Society.

method in connection with the Erie Canal enlargement of the 1850s; so Chesbrough would have known that the problems concomitant with raising the city's grade were surmountable. The Tremont Hotel was the first brick building that Pullman raised in Chicago; he reportedly received $45,000 for the job. Soon his method was used to raise all Chicago's brick buildings. The method placed a building's foundation on a series of screws, and then, by simultaneously turning these screws, the entire building was lifted to the new, desired level. The work required years. No one knows the cost, but it has been estimated at $10 million.[30] At $45,000 per brick building, $10 million will raise over 200 buildings. This is probably an overestimate of the number of buildings raised, but the large number of other expenditures, including Chicago River dredging and legal expenses, suggest that $10 million may be an underestimate.

The city's raising was not entirely satisfactory. In many neighborhoods the sewers were so near the pavement that they were above the area's cellars. During heavy rainstorms, the water rose until the sewers were full. This plumbing arrangement allowed the filthy sewer water to run backwards; it ran from the sewer's high level to the adjoining cellar's low level. Some areas were so poor that they could not afford to raise area homes, and, as late as 1950, it was not uncommon to see a home that had steps leading down from the street to a lower-level door, or to see steps leading up to a second-floor door. Some have survived to this day.

The city on two levels, taken in 1968. Photo by Gustav Frank. Chicago Historical Society.

The sewage system was constructed substantially according to the 1855 report's recommendations, with two principal exceptions. First, the proposed Sixteenth Street flushing canal was never constructed, and, consequently, the South Branch of the Chicago River became quite polluted shortly after sewage was admitted into it. As early as 1858, however, Chicagoans began to realize the sewage disposal potentialities of the Illinois and Michigan Canal. The canal's pumps (see map 5) utilized Chicago River water to maintain the water level in the canal, and, by doing so, the pumps relieved a portion of the South Branch's pollution load. In 1863, the Board of Public Works issued Chesbrough's report on purifying the Chicago River. Chesbrough recommended the construction of the Fullerton Avenue and Sixteenth Street flushing canals and noted that the Illinois and Michigan Canal's effect served as a proxy to the probable effect of the proposed Sixteenth Street canal.[31] Therefore, although the Illinois and Michigan Canal's potentialities were realized, and Chesbrough argued in favor of using them, city officials evidently were not ready to pursue them completely in the early 1860s.[32]

Over time, the Illinois and Michigan Canal's pumps were used regularly to relieve the pollution load, the canal itself was deepened, and additional pumps were installed to increase the canal's capacity for handling sewage. Finally, the Sanitary District of Chicago was formed in 1889 for the express purpose of constructing a new and enlarged canal to service Chicago's sewage disposal needs. The through-cut steamboat canal, Chesbrough's fourth alternative, materialized over four decades later as the Chicago Sanitary District's Main Channel (see map 7 in Chapter 4).

The second exception to the original plan was the abandonment of continuous sewer flushing. Chesbrough developed a sixty-barrel capacity, wheeled flush tank which was drawn by four horses. One tankful poured into a manhole effectively flushed a sewer—"more effectively than a constant flow," Randolph claimed.[33] In later years an automatic flush tank was devised, but as late as 1940 horse-drawn tanks were still utilized for certain sewers in downtown Chicago.

In the short run, Chicago's decision to raise the city's grade, concomitant with sewer installation, was one which solved the drainage, waste disposal, and road building problems in the context of the city's existing topography and future necessities (see map 5). As it was, the selected alternative presented the city with the need to review the efficacy of Chesbrough's approach for several years thereafter. This was true because Chicago's continued growth made the discharged wastes a threat to the city's Lake Michigan water supply.

THE DEVELOPMENT OF CHICAGO'S SEWER SYSTEM

Approximately fifty-four miles of sewers were constructed under the Board of Sewage Commissioners' authority.[34] This figure is broken down by year in table 4. In 1861 the Board of Public Works was formed, and it incorporated the duties of the Board of Sewerage Commissioners, the Board of Water Commissioners, and other miscellaneous departments. E. S. Chesbrough was named Chief Engineer of the new board. Chesbrough inherited the "vicious circle" created by Lake Michigan's dual role as water supplier and, eventually, sewage disposer. Chesbrough's water-supply plan, adopted by the Board of Public Works in 1863, is the subject of the next chapter.

The first year in which sewer construction was under the Board of Public Works' control was 1861. During that year only one-half mile of sewer was laid, and three-fourths of that was the result of private efforts. The new board had no resources from which they could draw, and "suit was commenced against the Sewerage Commissioners for $58,882.84."[35] In 1862 almost three miles of brick sewers were laid, but the Sewerage Commissioners' funds were not yet available. The city's finances were "embarrassed" in 1863, but after that time sewer construction and the sewer system's growth progressed rapidly.

Table 4. *Sewer Construction, 1856–1861*

Year	Miles Constructed
1856	6.02
1857	4.86
1858	19.29
1859	10.45
1860	13.07
1861	0.53

Source: A. T. Andreas, *History of Chicago from the Earliest Period to the Present Time*, vol. 2, p. 65.
B. L. Pierce, *A History of Chicago*, vol. 2, pp. 330, 331.

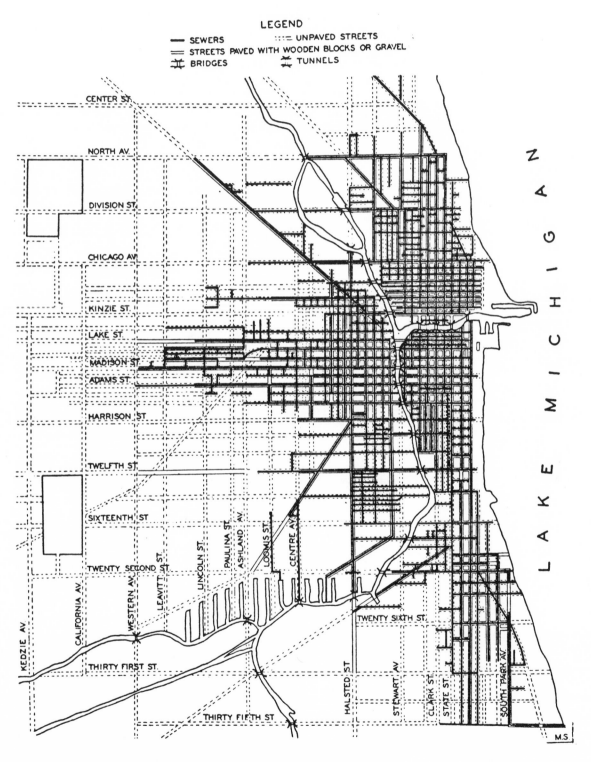

LEGEND

— SEWERS   ⋯⋯ UNPAVED STREETS
═ STREETS PAVED WITH WOODEN BLOCKS OR GRAVEL
⌶ BRIDGES   ⋈ TUNNELS

Chicago's sewerage system, 1873, before the Sanitary District of Chicago. From Homer Hoyt, *One Hundred Years of Land Values in Chicago.* Copyright 1933 by the University of Chicago.

Map 5.

The sewers were financed by special assessments and bond issues.[36] Bond issues were the more common method of financing, but the interest was high; in 1870, interest payments equalled ten miles of sewers. Some bonds found their way to the East, but, allegedly, most remained in the Chicago area. Despite the bonds' expense, the city preferred them to special assessments because they felt the latter "would be unjust taxation and inadequate to pay off the existing debt."[37] This position was manifested by a city council vote in February 1871. Two months later, the Illinois legislature passed a bill which allowed cities to tax real and personal property, suitably defined, up to

Table 5. *Sewer Construction, 1861–1871*

Year	Feet Constructed	Cost
1861	283,586	$ 665,188.46
1862	2,856	3,617.31
1863	15,676	57,264.51
1864	39,605	169,299.29
1865	25,021	87,221.48
1866	29,948	137,643.02
1867	48,127	225,564.53
1868	89,661	416,730.51
1869	47,841	197,152.92
1870	139,705	654,141.26
1871	78,166	258,664.70
Total	800,192	$2,872,487.99

800,192 feet = 151.52[+] miles.

Source: A. T. Andreas, *History of Chicago from the Earliest Period to the Present Time*, vol. 2, p. 65.

Table 6. *Sewer Construction, 1871–1884*

Year	Feet Constructed	Cost
1871*	50,716	$ 153,295.36
1872	47,342	173,255.76
1873	146,702	450,222.90
1874	222,322	587,507.38
1875	120,971	342,932.89
1876	15,248	79,545.28
1877	64,666	291,829.63
1878	88,031	37,264.97
1879	145,381	130,840.50
1880	79,128	92,544.08
1881	132,076	452,310.06
1882	98,515	224,450.16
1883	75,364	232,084.33
1884	101,547	258,020.91
Total	1,388,009	$3,506,104.21

1,388,009 feet = 262.8[+] miles.

*1871 data in table 5 include construction and improvements.

Source: A. T. Andreas, *History of Chicago from the Earliest Period to the Present Time*, vol. 3, p. 135.

one mill per dollar for sewer construction, thereby relieving some of the board's financial difficulty. More information on the financing of the sewer system can be found in Appendix 1.

Table 5 summarizes sewer construction and expenditures for the period between 1861, when the Board of Public Works assumed responsibility, and 1871, the year of the great Chicago Fire. The 1861 figure includes the total construction and costs incurred by the Board of Sewerage Commissioners. Figures for the following years give the construction and expenditure during the preceding year.

The Chicago Fire did comparatively light damage to the sewer system. The principal difficulties encountered were injuries to manhole and catchbasin covers, and the extra expenses that were needed to clean sewers and basins, which were fouled by lime deposits and other debris from the burned buildings. The estimated loss to the sewer system was $42,000.[38] Table 6 summarizes sewer construction and expenditures for the period between 1871 and 1884. In 1861 Chicago had approximately 54 miles of sewers whose discharge threatened the city's Lake Michigan water supply. In the next quarter century this figure increased over eight-fold, and still the sewers discharged into the Chicago River and Lake Michigan.

NOTES

1. A. T. Andreas, *History of Chicago from the Earliest Period to the Present Time,* 1:190.

2. "Up from the Mud: An Account of How Chicago's Streets and Buildings were Raised," compiled by Workers of the Writer's Program, W.P.A., in Illinois for Board of Education, 1941.

3. Bessie Louise Pierce, *A History of Chicago,* 2:318.

4. Chicago's charter gave the city council the power to build and maintain streets within one mile of the city's center. Ditches that sloped toward the river were dug at the sides of the streets in an attempt to drain them.

5. "Up from the Mud." See also Pierce, *History of Chicago,* 2:317. The most famous reference to roving bands of pigs is Mrs. Frances Trollope's experience in Cincinnati, set down in her *Domestic Manners of the Americans,* ed. Donald Smalley (New York: Alfred A. Knopf, 1949), p. 39.

6. Andreas, *History of Chicago,* 1:190. See also Pierce, *A History of Chicago,* 1:348.

7. Andreas, *History of Chicago,* 1:190. Sidewalk construction was also subject to assessment.

8. George A. Soper, John D. Watson, and Arthur J. Martin, *A Report to the Chicago Real Estate Board on the Disposal of the Sewage and Protection of the Water Supply of Chicago, Illinois* (hereafter *CREB Report*), 1915, p. 68.

9. Andreas, *History of Chicago,* 1:190. See also Pierce, *A History of Chicago,* 2:317.

10. Quoted in Andreas, *History of Chicago,* 1:190.

11. Andreas, *History of Chicago,* 1:190.

12. *Gem of the Prairie,* August 1850.

13. This is the same man who played a crucial role in the city's major water supply decision eight years later. See Louis P. Cain, "Ellis Sylvester Chesbrough and Chicago's First Sanitation System," *Technology and Culture,* July 1972, pp. 353–72, for a discussion of Chesbrough's sources and the contribution of other non-Chicagoans. Many of the problems experienced later with this plan are attributable to utilizing traditional engineering technology under inappropriate conditions.

14. G. P. Brown, *Drainage Channel and Waterway* (Chicago: R. R. Donnelley & Sons, Co., 1884), p. 53.

15. *Report and Plan of Sewerage for the City of Chicago, Illinois,* adopted by the Board of Sewerage Commissioners, 31 December 1855 (hereafter *1855 Report*).

16. Langdon Pearse, "Chicago's Quest for Potable Water," *Water and Sewage Works,* May 1955, reprinted, p. 3.

17. *1855 Report.* Also quoted in Andreas, *History of Chicago,* 1:191.

18. *CREB Report,* p. 72. See also Pearse, "Chicago's Quest," p. 3.

19. *CREB Report,* p. 72. See also Pearse, "Chicago's Quest," p. 3.

20. G. P. Brown, *Drainage Channel and Waterway,* p. 53.

21. *1855 Report.* Also quoted in Brown, *Drainage Channel and Waterway,* p. 55, and *CREB Report,* p. 72.

22. *1855 Report.* See also Andreas, *History of Chicago,* 1:191.

23. R. Isham Randolph, "The History of Sanitation in Chicago," *Journal of the Western Society of Engineers,* October 1939, p. 229; Richard S. Kirby and Philip G. Laurson, *The Early Years of Modern Civil Engineering* (New Haven: Yale University Press, 1932), p. 234; and George W. Rafter and M. N. Baker, *Sewage Disposal in the United States* (New York: D. Van Nostrand Co., 1894), pp. 169–70.

24. *CREB Report,* p. 69.

25. Ibid., p. 70.

26. Ibid., p. 70. See also "Up from the Mud."

27. Randolph, "Sanitation in Chicago," p. 229.

28. "Up from the Mud."

29. Ibid.

30. Wendt and Kogan, *Give the Lady What She Wants* (Chicago: Rand McNally, 1952), p. 57. Wendt and Kogan do not say how they arrived at this number, and it is not referenced.

31. Nevertheless, in 1863, the Board of Public Works issued a report on purifying the Chicago River. *Second Annual Report of the Board of Public Works to the Common Council of the City of Chicago,* 1 April 1863. This is discussed in Brown, *Drainage Channel and Waterway,* chap. 6.

32. The evidence that the canal was capable of handling sewage is found in Chesbrough, "Report of the results of Examinations made in Relation to Sewerage in several European Cities, in the winter of 1856–57," published in Chicago by the Board of Sewerage Commissioners, 1858, p. 94.

33. Randolph, "Sanitation in Chicago," p. 231.

34. Pierce, *A History of Chicago,* 2:330, 331. Andreas, *History of Chicago,* 2:65.

35. Andreas, *History of Chicago,* 2:65.

36. Pierce, *A History of Chicago,* 2:331.

37. Ibid.

38. Andreas, *History of Chicago,* 3:134.

3

The Water Supply Decision of 1863

In the beginning, Chicago's water was supplied by individual initiative and private enterprise, but, eventually, the need for a public waterworks was recognized. The public water supply of the 1850s was pumped from an inlet basin at the foot of Chicago Avenue, 3,000 feet from the Chicago River's mouth. The city was growing rapidly, both in population and industry, and soon there were loud complaints about the public water supply. By 1860, Chicago was a city of over 100,000 people, where almost 2,000 head of cattle, sheep, and hogs were slaughtered daily.[1]

Lake Michigan was contaminated some distance from shore by the influx of these pollutants. In 1860 the lake was contaminated some distance from the shore, and the city's waterworks pumped this contaminated water into the main distribution system. As cold weather approached, millions of tiny minnows sought the warmth of the waterwork's breakwater. As a consequence, these fish made their way, with the water, into the city reservoirs. Every drop of water was highly flavored with fish. One was obliged to look twice to make sure that his water glass did not contain a minnow, alive and swimming around. These minnows proved to be a tremendous problem. Housewives sometimes found it impossible to keep the fish out of the cooking pot, and many a dish had "an unwanted piscatorial flavor." Even the temperate were ready to cook with beer, as opposed to water. Bathing was considered a fisherman's pastime. Milk often tasted fishy. There was one dubious benefit: a liquor dealer accused of watering-down his supply was caught when bottles he offered for sale were found to contain pickled minnows.

When the wind blew from the west or southwest, "fetid accumulations from the slaughter houses, tanneries, distilleries, and glue factories" were pushed into the lake, where they combined with the minnows to supply Chicagoans "a brackish, glutinous, dirty, odoriferous fluid," which was considered "fit only for the purposes of cleansing the dirtiest of Augaean stables."[2]

Further, the average Chicagoan in 1860 didn't possess even this questionable benefit. He used the backyard pump, and like the original wells that provided the city's first water supplies, these were dug ten to twelve feet deep into the sand and clay.[3] Excrements were emptied into privy vaults sunk into the same soil, often in close proximity to the water wells. The vaults were seldom tight. Dishwater and other refuse were commonly thrown on the individual premises. Therefore, it is not surprising that these supplies were often contaminated. Cholera and dysentery were frequent problems, and the advice that

Water Supply of early Chicago.

A water supply cart of the 1840s. Chicago Historical Society.

bathing and clean clothes were an effective preventive frequently fell on helpless ears.[4] It was clear that waterworks improvements were necessary.

THE BACKGROUND

Chicago's first effort to obtain a water supply was in 1834 when the city expended $95.50 to dig a public well. Chicagoans, however, favored the Lake Michigan supply over well water and that which could be obtained from the sluggish Chicago River. Some citizens traveled daily to Lake Michigan for a pail of lake water. Private enterprise, in the form of water carts, helped satisfy a part of the demand for water. These carts customarily were horse-drawn, two-wheeled contraptions that held a large keg. The waterman would back his cart into the lake, fill the keg with a pail, and then deliver water door to door. The price of cart water varied between five and ten cents per barrel, depending on the competition. Eventually this method was considered too primitive, and Chicagoans demanded more modern waterworks.

The principal disadvantage of a Lake Michigan water supply was its physical quality. The greater mineral content or hardness of the ground water was accepted in some contexts because of the impurities in the lake supply; however, the costs of a hard water supply are generally greater.[5] This was important for Chicago's industrial development. In several cases, industrial concerns found it necessary to supply their own water, but this would have been true no matter which supply had been selected. Lake Michigan water is rated as moderately hard; yet few communities with ground water supplies shifted to the lake supply. Municipal softening was just as scarce. As such, these communities incurred additional costs from using the harder ground water supplies.

In the 1920s many Chicagoans employed their own rainwater cisterns or softeners. The annual cost of a cistern, all things included, was around $30 a year, and a softener was around $35 a year. This was a much larger amount than the average individual then paid for lake water. In one town a merchant reported commercial home water softener sales fell from 180 cans the week preceding the start of municipal softening to 14 cans the following week. Consequently, there was a strong impetus to use Lake Michigan as the water supply, because its water was softer than the available ground supplies. It was estimated that in the 1930s, due to the physical quality of Lake Michigan's water, Chicagoans spent $5 million annually for bottled drinking water and an additional $1 million for the operation and maintenance of private filters. It was concurrently estimated that Chicago's total annual cost for public water filtration would not be substantially greater than the $6 million spent for bottled water and private filtration.[6] Before the 1930s ended, the first step toward public filtration was taken, but that was not a concern in 1860. The point is that there was good reason to prefer the Lake Michigan water supply. Whether or not Chicagoans of the 1850s and 1860s could accurately judge hardness is a moot point. It is fair to argue that they could discern that Lake Michigan water was softer and, therefore, the less expensive of the two alternatives on that basis.

In January 1836, the Illinois legislature passed a special act incorporating the Chicago Hydraulic Company.[7] Its capital stock was limited to $250,000, with the charter to run for seventy years. The incorporating act permitted the company to construct mains through city streets without obtaining the consent of Chicago's trustees. The company was given four years to construct the necessary works. The Panic of 1837, which disrupted so many other projects, postponed construction until 1840, and it was not until 1842 that the works were finally operative. This delay led some citizens to hope that the city would take advantage of newly granted powers and care for its own water supply.[8] When the Chicago Hydraulic Company's initial supply was considered remarkably pure and transparent, the public water supply question was dropped for the time being.[9]

A twenty-five horsepower engine ran the pumping works which were located at the foot of Lake Street; the eighteen-inch diameter inlet pipe extended seven hundred feet into Lake Michigan. The works were capable of pumping twenty-five barrels of water per minute, thirty-five feet above the lake level. Two 7,250 barrel reservoirs were planned, but only one was included in the company's calculation of approximately $24,000 in total expenses. Several miles of six-inch diameter pinewood logs, bound with iron hoops, were laid as mains, and these appeared to be still functional twenty-five years later when sewer and iron water-main excavation took place.

The Chicago Hydraulic Company published its rates in the spring of 1842. They ranged from $10 a year for a private family of five persons or less, to between $15 and $125 a year for a private boarding-house, "provided that no bath or bath houses shall be annexed to, or connected therewith." From $50 to $200 a year was the tavern and hotel rate. Lastly, the company charged up to $500 a year for large manufacturing requirements. The pipes between the Hydraulic Company's mains and a supplied building were additional.[10]

In 1842 James Long offered the Chicago Hydraulic Company an arrangement by which he would attend to the company's pumping operations for ten years without cost to the company, in exchange for the free use of their engine's surplus power. Their mutual agreement proved profitable to both parties. Long used the pump's excess power to erect the "Hydraulic Mills" on the corner of Lake Street and Michigan Avenue. The building, which cost about $12,000, did a good milling business. When new waterworks were constructed in 1853, the milling enterprise was abandoned.[11]

Expectations for a pure water supply were not realized in the 1840s, or even the 1850s. In 1845, the Chicago Hydraulic Company was joined by a second private, state-chartered water company. This second company, the Lake Michigan Hydraulic Company, enjoyed the same freedoms that the state legislature had given its competitor. The Lake Michigan Hydraulic Company's charter was limited to supplying water to Chicago's north division, but the company never did supply water. During the fall of 1847 the Chicago Hydraulic Company's supply was particularly polluted. The city's agent, Philip Dean, had the waterworks cleaned and repaired; however, Chicagoans already held the opinion that little could be accomplished unless the intake pipe was extended farther into Lake Michigan. The intake pipe, as originally laid, was some three or four feet below the lake's surface; however, in 1842–1843, Lake Michigan had receded so far that a south wind could leave the intake pipe's lake end out of the water.[12]

The matter became an important topic in Chicago's conversation. In the spring of 1848 the Chicago press was editorially active in condemning the "primitive system of supply under which the city was suffering." Parenthetically, a cholera epidemic began the next year. The Chicago Mechanics' Institute referred the problem to a committee which was to develop a plan for obtaining an unpolluted lake water supply.

The Mechanic's Institute committee report was presented in May 1848. It proposed that pipe be laid three feet below Lake Michigan's low-water mark. The pipe was to extend between a point in the lake sufficient to avoid muddy water and a point on Chicago's western boundary. The pipe was to be laid down the middle of First Street, and lateral branches constructed where alternative streets crossed. The wooden pipes were estimated to cost $2,000 per mile. The committee proposed that the pipe be extended into twenty feet of water, where a ten-foot elbow pipe would be attached. At such a point water could be

drawn which would avoid both floating impurities and bottom distur-
bances. The drawn water would be deposited in two 20,000 cubic-foot
reservoirs. The water would be deposited in one reservoir, then tapped
at the top of the first and deposited at the bottom of the second
through an elbow connection. Finally, the city's water supply would be
drawn from the top of the second reservoir. By comparison, the Chicago Hydraulic Company's works deposited into their reservoirs 28,000
cubic feet of water every twelve hours. This water was drawn from the
bottom of the lake, poured into the top of the reservoir, and taken from
the bottom, replete with sediment.

In addition to poor water quality, other forces were at work to end
the Chicago Hydraulic Company's corporate existence. A portion of
the South Side, a smaller portion of the West Side, and almost none of
the North Side were being supplied with water. The rest of the city was
still dependent on private wells or the waterman and his cart. Chicago's poorer citizens were not able to avail themselves of even these
niceties and drew their water supply by the bucketful from the polluted
Chicago River. It was estimated that not more than one-fifth of Chicago was being supplied by the city's only operative supplier, the Chicago Hydraulic Company. For a large and rapidly growing city this was a
serious situation; the general health of the population was suffering.
The cholera epidemic of the early 1850s originated in wells contaminated by sewage leaks from privy vaults. One reason for the public
company was to make Lake Michigan the only water supply source,
thus ending the dependence on polluted ground water and river water.
A second reason for the public company was that it was expected to
guarantee a water supply for fire fighting.

In April 1850, Chicagoans moved into action. A meeting was held
to devise a scheme by which the city could obtain pure and whole-
some water. These efforts led to a state act in February 1851, which
incorporated the Chicago City Hydraulic Company and provided for a
Board of Water Commissioners.[13] In July 1851 an enumeration was
made of the first buildings in which water pipes would be laid. This was
an attempt on the commissioners' part to justify the expense of the
planned construction. Water was to be taken from Lake Michigan, 600
feet east of the Chicago Avenue beach. Three reservoirs were required, one for each of the city's geographic sections. The water would
travel from the inlet pipe to a well inside the engine house. This building was to be located on the beach and was to contain a 170-horse-
power noncondensing engine. The pipes were to be iron; the reservoirs were to be iron tanks. This plan was based on the assumption
that Chicago's 1875 population would be 162,000. In fact, by 1875
there was a population of 408,000 tributary to Chicago's waterworks.
The estimated cost of $570,000 included forty-eight miles of iron distri-
bution pipe, sufficient to supply 100,000 people. The total estimated
collections for the first complete year's operation were $37,366. The
system was considered ample to provide for future growth, and was
considered by many to be extravagant. Chicago's second waterworks
were constructed as planned, but the plans underestimated Chicago's
future needs.

The water commissioners went to New York and marketed $400,000 in bonds. The first loan, $250,000 payable in twenty years, was negotiated in April 1852. By June 1852 the demand for these bonds, "the Chicago City Six's," was quickly exhausting the dealer's supply. The rate was advanced to 97 1/2, plus accrued interest, and it was claimed that the bonds sold faster than the city officers could execute and forward them.[14] Two additional loans were negotiated in April and August 1855; $361,280 was realized from the sale of $400,000, 6 percent, twenty-five-year bonds.[15]

Construction began in the summer of 1852. The new works were located on the North Side at the Chicago Avenue beach. During 1852, the pump well was built, a portion of the thirty-inch wooden inlet pipe was laid, and the foundations were laid for the building and tower. During 1853 the building and tower were completed, and several attempts were made to complete laying the inlet pipe. This pipe had been designed to extend 600 feet into the lake and terminate in a wooden crib, but the lake proved too rough and prohibited securing the crib. Consequently, efforts to do so were abandoned. The water that was pumped came from a pipe close to the shore. In the fall the standpipe and the condensing and noncondensing engines were erected. The condensing engine was put into operation in December 1853, and the Chicago City Hydraulic Company first supplied Chicago in February 1854.

For the first four months water was supplied nine hours a day. None was supplied on Sunday, except when a fire necessitated pumping. After July 1854, water was pumped twenty-four hours a day. There were few customers and no reservoir; water was allowed to run wasted through the fire hydrants in order to keep the small engine running.

The old hydraulic company did not allow the public company to commence operations without a fight. The Chicago Hydraulic Company claimed they held exclusive rights, and that these rights would have to be purchased. The older company claimed that without their then-current water-rent the new company's revenue estimates would be smaller by $15,000 yearly.

The Chicago Hydraulic Company was not opposed to the Chicago City Hydraulic Company. It showed the city the advantages that could be gained by purchasing their works. Nevertheless, the Chicago Hydraulic Company intimated that unless matters could be settled, in the manner which they suggested, an injunction would be sought to prohibit the construction of the Chicago City Hydraulic Company's new works.

In 1853 the Chicago Hydraulic Company requested an injunction, which the court denied. Finally, the matter was settled when the city agreed to purchase the older company's franchise for $15,000 plus interest, to be paid on 1 May 1855. The transfer evidently didn't take place as quickly as had been planned, because, in 1855, the state legislature extended the Chicago Hydraulic Company's corporate powers until such time when its affairs could be concluded.

Early in 1856, water pumping was approaching the engine's maximum capacity. Plans were made to replace the original engine with a larger one. A contract was reached, and the second engine was constructed, installed, and operating by July 1857. The original engine had a daily capacity of 7 million gallons and cost (engine and one boiler) $24,500. The second engine had a daily capacity of 13 million gallons and cost (engine and two boilers) $59,000.[16] These latter costs take into consideration the fact that some engine parts were constructed to conform with the building's contour. The water tower's position was such that the valve gear, customarily the front of the engine, was placed on the side to avoid cutting into the tower.

In December 1853, water was pumped into the pipes to test them, and the first hydrant was opened (near the North Clark Street bridge). North and West Side residents were granted the first permits to draw water from the distribution pipes. By 1 May 1857 the works were supplying 7,053 buildings with water, and had annual receipts of $85,012. The company established a rate structure based on anticipated demand. Private homes paid the lowest rate, with boardinghouses, hotels, and manufacturing firms following in order of increasing rates. The rates apparently reflected the average cost of supplying water. The finances for the first four years are summarized in table 7. More information on the financing of the water system can be found in Appendix 1.

Table 7. *Chicago City Hydraulic Company "Finances," 1854–1857*

Year	Cost of Works	Operation Expense and Interest	Revenue
1854	$393,045.32	$38,128.51	$26,808.50
1855	496,849.64	59,051.27	54,739.19
1856	641,509.93	73,087.23	76,806.36
1857	738,436.51	85,170.61	97,008.55

Source: A. T. Andreas, *History of Chicago from the Earliest Period to the Present Time*, vol. 1, p. 189.

As noted earlier, the Board of Water Commissioners was absorbed into the new Board of Public Works in 1861. The new board's chief engineer, E. S. Chesbrough, inherited the water supply problem in addition to his sewerage responsibilities. Chesbrough's water supply plan, adopted by the board in 1863, was as unique and imaginative as his sewage disposal plan.[17] The presence of Chesbrough in these deliberations and the merger of the Sewerage and Water Commissioners into a Board of Public Works are evidence that Chicago was beginning to recognize the interdependence of water supply and sewage disposal problems.

THE RESEARCH

In 1859 one of Chicago's Water Commissioners "proposed to sink a wrought iron pipe . . . one mile out into the lake, to obtain the supply from a point which could not be affected by the river."[18] Chesbrough was asked to study and report on this plan, and to do the same on "erecting additional pumping works, in such locality as shall secure a supply of pure water." His report discussed several possible methods without making a specific recommendation; however, even at this early date he considered a tunnel under the lake to be the most desirable alternative.

Shortly after its formation in 1861, the Board of Public Works adopted as its goal the acquisition of an unpolluted water supply. Consequently, the board requested Chesbrough to make a canvass of the various water-supply possibilities and to investigate several filtration methods. Chesbrough dismissed the existing filtration methods as inadequate; his studied opinion was that the tunnel method was the most desirable:

> The engineer of the Board [E. S. Chesbrough], after much doubt and careful examination of the whole subject, became more inclined to the tunnel plan than any other, as combining great directness to the nearest inexhaustible supply of pure water, with permanency of structure and ease of maintenance. The probability of meeting insuperable difficulties in the nature of soil, or storms, or ice on the lake, were fully considered. One by one the objections appeared to be overcome, either by providing against them, or discovering that they had no real foundation.[19]

Chesbrough continued to explore the tunnel alternative's potential, and when he had worked out the details, a tunnel proposal was submitted to several engineers, all of whom considered the tunnel plan to be feasible. Nevertheless, the 1861 board was against adopting the project. After a new board was elected in 1863, and additional soil examinations had been made, the tunnel plan was favorably reported to the Chicago City Council, which accepted it and submitted it to competitive bid. The board reported that

> . . . what is most to be desired by the city, is that the supply should be drawn from the deep water of the lake, two miles out from the present water works . . .
> The careful investigation of the subject has satisfied us sufficiently to say, that with our present knowledge, we consider it practicable to extend a tunnel of five feet diameter the required distance under the bed of the lake, the mouth or inlet to such a conduit being the outmost shaft, protected by a pier [crib], which will be used in the construction of the tunnel.[20]

In their 1863 report, the Board of Public Works noted that three alternatives had been considered, any one of which would have afforded Chicago a healthier and better protected water supply. These three, with cost estimates in parentheses, were: (1) a two-mile lake tunnel ($307,552 exclusive of a lighthouse); (2) a filtering or settling basin ($300,575); and (3) a one-mile lake tunnel located five miles to the north ($380,000).[21] The board had two principal objections to the second alternative. First, they commented:

> For settling and filtering the water from sediment, we are of the opinion that the basin would be found effective, and would continue to be so, but that for filtration it is not safe to rely upon it. There have been filtering basins of this character in other places. Some of them appear to have continued to work during long use, and others have failed and become useless.[22]

Second, the board objected to the basin scheme because the water supply intake would still be in the shallow water close to shore and would not be located in a deeper point where the water was considered to be better. The policy of attempting to avoid pollution by taking the water from a distant lake point is a common one. Lakefront cities are forced to consider alternatives which will minimize the interdependencies created by using the lake for both water supply and sewage disposal. Chicago adopted that policy in making this decision and adhered to it until further extensions of the intake point were no longer feasible. For example, by 1915, the desirable depth for a water intake was fifty feet, but this would have placed the intake point ten to fifteen miles from shore.[23]

Chesbrough's 1863 report, included in the board's report, acknowledged that the board had considered the three most promising alternatives that provided the city with a pure water supply and had rejected one; he (Chesbrough) was to assess the remaining two. Almost immediately he dismissed any project that required moving the existing waterworks, such as the board's third alternative.

> Other projects, such as erecting new pumping works at Winnetka, or going to Crystal Lake and bringing a supply thence by simple gravitation, as is done for the cities of New York, Boston, Baltimore, and Albany, have been considered, but their great cost, as compared with that of obtaining an abundant supply of good and wholesome water at points much nearer the city, is deemed a sufficient apology for not discussing their details here.[24]

Chesbrough concerned himself only with those alternatives that would bring water from a point two miles east of the existing Chicago Avenue Water Works, and there were two of these:

> Of the plans proposed for obtaining water from the lake, where it will be free from not only the wash of the shore, but from the effects of the river, two classes only have been considered: one, an *iron pipe with flexible joints; and the other, a tunnel under the bottom of the lake.*[25]

Although the cost of the iron-pipe project ($250,000) was slightly less than the tunnel project, ($307,552), Chesbrough chose between them on other than an initial cost basis:

> In consequence of the possibility of such a pipe being injured, by anchors, by the sinking of a heavily loaded vessel over it, or by the effect of an unusual current in the lake moving it from its place, it has been thought preferable to attempt the construction of a tunnel under the bottom of the lake.[26]

His research had convinced him that the tunnel's construction would be less difficult than was generally supposed. Lill and Diversey's brewery, adjacent to the waterworks, was the site of artesian borings which showed that, between 25 and 100 feet deep, the ground at the lakeshore was a clay that was also found on the lake bottom where the water was 25 feet deep. A tunnel easily could be constructed in this type of clay, if it were continuous. Chesbrough was confident that the clay was continuous, but he admitted he was uncertain whether beds of sand might not be interspersed with the clay.

Other alternatives had been considered, such as extending the intake one mile into the lake or building a one-mile lake tunnel, but they were not deemed as favorable as the same projects with the intake point two miles in the lake.[27] Apparently a pure water supply was the principal objective; cost entered only as a constraining factor.

This impression is furthered by the Public Works Commissioners' actions when they opened the tunnel project bids. Submitting this project to competitive bid was unusual, since work of this type had never been attempted, and it is doubtful that any contractor could have given a realistic estimate of his construction costs. The commissioners must have realized this, because they elected not to award the contract to the lowest bidder, but rather to a contractor in whom they had confidence. In short, the commissioners were concerned primarily that quality construction be done and that the finished works provide Chicagoans an unpolluted water supply.

As noted, the sewerage decision of 1855 was made with little regard for water supply considerations. The question which then arises concerns the effect that the sewerage decision played on the water supply decision. Chesbrough's sewer system appears to have been chosen, at least partially, on a least-cost basis. In the water supply decision of 1863 cost did not appear to be the deciding factor. The decision was made as to which alternative, with a realistic cost, offered the purest, and best protected, water supply subject to the constraint presented by Chesbrough's sewerage system. It can be asserted that, after their initial experiences, the commissioners became aware that economizing on these public works actually might increase the city's total cost through a greater incidence of disease and various attempts to circumvent the city's polluted water supply. Contemporary writers in appraising any improvement in the water supply-sewage disposal-drainage strategy would invariably recite cholera statistics as a leading indicator of the improvement's effectiveness. Industry could either dig ground wells and purify the water to suit their own needs, or they could avoid the area altogether. Private homes could either boil the city's water, purchase bottled water, or dig their own wells. The average citizen, however, was stuck with the existing water supply.

There is, therefore, a strong suggestion that the commissioners, voting in the aftermath of the sewerage decision, moved to minimize the total social cost of the water supply decision, as opposed to the total monetary cost as had been done in the sewerage decision eight years earlier.[28] The objective of the earlier decision, drainage and waste disposal, entered the latter decision as a constraint; in turn, the objective of the latter decision, a pure water supply, became a constraint in all future decisions.

THE ADOPTED APPROACH

The 1863 Board of Public Works plan, approved by Chicago's Common Council, was to secure a pure water supply by constructing a two-mile lake tunnel and drawing the water from there (see map 6). As conceived, the task was to dig a shaft near the lake shore to a depth significantly below the lake bottom and then burrow eastward toward the intake point. At the intake point, a similar shaft was to be dug, and

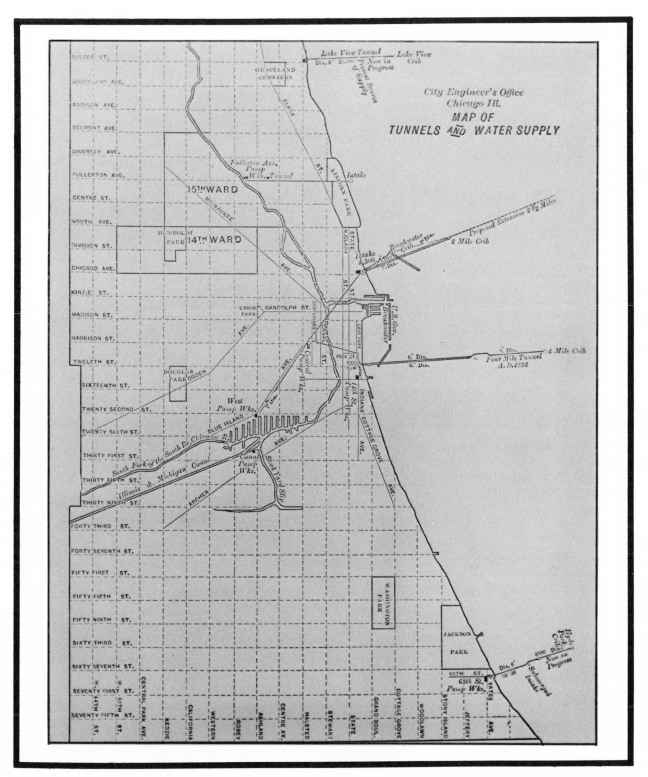

Chicago's water supply system in 1892. The 2 Mile Crib and Tunnel were erected as part of Chesbrough's 1863 water supply system. Chicago Historical Society.

Map 6.

Chicago's waterworks, 1865, prior to the completion of the water tower. Chicago Historical Society.

workers starting at that point were to burrow westward. A crib would be installed at the intake point to house workers during construction, aid in repairs, and protect the tunnel system where the water supply intake was to be located. As noted, bids had been requested and were opened on 9 September 1863.[29] The contract was awarded to a well-known engineering firm, Duel and Gowan of Harrisburg, Pennsylvania, for a bid of $315,139. Although theirs was not the lowest bid, Duel and Gowan assumed all risks. In October 1863, the Common Council granted all necessary authority for constructing the tunnel and ordered that the requisite bonds be issued. The contract specified that the work should be completed by 1 November 1865, but this was to be a far more complex project than had been imagined. The last stone would not be laid until a year after the contracted completion date.

The main shaft, nine feet in diameter, was located on the Chicago City Hydraulic Company's site, at the Chicago Avenue beach. The original plan called for this shaft to be sixty-nine feet deep with brick walls; however, "shifting quicksand" a few feet below the shore level required that an iron shaft be sunk for the first twenty-six feet.[30] A building was erected over the shore shaft, which contained an office, a toolshed, and a powerful steam engine. An elevator was constructed inside the shaft to transport construction workers and remove excavated clay. When water began to ooze through the bottom, a pump, run by the steam engine, was employed to dry the shaft. Later this became the pumping station, a building that still stands, even though subsequent landfill to the east has placed it several blocks inland. The lake end was fixed by soundings, and the spot marked with buoys.

The engineering problem was to connect the shore and lake points by a straight line, sixty-nine feet below the surface of Lake Michigan. Contemporary compasses could not be used, since local attraction rendered them inaccurate below ground level. To a worker in the tunnel, the only place where the direction of the line drawn between the two shafts could be observed was at the top of either shaft. Consequently, when the engineers attempted to run the tunnel axis parallel to this imaginary line, they ran into difficulties that affected the turn from shaft to tunnel.[31]

When the iron cylinder lake shaft was completed, workers were lowered to begin burrowing westward to meet with the other workers burrowing eastward. The tunnel was sloped two feet per mile from the lake end to the shore so that it could be emptied should repairs prove necessary; the water would be shut off at the lake end. Although the methods were primitive (the tunnel was dug entirely by manual labor), it was claimed that the workers caused the two tunnel sections to meet within one inch of achieving a perfectly smooth wall.[32]

Only two men could excavate at one time. Work was performed on a twenty-four-hour basis; fourteen to twenty feet was considered a good day's work. A large bellows attached to perforated stove pipe provided ventilation. Rails were laid to transport the excavated clay. At first, the carts were propelled by the workers, but as distances increased, two mules were trained, then lowered, to aid with this work.

No expense was spared in making the crib strong.[33] It was launched in June 1865 and tugged to its lake mooring. The cost was an estimated $100,000, which included the huge timbers and tons of iron used in its construction. This figure was much higher than would have been the case had construction not taken place during the Civil War. The materials used were in great demand and short supply. In fact, this crib was a structure as big as the original Palmer House. Forty and one-half feet high, it was pentagonal, with a diameter of ninety-eight and one-half feet. When the crib was in place, it was loaded with stones, except for the center compartment which the lake shaft occupied. Mitchell's marine mooring screws, used in the Thames River tunnels, had been imbedded in the lake bottom; cables connected the five crib corners to these screws. Consequently, the crib reached the lake's clay bottom, thirty-one feet below the surface.

The total estimated expenditure on the tunnel project was close to $600,000. This included the $100,000 expended on the crib, $55,000 for the new building constructed on the old waterworks' site; and

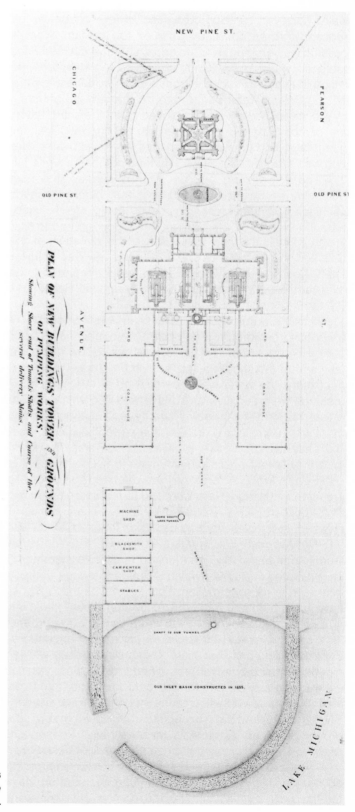

Plans for shore buildings, Chesbrough's waterworks. From *8th Annual Report of the Board of Public Works,* 1869. Chicago Historical Society.

$100,000 for a new engine which was capable of pumping 18 million gallons of water daily.[34]

All things considered, the first lake tunnel sufficed only until 1872. This tunnel demonstrated the feasibility of the approach, but a second tunnel was needed to provide the ever-increasing population with water. Chicago's population more than doubled in the decade of the 1860s and continued to grow at approximately that rate for the remainder of the 1800s. By 1914 the city's population was 2.40 million, and growing at an annual rate of 0.15 million.[35]

Provision for a second tunnel had been made when the first tunnel was constructed; the crib allowed space for a second connection. The two tunnels were constructed nearly parallel, at the same depth, sixty-three feet apart. The second tunnel was larger, seven feet wide and seven feet, two inches high. The first was five feet wide and five feet, two inches high. The contract price of the second tunnel was $29.50 per foot, slightly more than $310,000 for a two-mile tunnel.[36] Although this was close to the contract price of the first tunnel, the price of the second tunnel did not include the crib and other items which would not have to be duplicated.

The water was distributed from the pumping works through a system of mains and pipes; the force was obtained from the standpipe into which the engines lifted the water. This system also proved inadequate as the city grew. In order to overcome the water supply shortage in those sections of Chicago which were a significant distance from the original pumping works, it was decided to excavate a tunnel under the city. This tunnel went from the pumping works, at East Chicago Avenue and North Michigan Avenue, to a point on the Chicago River's South Branch near its intersection with West Twenty-second Street. Auxiliary pumping works were erected on the latter site to supply the southwest side with water. The cost of this tunnel was estimated at approximately $1 million, the most expensive project Chicago had ever undertaken.[37] Work on both the second lake tunnel and the city tunnel began in 1869. Parenthetically, it is interesting to note the following, written in 1874:

> This tunnel [under the city], it is expected, will complete for many years at least, the water system of Chicago. To say that it will be the most unique and perfect system in the world, will be only to corroborate the opinions of all scientific men on the subject.[38]

In fact, the next addition to Chicago's waterworks did not come for thirteen years.

The cost of the water system to 31 March 1869, including the expenditures for work in progress, was in excess of $3 million. These expenditures had been financed by bond issues totaling over $2.5 million, and by water rents—flat, yearly charges based on expected water use. In 1861, meters had been installed to monitor the water usage of large consumers. This practice was not unique to Chicago, and the practice of metering only large customers continues to this day in several cities, including Chicago. The rate structure of the Chicago Hydraulic Company ranged from $10 a year for a private family to

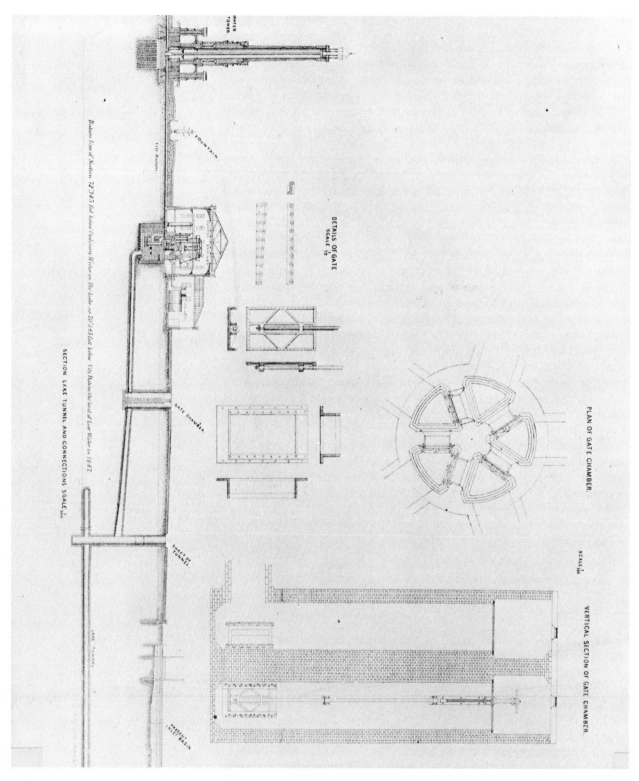

Cross-section of shore section, Chesbrough's waterworks. From *8th Annual Report of the Board of Public Works,* 1869. Chicago Historical Society.

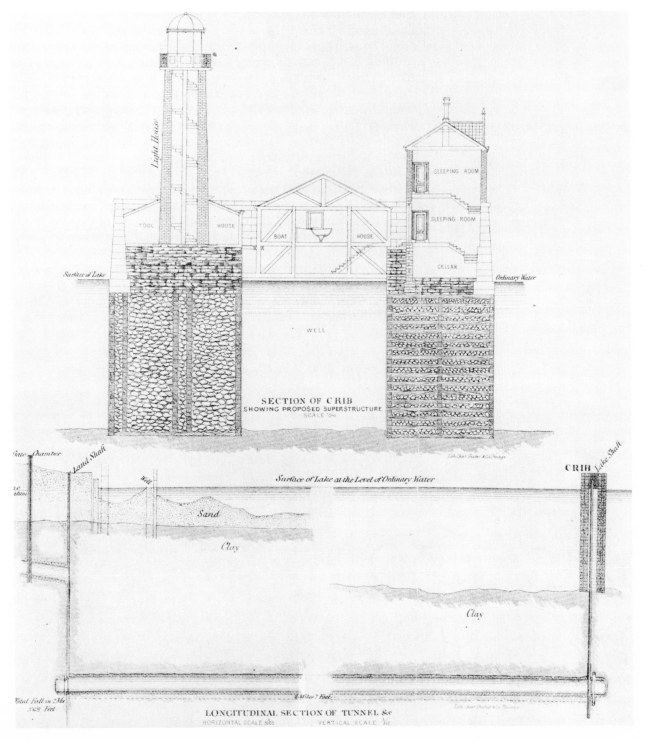

Plan of crib and tunnel, Chesbrough's waterworks. From *8th Annual Report of the Board of Public Works,* 1869. Chicago Historical Society.

$500 a year for a large manufacturer. Manufacturers quite likely used more than fifty times the amount of water of private families; hence manufacturers were subsidized. The use of water meters enabled the city to assess a charge for water use which more accurately reflected actual consumption than the broad classifications of the water rent structure. Yet if metered charges embodied lower rates for large consumers, there is a subsidy in this case as well. The use of meters helps make these subsidies more explicit and differentiates the subsidy by usage. Whether or not meters are used, water pricing and consumption appears to resemble a regressive tax; that is, the percentage of income spent on water declines as income increases. This appears to be true of both cases above and of a case where metered systems assess a flat minimum charge. To the extent that the principal and interest on bond issues were paid from property tax revenues, regression would still be present. To the extent they were paid from income taxes, the conclusion would be less clear. The impact of the rate structure, with and without meters, is a subject that needs considerably more study.

By April 1870, approximately 240 miles of water pipes were supplying Chicago. Operating expenses were $190,000; the cost of servicing the water debt was $200,000 a year. Water rents furnished $477,000 in revenue, which left an $87,000 surplus to provide for fu-

New Sixty-eighth Street water supply crib, 1908. Chicago Historical Society.

Exterior of the Sixty-eighth Street crib, 1916. Photo by Fred Fuller. Chicago Historical Society.

ture growth (see Appendix 1).[39] Tables 8 and 9 summarize the position of Chicago's water supply system prior to the Chicago Fire in 1871.

The fire caused considerable damage to the water system. The pumping works suffered extensive damage, but the Water Tower across the street was unharmed. While the walls of the pumping works escaped serious damage, the roof, floors, and other parts of the building were completely destroyed. The loss on machinery and buildings, principally buildings, totaled $75,000. The machine shop was almost a

Table 8. *Tax Assessments for Chicago's Waterworks System's Maintenance*

Year	Assessment
1862	$ 42,635.49
1863	46,493.67
1864	389,169.31
1865	103,576.35
1866	802,574.56
1867	317,206.18
1868	1,354,436.48
1869	2,395,683.03
1870	2,836,852.48
1871	2,359,835.89
Total	$10,648,463.44

Assessments made by the Board of Public Works. Their fiscal period ended on 1 April.

Source: A. T. Andreas, *History of Chicago from the Earliest Period to the Present Time*, vol. 2, p. 70.

The Chicago Water Tower with pumping works in the background, before 1871.
Chicago Historical Society.

Table 9. *Chicago Water System Statistics, 1858–1871*

Year	Daily Supply in Gallons	Daily Capacity of Works in Mil. Gal.	Revenue	Miles of Pipe Laid	Miles of Pipe in Use
1858	2,991,413	20	$102,179	—	72.4
1859	3,877,119	20	122,753	12.7	85.1
1860	4,703,525	20	131,162	5.9	91.0
1861	4,841,520	20	150,290	4.3	95.3
1862	6,074,739	20	150,920	9.6	104.9
1863	6,400,298	20	192,246	10.5	115.4
1864	6,913,259	20	224,902	11.9	127.3
1865	7,610,459	20	253,114	13.9	141.2
1866	8,681,536	20	302,017	11.0	152.2
1867	11,562,273	27	338,929	22.6	174.8
1868	14,724,999	35	420,686	33.8	208.6
1869	18,633,278	35	476,968	31.3	239.9
1870	21,766,260	35	539,180	32.5	272.4
1871	23,464,877	35	445,834	15.3	287.7

Source: A. T. Andreas, *History of Chicago from the Earliest Period to the Present Time,* vol. 2, p. 70.

A Statistical Supplement to the 1966 Annual Report of the Department of Water and Sewers, City of Chicago, p. 3.

total loss. Damage to the North and South Division reservoirs was sufficient to discontinue their use permanently. Fifteen thousand water service pipes melted, or were otherwise damaged, and this led to a serious water shortage. Vast amounts of water were wasted. The amount pumped during the six months ending 1 April 1872 was larger than that pumped during any previous six-month period, or for more than ten years thereafter. This wasted water cost the city almost $100,000; the entire loss was set at slightly less than $250,000. Additional trouble stemmed from the fact that the water books were lost, and a set of water maps, which outlined the location of water mains, and the detailed drawing of the lake tunnel were destroyed. The entire loss was set at $248,910.[40] Those portions of the system which were destroyed by the fire were quickly replaced. There were no significant changes in the water supply strategy after 1863, although the system was enlarged and improved. Chicago did not adopt filtration of the water supply until 1947. Before then the water was subjected only to settlement and, after 1912, chlorination.[41] The raising of the city with the construction of the sewer system during the 1850s solved the drainage problem. The interdependency between the water supply and sewage disposal problem was recognized in the water supply decision of 1863, but the water supply problem could not be termed solved in any final sense as long as sewage pollution threatened Lake Michigan. The 1863 decision was crucial, however, because in future years the conservation of the lake water supply was a constraint on sewage disposal decisions. In the evolution of Chicago's sanitation strategy, the water supply decision can be termed "solved" in 1863; thereafter, the city concentrated its efforts on the sewage disposal problem.

NOTES

1. George A. Soper, John D. Watson, and Arthur J. Martin, *A Report to the Chicago*

Real Estate Board on the Disposal of the Sewage and Protection of the Water Supply of Chicago, Illinois (hereafter *CREB Report*), 1915, p. 51.

2. Bessie Louise Pierce, *A History of Chicago,* 2:333.

3. *CREB Report,* p. 50.

4. Pierce, *A History of Chicago,* 2:333.

5. The costs associated with hard water supplies are well known. See Max R. White, *Water Supply Organization in the Chicago Region* (Chicago: University of Chicago Press, 1934), pp. 37–39. See also A. T. Andreas, *History of Chicago,* 1:185.

6. White, *Water Supply Organization,* pp. 34–43.

7. Pierce, *A History of Chicago,* 1:342.

8. Ibid., p. 352.

9. See Andreas, *History of Chicago,* 1:185.

10. The rates were quoted in Andreas, *History of Chicago,* 1:186, and Pierce, *A History of Chicago,* 1:352.

11. Andreas, *History of Chicago,* 1:186.

12. Andreas, *History of Chicago,* 1:186.

13. Andreas, *History of Chicago,* 1:186.

14. Ibid., p. 187.

15. Pierce, *A History of Chicago,* 2:322. This was consistent with the nineteenth section of the act incorporating the new water company.

16. Andreas, *History of Chicago,* 1:189.

17. Cain, "Ellis Sylvester Chesbrough and Chicago's First Sanitation System," *Technology and Culture,* July 1972, pp. 353–72.

18. G. P. Brown, *Drainage Channel and Waterway,* p. 32.

19. Reported in Brown, *Drainage Channel and Waterway,* p. 33.

20. *Second Annual Report of the Board of Public Works to the Common Council of the City of Chicago,* 1 April 1863 (hereafter the *1863 Report*), p. 5.

21. *1863 Report,* p. 9.

22. Ibid., p. 8.

23. *CREB Report,* p. 52.

24. *1863 Report,* p. 39.

25. Ibid.

26. Ibid., pp. 40, 41.

27. *CREB Report,* p. 51.

28. Social cost is an economic concept that measures the value of the best alternative resource utilization available to a society, as evaluated by that society. Social cost is distinguished from private cost, the value of the best alternative resource utilization available to a producer as evaluated by the producing firm. See, for example, R. G. Lipsey and P. O. Steiner, *Economics,* 3d ed. (New York: Harper & Row, 1972), pp. 221–29.

29. See J. M. Wing, *The Tunnels and Water System of Chicago* (Chicago: J. M. Wing and Co., 1874), p. 27.

30. Ibid., p. 31.

31. Ibid., p. 33.

32. Ibid., p. 76.

33. Ibid., p. 40.

34. Ibid., p. 80. See also Andreas, *History of Chicago,* 2:68, 69, and 3:133.

35. *CREB Report,* p. 30.

36. Wing, *The Tunnels and Water System of Chicago,* p. 93.

37. Ibid., p. 98.

38. Ibid., p. 99.

39. Pierce, *A History of Chicago,* 2:334. See also Appendix 1.

40. Andreas, *History of Chicago,* 3:133.

41. For more recent material on the Chicago water system, the best source is Carl W. Condit, *Chicago, 1910–1929,* pp. 16–18, 248, and *Chicago, 1930–1970,* (Chicago: University of Chicago Press, 1974), pp. 26–27, 45, 253–54, 267.

4
The Sewage Disposal Decision of 1886

By 1880 the sewage disposal problem was well defined: remove the sewage sediment from the Chicago River without its passing into Lake Michigan. The approach Chicago adopted discharged the sewage through the Illinois and Michigan Canal. In the process, the natural flow of the South Branch toward Lake Michigan was reversed, and the flow of the North Branch toward Lake Michigan was adjusted so that it discharged through the reversed South Branch toward the canal. To accomplish this, two sets of pumping works were erected. Twin pumping works were installed at the canal's entrance at Bridgeport in 1883 at a cost of $258,000. These works took the polluted river water and poured it into a supplementary canal basin; this constant water removal created a strong current flowing away from Lake Michigan. The second set of pumping works was erected on the North Branch, at Fullerton Avenue in 1880 at a cost of $564,000. Forcing lake water into the river created a strong, southerly, cleansing current (see maps 6 and 7).[1]

The sewage disposal-drainage scheme which had evolved worked as follows: In the dry seasons when water levels were low, and the Chicago River's current was practically nonexistent, the Fullerton Avenue pumping works were utilized to swell the water volume and increase the North Branch's current. Simultaneously, the Bridgeport pumping works lifted polluted water from the South Branch and emptied it into the supplementary canal basin, thus augmenting the southerly current.

On the occasion of an easterly gale, the lake would rise from eighteen inches to two feet. Consequently, water would flow into the Chicago River, raising it from twelve to eighteen inches and creating a strong current down the South Branch and up the North Branch. When such a situation existed, Bridgeport pumping was suspended, the canal locks were opened, and the polluted river water was allowed to discharge directly into the canal. The Fullerton Avenue pumps were reversed, and the polluted water forced up the North Branch was pumped through the conduit into Lake Michigan.

The condition of the Chicago River in the late 1880s was predictable under the circumstances. Ninety sewers discharged into the river, bringing the sewage and drainage from 7,100 acres. On the South Side, 1,400 acres east of State Street still drained directly into Lake Michigan, according to Chesbrough's 1855 sewerage scheme.[2] The last two sewer outlets into the lake were closed when an intercepting sewer along the lakeshore was completed in 1907. The river's Main Branch was relatively free of pollutants and had little odor. The North

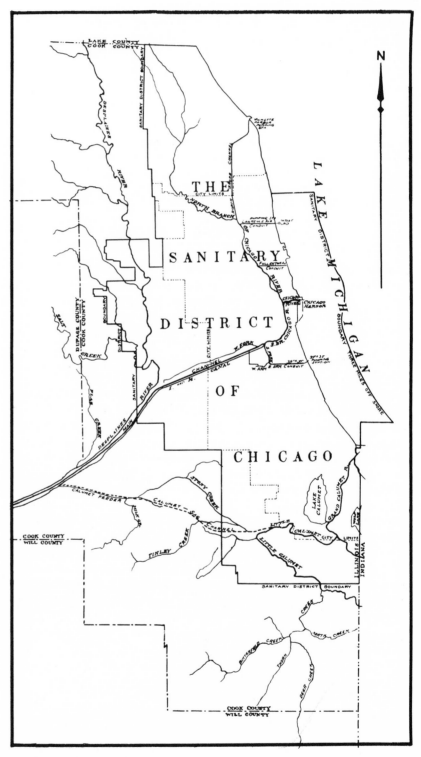

Map 7.

The Sanitary District of Chicago, 1917. From *Diversion of Water from the Great Lakes and Niagara River,* atlas vol. U.S. Government Printing Office, 1921.

Branch was often highly discolored and had a considerable odor. The West Fork of the South Branch, near the Bridgeport pumping works, was relatively pure, with little odor; the South Fork, the infamous "Bubbly Creek" adjacent to the stockyards, was extremely foul and possessed a very offensive odor. The South Fork extended from the Bridgeport pumping works to Thirty-ninth Street; it was a cesspool for the stockyard's refuse and offal. It defied cleaning, and became a public nuisance.

Andreas's conclusion well summarized the situation in the late 1880s:

> While the highest engineering skill obtainable has been brought to bear on the question of the disposal of the public sewage of Chicago, and while money has been spent lavishly in building the most improved machinery for rendering the river an available and efficient agent for this purpose, it must be conceded that thus far only indifferent results have been attained; and as the population of Chicago shall double and quadruple, it will be found imperatively necessary to push to a successful solution of this perplexing problem.[3]

Chesbrough's sewers effectively solved Chicago's drainage problem, but they only partially solved the sewage disposal problem. Although Chicago had come a long way from the sewage ditches and muddy streets that characterized the city's early years, the fact remained that the Chicago River and often Lake Michigan were still polluted. By 1871 engineers reversed the current of the Chicago River under normal conditions. This is contrary to the commonly held view that the Sanitary District of Chicago was responsible for reversing the Chicago River at the turn of the century. In the nineteenth century, the reversal could not be maintained under adverse weather conditions, thus endangering the city's Lake Michigan water supply. In the 1880s Chicago decided to improve the effectiveness of its sewage disposal strategy; the objective of this decision was to find a sewage disposal technique that would conserve the city's water supply. If the reversal could be insured under all, or almost all, weather conditions, the Lake Michigan water supply would be conserved and the existing water supply strategy would be appropriate. The Sanitary District of Chicago was created to implement a scheme designed to accomplish that end. As such, the Sanitary District and its concomitant engineering plans were not revolutionary in method, just more effective and more flexible in meeting Chicago's ever-growing sewage disposal demands.

THE BACKGROUND

The condition of the Chicago River was evidently innocuous for the first few years after Chesbrough's sewers were installed. In July 1860, however, the sewerage commissioners called Chesbrough's attention to the "possibility and probability of an enlargement and deepening of the Illinois and Michigan Canal to such an extent as to create a constant current from the lake to the Illinois River, making a new channel through Mud Lake to the Des Plaines River."[4] In 1860 Chesbrough still considered a "through steamboat canal" unadvisable. On 17 July 1861, three city aldermen had been appointed to confer with the general superintendent of the Illinois and Michigan Canal, for the river was extremely offensive.

In 1864 a committee of men representing both sanitary and commercial interests, including Chesbrough, was appointed to investigate methods of cleansing the Chicago River. The committee's report was issued in March 1865, and their recommendations included three principal proposals.

First, it was proposed that a series of intercepting sewers be constructed that would receive sewage intended for the river and divert it to machinery located along the shore. The machines would then pump the sewage into Lake Michigan some distance from the water supply intake. Second, covered sewers were to be cut between the Chicago River's two branches and Lake Michigan. Pumping works would then be erected which could either pump lake water into or filthy water out of the river, thus artificially creating the constant and sufficient current which natural forces could not guarantee. It is interesting to note the similarities between these first two recommendations and the alternatives which had been rejected earlier. This proposal eventually was abandoned as well. The flushing canal and pumping works had been included in Chesbrough's original sewage plan, but they had never been erected.

Third, the committee recommended that the summit level of the Illinois and Michigan Canal be reduced below the lake level at a cost of $21 million.[5] The committee hoped that the lowered canal would draw a sufficient quantity of lake water through the Chicago River to create the necessary purifying current. The canal was to be deepened over the twenty-six miles between Bridgeport and Lockport. Prior to completion, the Bridgeport pumping facilities were to be made available to the Board of Public Works.

The Illinois and Michigan Canal had been intended for shallow navigation only. It was fed by the Des Plaines and Calumet rivers and the South Branch through a lift wheel at Bridgeport. The Des Plaines and Calumet rivers supplied little water during the summer, and, consequently, the summit level was fed primarily by the South Branch and the Bridgeport pumps. It can only be surmised that canal workers discovered that this pumping removed considerable quantities of sewage in the river. No one knows for sure how the discovery was made, or who made it. That the suspended sewage would flow into the canal along with the water seems self-evident today. To what extent was the decision to use the Illinois and Michigan Canal for Chicago's sewage disposal predicated upon this "accidental" discovery that South Branch water pumped to increase the canal's volume and current simultaneously lessened the river's pollution load? As it was reported, the Bridgeport pumps were called into extra duty simply to feed the canal; sewage disposal had no role in choosing this action. Nevertheless, future decisions regarding Chicago's sewage disposal strategy were based on the open sewer potentialities of the Illinois and Michigan Canal, and one can only speculate whether this alternative would have been considered at all if the Des Plaines and Calumet rivers had proved to be satisfactory feeders. If they had been, Chicago's sewage disposal history might have been radically different. Thus, this "accidental" discovery was the key to Chicago's sanitary future.

The summer of 1865, following the pumping agreement, was sufficiently rainy, and nature provided an adequate current. In 1866 the pumps were run from mid-June to mid-September. Freshets in the springs of 1867 and 1868 greatly assisted in cleansing the Main and South branches, but the North Branch was relatively unaffected by either the freshets or the pumping and became offensive. In 1869 the river was exceptionally mephitic, and, by 1870, both pumps running at full capacity were unable to keep the river clean. It was discovered that when there had been little rainfall, the pumping operations caused the Main and South branches' flow to act as a barrier to the North Branch's outlet.

The deepening of the Illinois and Michigan Canal began in February 1866 and was completed in July 1871. Andreas reported that

> By the cutting of the temporary dam across the canal at Bridgeport quite a current was at once created, and an entire change of the water in the main river and South Branch was affected [*sic*] in about thirty-six hours. Also, this had a good effect upon the North Branch, although more benefit was derived by abstaining from throwing garbage, offal, and distillery filth into the Branch. The cost of deepening, from its inception up to April 1, 1871, exclusive of interest, was $2,982,437.12.[6]

Putnam summarized the canal deepening project, and foreshadowed its results:

> As early as 1865 the problem of sewage disposal led the city to obtain from the state the permission to lower the summit level of the canal sufficiently to insure such flow of water from Lake Michigan as would carry the sewage from the Chicago River through the canal into the Des Plaines. This improvement, completed in 1871 at an expenditure of approximately $3,000,000 (after the fire in 1871, the state reimbursed the city $2,955,340 for this expenditure), met the sanitary requirements for nearly a decade. By 1881, however, the collection of debris in the prism of the canal, the lowering of the lake level, and the increasing amount of sewage to be carried, combined to render the canal ineffective as an outlet. The putrid condition of the sewage-laden water passing sluggishly through the canal became a menace to the health of the people living along the course of the canal and the Des Plaines and upper Illinois Rivers. To obviate this danger, the General Assembly, in 1881, required the city to reestablish the pumping works at Bridgeport in order to augment the flow of water through the canal. The expedient, however, proved unsatisfactory. Local floods frequently polluted the water supply of the city by carrying the accumulating sewage from the river into the lake.[7]

During the summer of 1879, the Chicago River discharged into Lake Michigan for thirty consecutive days, befouling the city's water supply with sewage pollution.[8] In 1880 the Citizens' Association of Chicago sponsored the the formation of a committee whose mandate was "to devise a plan to dispose of the sewage of the city without contaminating the city water supply."[9] Contingent upon future expansion, the committee recommended a new canal with dimensions comparable to those of the Chicago River.

Like the Illinois and Michigan Canal, the new canal would carry the city's sewage and drainage over the divide, away from Lake Michigan. The committee further recommended that all the city's sewage be emptied into the Chicago River and its branches. The river, and especially the South Branch, would be cleansed, as its current was attracted by the strong current created by this "new river's" outflow.

The committee made a second report in 1885, following an unprecedented Des Plaines River flood which overflowed into the Chicago River and carried vast amounts of accumulated filth into Lake Michigan and the city's water supply. This report "amplified and urged" the 1880 proposal as

> . . . a public necessity which should receive the attention of a commission of experts to be created for the purpose of devising a comprehensive system for disposing of the sewage of the city and putting a stop for all time to the unsanitary condition which then existed.[10]

The South Branch was described as being "in an abominable condition of filth beyond the power of the pen to describe"; the city's water supply was polluted by the Chicago River's discharge; and the city was considered to be in danger whenever the Des Plaines River flooded. Surely, the "new river" was a proposal that needed close and expert scrutiny. The committee's second report noted that it was

> . . . practicable to restore the ancient outlet of the Great Lakes by opening a channel across the Chicago Divide, thereby creating a waterway to the Gulf of Mexico. The most practicable route was from Lake Michigan through the Chicago and Des Plaines Rivers to the head of navigation on the Illinois River at Utica.[11]

THE RESEARCH

A heavy storm in August 1885 flushed the city's wastes well into the lake, beyond the water supply intake. The resultant outbreak of cholera, typhoid, and other waterborne diseases killed approximately 12 percent of Chicago's population. The concerted efforts of leading citizens, plus the works of the Citizens' Association, caused the Chicago City Council to create the Drainage and Water Supply Commission in the spring of 1886, upon whose recommendation the "new river" project was instituted. The committee, composed of Rudolf Hering of New York, chief engineer, and Benesette Williams and Samuel Artingstall of Chicago, consulting engineers, was asked to

> . . . report on the whole matter committed to it in the most full and comprehensive manner, with maps, plans and diagrams complete, and accompany the report with estimates of first cost and annual requirements for the maintenance of the system proposed.[12]

The commission discovered that their mandate required the solution to two problems: the protection of the city's water supply, and the abatement of the river's objectionable condition. There does not seem to have been any question about the city's ultimate water supply source. Lake Michigan was it; no other alternative was considered. Thus, the problem was to keep the pollution out of the lake and to keep it from accumulating in the Chicago River.

Fifty thousand dollars was allocated to the commission. Its report was due no later than January 1887, and the commission made what was termed a preliminary report at that time. This was the only report the commission made. Its work was never completed, because the city council failed to make additional funds available. The intent of the preliminary report was to indicate the character of the legislation that would be necessary to implement any of several projects. The commissioners planned to leave the detailed features of the preferred project results to the final report.

The commission's recommendation to pursue the existing water supply strategy reflected the confidence that they had in their sewage disposal recommendations. New tunnels, cribs, buildings, and machinery were recommended, and the city was "urged to decide upon the location of the new works as soon as possible." Two South Division pumping stations were recommended, one between Harrison and Twelfth streets and the other opposite the stockyards, with additional pumping stations in the planning stage to accommodate future growth. The commission's report claimed:

> With the sewage kept out of the lake, there is no need of locating the intake farther than two miles from the shore, where water can be obtained sufficiently free from suspended earthy matter, and where a depth of about thirty feet is generally found, which is the least depth desirable for a submerged outlet.[13]

Three alternatives were considered by the commission: (1) to discharge the sewage into Lake Michigan, as far removed from the water-supply intakes as possible; (2) to discharge the sewage on a "sewage farm"; (3) to discharge the sewage into the Des Plaines River, from which the sewage would pass into the Illinois and Mississippi rivers. The study of these alternatives was divided into three classifications: topographic, hydrographic, and miscellaneous. The topographic work consisted of surveys whose intent was to determine the third alternative's feasibility. The hydrographic work largely consisted of determining the rate of flow of the Des Plaines River, and the probable effects upon it if diluted sewage were to be diverted into it. The commission also investigated Lake Michigan currents and levels, plus lake and river deposits under the existing sewage system. Among the miscellaneous studies were an inquiry into the feasibility of sewage purification through filtration, and the estimated growth and distribution of the metropolitan Chicago population.

The commission reported that diverting the sewage into the Des Plaines River was the only practical alternative. In rejecting sewage disposal in Lake Michigan, the commission said:

> The proper place from which to bring the water would be opposite Grosse Point and the sewage discharge should be east of Hyde Park. While it might be practicable to allow the sewage to enter the lake in crude form under such conditions for many years, the necessity would arise later for clarifying it, at least partially, previous to its discharge. It could not be allowed to run into the rivers as at present, but the dry-weather flow and a considerable amount of storm-water would have to be intercepted and carried to the outfall through many miles of special

conduits, and this entire quantity would have to be raised by pumping in order to get sufficient lead to empty the lake.

> The water-supply would have to be brought from Grosse Point in large conduits to the several pumping stations scattered over the city and its present surburbs. The circulation of water in the Chicago River and its branches would have to be maintained practically as it is at present because the removal merely of the dry-weather flow would not altogether prevent its pollution.[14]

Since other large Great Lakes cities had adopted the procedure of locating the water supply intake and sewage discharge pipe at opposite ends of the city, the commission's rejection of this alternative has to be viewed as rejection in favor of a preferred alternative.

The sewage farm alternative was to be accomplished through intermittent filtration rather than irrigation. Discussing this alternative, the report noted that

> . . . as the amount of land required to purify sewage can only be determined by experience, and this has been very limited in our own country, we are forced to rely mainly on that of Europe. . . . We will simply state that . . . from 10,000 to 15,000 acres of land would be required to dispose of the sewage from the entire metropolitan area. The only available territory for sewage filtration in the neighborhood of Chicago consists of two sandy ridges in the town of Thornton and extending across the State line into Indiana, and a sandy ridge crossing the town of Niles. The soil is quite favorable, but the character of the surface is such that the necessary preparation to make it suitable for filtration beds would be comparatively expensive. An enormous cost is, however, represented by the fact that the sewage would have to be collected by large intercepting sewers, lifted altogether some 90 feet and carried about twenty miles before reaching the farms. We therefore [sic] consider such a project entirely impracticable.[15]

In 1896, B. A. Eckhart, the president of the Chicago Sanitary District's board of trustees, reviewed the commission's deliberations in remarks he made to the International Conference of the State Boards of Health. After discussing the rejected alternatives, Eckhart concluded that

> . . . the vital defect of all these methods of sewage disposal was, that they provided only for the dry weather flow of sewage. When the heavy rains came, the greater portion of the floods, laden with surface accumulations of filth, would still find the way into the river and its branches. The Des Plaines River . . . would still make its way to the Chicago River, sweeping its population into the lake, and carrying it out towards our source of water supply. Moreover, the volume of the storm flow is far in excess of the dry weather flow. It was evident to the Commission that any method adopted which should not also take care of this storm flow would be but partial, and would leave our water supply unprotected.[16]

Thus, discharging the sewage into the Des Plaines River, the alternative that Chesbrough had termed "too remote" in 1855, was the one recommended by the commission report. It claimed that this alternative was

> . . . rendered practicable by the fact that the divide between Lake Michi-

gan and the Mississippi valley lies about ten miles west of Chicago, with so slight an elevation that it is not difficult to carry the sewage westward into the Des Plaines River and thence into the Mississippi River. The method of disposal . . . is in fact mainly the present one, most of the sewage now being carried across the divide by the Illinois and Michigan Canal.[17]

The commission felt that this method would avoid "all possible lake

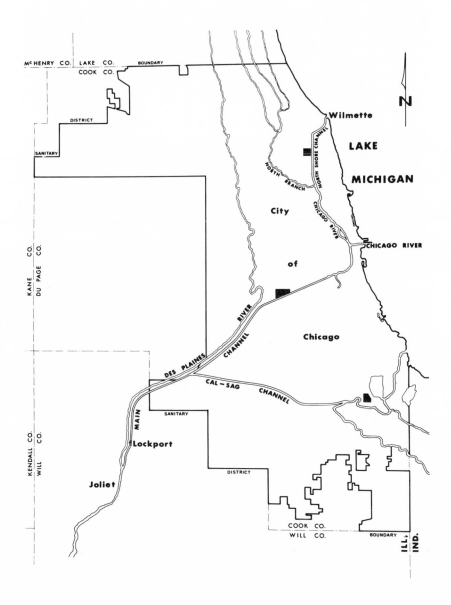

The channel system of the Sanitary District. Courtesy of the Metropolitan Sanitary District of Greater Chicago.

Map 8.

pollution and permit the supply of water to be drawn from any number of convenient points in front of the city."[18]

The method was to reverse the current of the Chicago River by connecting the South Branch with the Des Plaines River (see maps 7 and 8). The means was to be a canal of sufficient size to drain Chicago River storm waters, after some of the headwaters had been diverted. The maximum Chicago River flood flow was measured at 10,000 cubic feet per second (c.f.s.), and this was the important factor in determining the size of the proposed canal. The diversion was to be complete; all sewage was to be kept out of Lake Michigan.

Some dilution ratio had to be assumed if the commission was to estimate the proposed channel's size and cost. Four hundred c.f.s. per 100,000 population was taken as the working estimate, and it was planned that the channel should be designed for a total tributary population of 2.5 million. Taking these figures as given, the commission estimated the initial investment and the annual costs, including interest, for each project. These estimates are given in table 10.

Table 10. *Cost Estimates of the Drainage and Water Supply Commission*

Project	Initial Investment	Annual Cost
	(in millions of dollars)	
Lake Michigan Disposal	$37	$2.4
Land Disposal	58	3.0
Des Plaines River Disposal	23–28	1.3

Source: R. Isham Randolph, "The History of Sanitation in Chicago," *Journal of the Western Society of Engineers*, October 1939, p. 235.

Soper, Watson, and Martin, *A Report to the Chicago Real Estate Board on the Disposal of the Sewage and Protection of the Water Supply of Chicago, Illinois*, p. 86.

The proposed plan promised the specified benefits at least cost, in terms of both initial and annual costs. Also, the report noted that

> . . . the proposed canal will, from its regular discharge, produce a magnificent waterway between Chicago and the Mississippi River, suitable for the navigation of boats having as much as 2,000 tons burden.[19]

From this it is clear that hopes for a deep waterway between the Great Lakes and the Mississippi had not been abandoned in the Panic of 1837.[20] Further, the report argued that such a channel would be a significant waterpower source, which would be of great commercial value to the governmental body responsible for its operation. Finally, the report noted that, because it would lower the level of the Des Plaines River over some sections, the proposed channel would have the effect of raising the level of the low-lying prairies contiguous to those sections, thus making the prairie less susceptible to damaging floods.

When the existing method was functioning properly, the net results of both the existing and the proposed methods were identical: diluted sewage discharging into the Illinois River valley. The proposed method, therefore, should be looked upon as one which removed the offenses of its predecessor while affording a greater degree of protection to the Lake Michigan water supply. In spite of the fact that a new channel would be required, this proposed continuation and improvement of Chicago's traditional sewage disposal strategy proved to be the least costly. The possibilities of using existing facilities were undoubtedly a factor holding down the expense of the proposed method; for example, the existing sewer system could be utilized intact and no change was necessitated in the city's water supply strategy. In fact, stripped to its essentials, the commission's proposal called for little more than a new, larger channel.

The commission's report did not discuss many important topics. Among these were the probable effects on the health and utility of Des Plaines and Illinois river valley residents, should the sewage be discharged into the Des Plaines River. It did not discuss the possibility that this method might pollute St. Louis's water supply, as well as those of other Mississippi River towns.[21] Nothing was said about the possibility of filtering the water supply, even though slow sand filtration was an established, effective method. The report did not discuss how and where the sewage would enter the Chicago River, nor did it discuss the steps which should be taken to avoid sewage deposits, dead ends, and unsightly or malodorous conditions, except that the sewage was to be diluted with lake water, and that the dilution could be regulated to help with these problems. The commission withheld from this preliminary report its opinion as to the proper degree of dilution "to provide immunity from offense" until tests could be conducted under variable weather conditions and in comparable bodies of water. It did not discuss the potentially serious problems connected with the fact that industrial wastes were also being discharged into the Chicago River.[22] Finally, the commission's report made no mention of state and federal government interests with respect to drainage via the Des Plaines River and diverting Lake Michigan water. This last omission became more significant in the perspective of the long-running, continuous debate between the local authority, the Sanitary District of Chicago, and the federal government over the diversion of lake water to dilute the sewage which developed a few years later. Yet it must not be forgotten that the commission's preliminary report was intended only to give conclusions without answering all the questions raised by the recommendations. The problem they confronted was the interdependence of water supply and sewage disposal in the Chicago area. The benefits of all the alternatives considered by the commission were a better protected water supply and improved sewage disposal. Chicago again made its decision on the basis of the alternative which, at least cost, secured the benefits the city specified.

THE SANITARY DISTRICT OF CHICAGO

A direct result of the establishment of the Water and Drainage Commission was the Sanitary District Enabling Act of 29 May 1889, which went into effect 1 July 1889.[23] This act was necessary because natural drainage areas did not conform to political boundary lines, and, in particular, Chicago's proposed drainage and sewage disposal scheme involved an area beyond the city's limits. Yet Chicago and its suburbs had identical water supply and waste disposal problems. The enabling act permitted a governmental body to be created which would extend over the entire area benefitted by the proposed scheme. Sanitary districts could be created:

> . . . whenever any area of contiguous territory within the limits of a single county shall contain two or more cities, towns or villages, and shall be so situated that the maintenance of a common outlet for the drainage thereof will conduce to the preservation of the public health.[24]

This body was also necessary in order to finance, create, and administer the public utilities which the plan envisioned. The Illinois constitution limited a municipality's borrowing capacity to 5 percent of the total assessed taxable property within its corporate limits, and both Chicago and its suburbs were fully extended. Like most local governmental bodies, the new district's financing powers consisted of property taxation and bond issues. Parenthetically, the Sanitary District of Chicago financed its projects primarily by construction bonds, with the remainder coming from excess tax revenues. Operating expenses, bonded indebtedness, interest, and the like were paid out of district tax revenues (see Appendix 2). In November 1889, affected voters carried a referendum for the creation of the Chicago Sanitary District by a vote of 70,958 to 242.[25]

In addition to the Sanitary District, the act provided for the construction of the Main Channel and its necessary adjuncts, in order to collect the sewage and discharge it, with Lake Michigan diluting water, into the Des Plaines River. The channel was to be large enough to allow for a minimum continuous flow of 20,000 cubic feet of water per minute (c.f.m.) per 100,000 population. Provision was to be made for a total tributary population of 3 million people.[26] The 20,000 c.f.m. provision in the state law appears to be based more on expedience than on any definite knowledge. The Drainage and Water Supply Commission report had assumed 24,000 c.f.m. per 100,000 population, and had designed a channel based upon a total tributary population of 2.5 million. These figures, however, were assumed only for estimating costs. Officially, the commission withheld its opinion on the proper dilution until it could complete additional tests. Consequently, although the commission's preliminary report was thorough, there were several important questions regarding the channel's construction which had been left unsettled. If the funds had been available to prepare a final report, and had the commission been able to deal with all the questions referred to it, many costly future errors possibly could have been avoided.

The district's corporate authority was placed in a nine-member board of trustees, elected by the voters within the district. This body was given the power to pass ordinances relevant to their business, which, as defined by the act, was to

> . . . provide for the drainage of such district by laying out, establishing, constructing and maintaining one or more channels, drains, ditches, and outlets for carrying off and disposing of the drainage (including the sewage), of such district, together with such adjuncts and additions thereto

as may be necessary or proper to cause such channels or outlets to accomplish the end for which they are designed in a satisfactory manner.[27]

The original area encompassed by the Chicago Sanitary District was 185 square miles, but this increased greatly (see map 9). In 1903 large additions were made to the north, in the Chicago River drainage basin, and to the south, in the Calumet River drainage basin. These areas included the Calumet region and the North Shore suburbs. The Illinois legislature, as part of the measure which authorized these 1903 annexations, provided that the annexed lands should be drained by canals, through which the sewage would flow with dilution water at the same ratio that existed in the Main Channel. Authority also was granted, in language identical to that of the original enabling act, to construct and maintain adjuncts as would be "necessary or proper to cause such channels or outlets to accomplish the end for which they are designed in a satisfactory manner."[28] Later, some land was added to the west as well (compare map 7 with maps 8 and 9). By 1914 the area encompassed by the Sanitary District was 386 square miles, more than double its original area.

The channel proposed by the Water and Drainage Commission was the first construction work undertaken by the Sanitary District, and construction commenced in September 1892. This twenty-eight-mile long channel is known by one of three alternative names: the Drainage Canal, the Chicago Sanitary and Ship Canal, or, simply, the Main Channel. Construction had been delayed for two years by administrative snarls and political conflicts. There were disputes over routes, disputes with chief engineers (three were fired), and controversial deliberations about reducing the water capacity of the Main Channel by 42 percent and dropping the shipping functions of the canal as a cost-cutting "improvement." The shipping function was not dropped. By the end of November 1891 more than $650,000 had been spent, and nothing had been constructed.[29]

The Main Channel and the Illinois and Michigan Canal were practically parallel from Chicago to Lockport (see map 7). Both connected with the Chicago River and drew their water supply through the river from Lake Michigan. The inlet of the Main Channel was at Robey Street (now Damen Avenue) on the South Branch. The inlet of the Illinois and Michigan Canal was a half mile east, closer to Lake Michigan. The Main Channel's water supply, therefore, was drawn past the Illinois and Michigan Canal's inlet. Nevertheless, while these two were parallel, they were in no way connected to one another. Unlike the Illinois and Michigan Canal, the Main Channel had no locks within its own length; the water level was controlled by the Lockport works at the Des Plaines River end. At Lockport, the Sanitary District constructed controlling works and a power plant, which converted the channel's fall into electrical energy.

From the Main Channel the water route was by way of the Illinois and Michigan Canal, which followed the Illinois Valley to LaSalle, 63 miles below Lockport, where it joined the Illinois River. The diluted sewage carried in the Main Channel was discharged in the Des Plaines

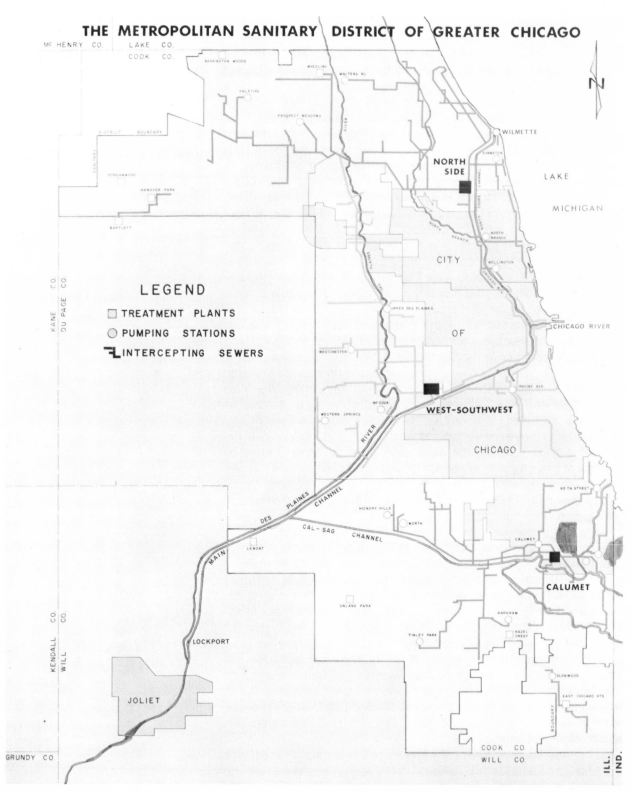

THE METROPOLITAN SANITARY DISTRICT OF GREATER CHICAGO

LEGEND
□ TREATMENT PLANTS
○ PUMPING STATIONS
⌐ INTERCEPTING SEWERS

Map 9.   The Sanitary District today. Courtesy of the Metropolitan Sanitary District of Greater Chicago.

A lock on the Illinois and Michigan Canal. The canal was approximately one-tenth the size of the Main Channel. Chicago Historical Society.

River, a small, sluggish stream at that point. The Illinois River, formed by the confluence of the Des Plaines and Kankakee rivers, 26 miles downstream from Lockport, empties into the Mississippi River approximately 250 miles to the southwest. Therefore, Chicago was using the Great Lakes drainage area for its water supply, and the Mississippi River drainage area for its sewage disposal.

When completed, the capacity of the Main Channel was 10,000 c.f.s., with a current of less than 2 mph. The channel had a navigable depth in excess of 20 feet; the width varied between 110 and 201 feet; the sides were either vertical or very slightly inclined. It was constructed in three distinct sections. An earth section between Robey Street and Summit, Illinois, was 7.8 miles long, 24 feet deep, and 162 feet wide at the bottom. An earth and rock section between Summit and Willow Springs was 5.3 miles long, 24 feet deep, and 202 feet wide at the bottom. Finally, a rock section from Willow Springs to Lockport was 14.95 miles long, 24 feet deep, and 160 feet wide at the bottom. Initially, the earth section was given a provisional width of 110 feet but was later widened to 160 feet. By 1915, only the earth and rock section was completed to its full-designed capacity.[30]

Construction of the Main Channel. Chicago Historical Society.

In fact, the constructed capacity of the southern rock section was 14,000 c.f.s., 40 percent greater than had been anticipated.[31] The 40 percent figure is interesting because it formed the basis for the Calumet-Sag Channel's proposed diversion a few years later; this will be discussed in the next chapter. While the Sanitary District first described the excess capacity to have been accidental, they claimed later that this was the designed capacity, and that the earth section and the earth and rock section were to have been increased to 14,000 c.f.s. capacity, when Chicago's population warranted this increase. Newspaper accounts as early as 1891 support the idea that the designed capacity of the rock section was 14,000 c.f.s. to accommodate the proposed channel.

A flow of 10,000 c.f.s. was considered to be the Chicago River's maximum runoff, and, therefore, the Main Channel was constructed to handle this volume. This was necessary to prevent the Chicago River from emptying into the Lake Michigan water supply. The engineers who designed the channel believed that no restriction existed upon the maximum quantity which could be diverted from Lake Michigan; con-

Construction of the Main Channel. Chicago Historical Society.

sequently, they chose to build a channel that would have a 10,000 c.f.s. capacity.[32] There were legitimate grounds for the assumption that no restrictions would be placed upon the diversion of Lake Michigan water. The Main Channel was an updated and enlarged edition of the Illinois and Michigan Canal. The assumption was predicated on the belief that, as the new Main Channel was a substitute for the old Illinois and Michigan Canal, it had all the rights granted to its predecessor. It was not their intention that the Main Channel would maintain such a flow rate at all times; they designed a channel which would comply with the enabling act's requirement that there be a minimum flow of 3 1/3 c.f.s. per 1,000 population. The designed capacity of the Main Channel was for a contiguous population of 3 million, although, at the dilution rates stated in the Drainage and Water Supply Commission Report (4 c.f.s. per 1,000 population), it was projected for only 2.5 million.

Section 17 of the Enabling Act empowered the Sanitary District to "enter upon, use, widen, deepen and improve any navigable or other waterway, canal or lake" when it proved necessary "in making any improvements which any district is authorized by this act to make."[33] The Main Channel could not operate properly unless improvements were made in the Chicago River. The Chicago River was only 17 feet deep in spite of having been dredged on numerous occasions, and it was less than 100 feet wide in several places. It was shallow, narrow, and tortuous. The river had to be enlarged if water was to pass be-

75

tween Lake Michigan and the Main Channel without creating a current obstructive to Chicago River navigation. As such, the Chicago River project was included in the district's plans from the outset, as the following resolution, passed by the Sanitary District trustees in April 1891, testifies:

> Resolved that this Board hereby ordains that the Sanitary District of Chicago do, forthwith, enter upon, use, widen, deepen and improve the Chicago River from its mouth at Lake Michigan to the south branch thereof, and also the south branch thereof together with the south and west forks thereof, so as to make the same a proper and sufficient supply channel for the main channel heretofore surveyed from the Chicago River to Joliet and further, that the action Chief Engineer be and he is hereby directed immediately to investigate and report upon the capacity of said river and its said south branch and forks for that purpose, and also as to any changes that should be made therein and that a copy of this resolution . . . transmitted to the mayor and common council of the City of Chicago, and the Secretary of War of the United States.[34]

The fact that the district waited until after the Main Channel was well under construction to begin the Chicago River improvements had serious ramifications for Chicago's sanitary history.

THE SANITARY DISTRICT AND THE FEDERAL GOVERNMENT

In May 1895, a federal commission was appointed to investigate the Main Channel's effect on lake and harbor levels. Its report, in October 1895, indicated that the proposed diversion from Lake Michigan would lower the levels of the Great Lakes by about six inches. The secretary of war, the chief of engineers, and Congress were all advised by this commission's report of the diversion's possible effect on lake levels and harbor navigation. The fact that the so-called lake-levels controversy played an important role in the Sanitary District's relationship with the federal government is sufficient reason to note at the outset that a diversion of 10,000 c.f.s. would lower the water surface in the Michigan and Huron basins by less than three inches, if all natural inflow into those basins were stopped for one year. This is the best current thinking. As Hough observed, "It appears that the observed low-water periods were caused by climatic variations rather than by diversion of water."[35]

In June 1896 the Sanitary District wrote the secretary of war requesting a permit to proceed with the proposed Chicago River improvements. With this request, the district enclosed full information and maps. Since the Chicago River was designated a federal harbor, the district had to obtain a federal permit for the necessary river improvements. The United States chief of engineers commented that

> As far as the work itself is concerned there can be no objection to it, as in every case the navigation channel of the Chicago River will be improved . . . I am unable to do otherwise than to recommend the granting of the authority sought.

> The question that must come up later for the action of the War Department, to-wit: Whether the improved channel of the Chicago River will be sufficient to carry 300,000 cubic feet of water per minute without lessen-

ing or destroying the navigability of the Chicago River or whether the City of Chicago will be allowed by the United States and Great Britain to take any water at all from the Great Lakes with the inevitable result of lowering their levels is not now under investigation. . . .

. . . that this authority shall not be interpreted as approval of the plans of the Sanitary District of Chicago to introduce a current into (the) Chicago River. This latter proposition must be hereafter submitted for consideration.[36]

A volume of 300,000 c.f.m. (5,000 c.f.s.) was to be the initial diversion from Lake Michigan. The term "diversion" as it will be used hereafter refers to the amount of water taken from the lake to provide a flow in the Sanitary District's works. It would be expanded to a maximum of 10,000 c.f.s., with increased demands upon the Main Channel. By comparison, the average flow today in the lower Mississippi River is in excess of 300,000 c.f.s. The flow in the enlarged Illinois and Michigan Canal was only 1,000 c.f.s. The chief of engineers authorized the river improvements, while simultaneously questioning the reason for the improvements.

In July 1896, the acting secretary of war granted the Chicago River an improvement permit subject to several conditions, the most important being that the authority was not to be construed as approval of the plan to induce a current in the Chicago River.[37] This was to be a matter which would be considered later. The government's opposition was apparently to the navigational features of the channel. Two reports, one by U.S. Army Engineer Captain W. L. Marshall in 1888 and another by U.S. Army Engineer D. C. Kingman in 1894, opposed the channel and argued that the current created for sewage would be injurious to navigation and that the costs of the project outweighed any transportation benefits. Kingman's report went on to note that improvements were necessary in the Mississippi River to make it navigable for deep-water ships and, in his opinion, these improvements were untenable. Improvements were also needed in the Illinois River and, parenthetically, it was not until 1939 when the last of five dams on the river was completed that the river became completely navigable.[38]

On 8 May 1899, the secretary of war, R. A. Alger, issued the permit that authorized the Sanitary District to open the Main Channel. The permit noted that the Sanitary District had been granted permission to make certain Chicago River improvements, and went on to observe:

Now therefore, the Chief of Engineers having consented thereto, this is to certify that the Secretary of War hereby gives permission to the said Sanitary District of Chicago to open the channel constructed and cause the water of the Chicago River to flow into the same, subject to the following conditions:

1. That it be distinctly understood that it is the intention of the Secretary of War to submit the questions connected with the work of the Sanitary District of Chicago to Congress for consideration and final action and that this permit shall be subject to such action as may be taken by Congress.

2. That if at any time it becomes apparent that the current created by said drainage work in the south and main branches of the Chicago River be unreasonably obstructive to navigation or injurious to property, the Secretary of War reserves the right to close said discharge through said channel or to modify it to such extent as may be demanded by navigation and property interests along said Chicago River and its south branch.

3. That the Sanitary District of Chicago must assume all responsibility for damages to property and navigation interests by reason of the introduction of a current in Chicago River.[39]

The secretary's only evident concern was the effect the diversion might have on the Chicago River. Referring indirectly to the lake levels question, Alger apparently was reluctant to choose sides, and hoped to pass the decisions to Congress. Congress took no action.

With the permit from Secretary Alger and tacit permission from Gov. John A. Tanner of Illinois, the Sanitary District turned water into the Main Channel on 2 January 1900. On 17 January 1900, with permits from both, the bear-trap dam at the Lockport controlling works was lowered, and, consequently, the Main Channel was opened for the 5,000 c.f.s. preliminary flow. This flow, however, was the one authorized by state law, and not by federal permit.

When the Main Channel was opened, a current was created in the Chicago River, due to its shallowness. Permits were issued for additional river improvements in July 1900. Nevertheless, because of an excessive current in the Chicago River, the secretary of war modified the district's original permit in December 1901, reducing the permissible diversion through the Chicago River from 5,000 c.f.s. to 4,167 c.f.s.[40] The Sanitary District later argued that "had there been no current created and had the Chicago River Channel been as wide and as deep as it was later created, there would have been no modification of the amount of the withdrawal."[41] In 1903 the permit was again modified to allow a maximum of 5,833 c.f.s. during the closed season of navigation.[42] These permits were to remain in force until 1925.

The Sanitary District of Chicago had been organized and its works planned and built with full knowledge on the part of any interested party as to the district's intentions. Yet the federal government did not assume any real authority until shortly before the completed channel was opened.[43] Then it entered on the basis of velocities in an unimproved section of the Chicago River and restricted the diversion to maintain a navigable velocity in that section, and this restricted diversion remained after the Main Branch and the South Branch had been widened and deepened.[44]

The Chicago River project was instituted for the purpose of making the Main Channel's operation possible, according to the requirements of the state law. It was instituted because the Chicago River, as it was, could not handle the maximum diversion for which the Main Channel was designed, 10,000 c.f.s. The Sanitary District spent in excess of $12 million improving the Chicago River, and it seemed reasonable to assume that if the river were improved so that the necessary water volume could be diverted through the river without creating a current "unreasonably obstructive to navigation or injurious to property," the federal government would offer no objection to the diversion required under the state law. Requests for a 10,000 c.f.s. flow were denied, however, and the secretary of war undertook legal action in 1908 and 1912 to prohibit any total diversion greater than that specified by the War Department permit. The Sanitary District never recognized the federal government's "right" to fix the Lake Michigan diversion. The permit only recognized a maximum withdrawal of 4,167 c.f.s through the Chicago River, but the federal government was now attempting to change the permit's interpretation. The Sanitary District had built a conduit along Thirty-ninth Street and had placed a pumping station at the lake end to flush the South Branch's south fork. The federal government always understood that the capacity of the Main Channel was the 10,000 c.f.s. minimum prescribed by state law. Public reports never mentioned a diversion less than 10,000 c.f.s. The Sanitary District had been diverting more water than 4,167 c.f.s from Lake Michigan and never denied that it was doing so. The district held that this was no violation of its federal permit, as no requirement ever existed.[45] The federal permit's restriction was on the diversion through the Chicago River, and not the diversion from Lake Michigan. If water could be pumped into the Main Channel through the Thirty-ninth Street pumping station into the South Branch, the Sanitary District could abide by both the federal permit and the state law.

The change in the War Department's emphasis from regulating only the flow through the Chicago River to regulating the total Lake Michigan diversion was influenced, undoubtedly, by the fact that several Great Lakes states had brought suits to the United States Supreme Court to restrain Chicago from diverting any Lake Michigan water. These states argued that the district's diversion "damaged their riparian rights, navigation, agriculture, horticulture, and climate."[46] The inclusion of Canada in this suit created an international controversy. The Sanitary District argued that the federal permit contained no condition

> . . . that there may be a limitation of the amount of flow because of the effect upon the surface elevation of the lake or damage to navigation by reason of diminishing lake levels. The permit is unlimited as to the amount of withdrawal except that it must be assumed that the limitation is the capacity of the main channel. . . . [47]

The district assumed that the Chicago River improvements would remove the necessity for federal restriction. It also assumed that the lake level issue would not be raised. Both assumptions seemed reasonable. The diversion limitations in the May 1899 permit were based on navigational dangers in the Chicago River, and not on the fear of lowering the levels of the Great Lakes. Over time, the secretary of war issued the additional permits as warranted, but each contained provisions similar to the May 1899 permit. Each permit was considered necessary to divert the sewage of the district's tributary area, and most of the works were unnecessary if the volume prescribed by the state law could not be diverted. In 1907 the War Department issued a permit for the North Shore Channel's construction, between the Wilmette lakeshore and the North Branch. In 1910 it issued a permit for the Calumet-Sag Channel's construction, between the Calumet River and the Main Channel (see maps 7 and 8).

The War Department had to have been aware that these improvements would cost a considerable amount, and no warning was given that such expenditures might prove to be useless. The expenditure on all the Sanitary District's works was more than $100 million. For the operation of these works, the Sanitary District ultimately diverted 7,250 c.f.s. through the Chicago River, 1,750 c.f.s. through the North Shore Channel, and 2,000 c.f.s. through the Thirty-ninth Street pumping station. These diversion figures indicate that the Sanitary District probably just completely ignored the federal permit. Inasmuch as the principal controversy had to do with the lake diversion, it is interesting to speculate how events might have been different had the Illinois and Michigan Canal been enlarged, as it was apparently possible to do without further application for authority or permits for the increased diversion.

THE SANITARY DISTRICT'S DOWNSTREAM PROBLEMS

The War Department was concerned with problems upstream from Lockport, not with problems created by flushing Chicago's sewage downstream. The Illinois River basin, into which the district's channel system emptied, contains about 50 percent of the area of Illinois, and, with Chicago, about 70 percent of the state's population. It is logical to suppose that Illinois River valley residents might object to polluted water being thrust upon them, but this does not seem to be the case. The only two Illinois cities to object were Joliet and Peoria. On several occasions legislators from those cities attempted to repeal the Sanitary District Enabling Act, but they failed.[48] The Illinois River was a commercial waterway and was little used for drinking water or recreation. Most river towns were constructed with their backs to the river. Chicago's diversion was welcomed in that the increased water volume would ensure against low-water navigational problems. Initially, there was some concern about airborne health hazards, but an Illinois Board of Health investigation laid such fears to rest.[49] While local people did not complain about the Sanitary District, St. Louis did.

The city of St. Louis felt that the Sanitary District's strategy posed a threat to the city's Mississippi River water supply, and there was a distinct possibility that St. Louis would bring suit to enjoin the district from opening the Main Channel. The district was eager to open its completed channel before St. Louis could undertake any action. Consequently, water was pumped into the Main Channel on the same day Governor Tanner authorized the opening, after receiving the commissioner's report that the channel was ready. There was no formal ceremony. The opening was kept quiet, for the district feared that any prior notice might hasten St. Louis's attempt to get a federal injunction. The opening of the Lockport Dam was a more formal occasion, but nonetheless hasty. St. Louis was aware of the channel's construction but procrastinated in seeking an injunction until the last possible moment.

While the Sanitary District did avoid an injunction, it still had to answer St. Louis's objections in court.

In late 1898 the mayor of St. Louis appointed a committee to investigate the potential effect of Chicago's sewage on the St. Louis water supply. This committee reported, in April 1899, that the Main Channel constituted a pollution threat. Consequently, in January 1900, the state of Missouri petitioned the U.S. Supreme Court to enjoin the state of Illinois and the Sanitary District of Chicago from discharging sewage into the Main Channel. Why action was not taken earlier to enjoin the use of the Illinois and Michigan Canal as a sewage carrier is not clear; the Main Channel merely seemed to intensify the threat.

In 1902 Professor Arthur W. Palmer, of the University of Illinois chemistry department, issued a report of his study, which was made to determine the effect of flow in the Main Channel on the Illinois and Mississippi rivers. The Illinois River oxidized the sewage as it flowed toward the Mississippi. In fact, the Illinois was clean by the time it reached Peoria and Pekin, where it was befouled once again by slaughterhouse and distillery wastes. It was these wastes, and not Chicago's, that were the principal polluters of the lower Illinois River. By the time the river reached the Mississippi River, the water was clean once again—"little more than a harmless salt remained to tell of the enormous pollution 320 miles above."[50] The water's physical appearance and the presence of a fishing industry also testified to the river's improvement. There can be little doubt that Palmer's investigation was carried out in an unprejudiced manner, in spite of the fact that its purpose was to support the hypothesis that Chicago's sewage was not polluting the St. Louis water supply.

Palmer's study was prompted by the litigation initiated by St. Louis. Many expert witnesses were called, and the case was ultimately dismissed without prejudice. St. Louis found that the water in the Illinois at its confluence with the Mississippi was purer than that in the latter river, and, subsequently, St. Louis constructed purification works to remove the turbidity in the Mississippi supply.[51] The Sanitary District also learned from this experience, as the following quote from Mason's text suggests:

> Very recently the investigations connected with the alleged pollution of the Illinois River by the opening of the Chicago drainage-canal have tended to again modify our views, and have caused us to admit that stream-purification is a fact provided the length of flow be sufficiently great.[52]

The dilution method utilized the oxygen in a moving body of water to purify sewage and was dependent upon two variables: the length of the body, and its volume of flow. This explains why the Sanitary District vigorously defended its right to divert the larger volume prescribed by state law.

Once implemented, the Sanitary District performed its duties as efficiently as its proponents had predicted, as long as the growth of the city's population was within the district's capacity. The performance of these duties, as prescribed by the state law under which the district was created, required that the district operate outside the limits prescribed by the federal government. This dichotomy in mandates between state and federal government created uncertainties with which the district contended for many years. The ultimate resolution of this dichotomy forced the Sanitary District to adopt a new strategy, but it, too, was a logical consequence of the city's previous sanitary decisions.

NOTES

1. A. T. Andreas, *History of Chicago from the Earliest Period to the Present Time,* 3:135.
2. See chapter 2, pp. 26–27.
3. Andreas, *History of Chicago,* 3:137.
4. Quoted in Andreas, *History of Chicago,* 3:553.
5. Andreas, *History of Chicago,* 2:554. Bessie Louise Pierce, *A History of Chicago,* 2:331. George Soper, John Watson, and Arthur Martin, *A Report to the Chicago Real Estate Board on the Disposal of the Sewage and Protection of the Water Supply of Chicago, Illinois* (hereafter *CREB Report*), 1915, p. 74. R. Isham Randolph, "The History of Sanitation in Chicago," *Journal of the Western Society of Engineers,* October 1939, p. 234. Langdon Pearse, "Chicago's Quest for Potable Water," *Water and Sewage Works,* May 1955, reprinted, pp. 3, 4. James William Putnam, *The Illinois and Michigan Canal,* p. 143. C. Arch Williams, *The Sanitary District of Chicago* (Chicago: Sanitary District of Chicago, 1919), pp. 34, 189ff.
6. Andreas, *History of Chicago,* 2:554.
7. Putnam, *The Illinois and Michigan Canal,* p. 143.
8. See James C. O'Connell, "Chicago's Quest for Pure Water," Public Works Historical Society, Essay Number 1, June 1976, p. 5.
9. Pearse, "Chicago's Quest," p. 4. See also O'Connell, "Chicago's Quest for Pure Water," pp. 6–7, for why the association spearheaded the canal movement.
10. Quoted in *CREB Report,* p. 76.
11. Pearse, "Chicago's Quest," p. 4. The report was written in part by Lyman E. Cooley, a prominent hydraulic engineer.
12. Quoted in *CREB Report,* p. 79.
13. Quoted in *CREB Report,* p. 81.
14. Quoted in Randolph, "Sanitation in Chicago," p. 235.
15. Quoted in Randolph, "Sanitation in Chicago," p. 235. The commissioners assumed a population of 2 million and an average sewage discharge of 150 gallons per capita per average dry-weather day. On these assumptions they reached the conclusion that 10 to 15 thousand acres would be required.
16. Quoted in Williams, *The Sanitary District of Chicago,* p. 35. The problem of storm flows is one that continues to vex the Sanitary District today.
17. Quoted in Randolph, "Sanitation in Chicago," p. 235.
18. Quoted in *CREB Report,* p. 84.
19. Quoted in Randolph, "Sanitation in Chicago," p. 235. Also in *CREB Report,* p. 86.
20. For more on the ship canal movement of the 1880s, see O'Connell, "Chicago's Quest for Pure Water," pp. 10–11.
21. See section on "The Sanitary District's Downstream Problems" below.
22. Randolph, "Sanitation in Chicago," p. 235.
23. Illinois, *Laws,* 1889, pp. 85–92. Two acts with similar purposes had been defeated in the previous legislature and sent to committees for further study. See O'Connell, "Chicago's Quest for Pure Water," pp. 10, 13. See also Louis P. Cain, "The Search for an Optimal Environmental Jurisdiction: Sanitary Districts in Illinois, 1889," Department of Economics, University of British Columbia, discussion paper No. 76–08.
24. Illinois, *Laws,* 1889, p. 91.
25. Randolph, "Sanitation in Chicago," p. 236.
26. *CREB Report,* p. 87.

27. Illinois, *Laws,* 1889, p. 87.

28. *CREB Report,* p. 44.

29. O'Connell, "Chicago's Quest for Pure Water," p. 14. See also G. P. Brown, *Drainage Channel and Waterway,* p. 415.

30. Sanitary District of Chicago, *Engineering Works,* August 1928, p. 15.

31. Sanitary District of Chicago, "Memorandum Concerning the Drainage and Sewerage Conditions in Chicago," December 1923, p. 37.

32. George E. Fuller, "The Sewage Disposal Problem of Chicago," Western Society of Engineers, paper read at Mid-winter Convocation at Chicago, 19 February 1925, p. 4. See also Louis P. Cain, "Unfouling the Public's Nest: Chicago's Sanitary Diversion of Lake Michigan Water," *Technology and Culture,* October 1974, pp. 594–613.

33. Illinois, *Laws,* 1889, p. 89.

34. Quoted in Williams, *The Sanitary District of Chicago,* p. 192.

35. Hough, *Geology of the Great Lakes,* p. 6. The earlier estimates can be found in Williams, *The Sanitary District of Chicago,* p. 193.

36. Quoted in Williams, *The Sanitary District of Chicago,* p. 195.

37. Williams, *The Sanitary District of Chicago,* p. 195.

38. O'Connell, "Chicago's Quest for Pure Water," p. 13, and Brown, *Drainage Channel and Waterway,* p. 292. An interesting perspective on the enlargement of the Illinois River to the size of the Main Channel and the other operations of the Lakes-to-Gulf Deep Waterway Association can be found in Joel A. Tarr, *A Study in Boss Politics: William Lorimer of Chicago* (Urbana: University of Illinois Press, 1971), pp. 163–71.

39. Quoted in Williams, *The Sanitary District of Chicago,* p. 195. See also Sanitary District of Chicago, "Drainage and Sewerage Conditions," p. 37.

40. Sanitary District of Chicago, *The Water Power Development of the Sanitary District of Chicago,* 12 November 1914, p. 1723.

41. Sanitary District of Chicago, "Drainage and Sewerage Conditions," p. 37.

42. Sanitary District of Chicago, *Report of Commission Appointed by Federal Emergency Administration of Public Works Revising Plans of West-Southwest Sewage Treatment Project of the Sanitary District of Chicago,* May 1934, p. 49.

43. See Langdon Pearse, *The Sanitary Situation of Chicago, Water Supply and Sewage Disposal* (Chicago: Sanitary District of Chicago, 29 January 1914), p. 3.

44. Randolph, "Sanitation in Chicago," p. 236.

45. Pearse, "Chicago's Quest," p. 7.

46. Randolph, "Sanitation in Chicago," p. 237.

47. Sanitary District brief, quoted in Williams, *The Sanitary District of Chicago,* p. 196.

48. O'Connell, "Chicago's Quest for Pure Water," p. 15.

49. See Williams, *The Sanitary District of Chicago,* pp. 35, 36.

50. *CREB Report,* p. 101.

51. James A. Egan, M.D., *Pollution of the Illinois River As Affected by the Drainage of Chicago and Other Cities* (Springfield, Ill.: Phillips Bros., 1901); see also *CREB Report,* pp. 117–25, and Pearse, "Chicago's Quest," p. 6.

52. William P. Mason, *Water Supply: Considered Principally from a Sanitary Standpoint,* 3d ed. (New York: John Wiley and Sons, 1909), p. 203.

5

The Calumet-Sag Channel and the Lake-Levels Controversy

Downstream problems proved much easier to resolve than those upstream, and the Sanitary District's growth brought new problems. The District originally encompassed 185 square miles, but this eventually increased to include almost all of Cook County (see map 9). The two largest additions, the North Shore suburbs in the Chicago River drainage basin and the Calumet region in the Calumet River drainage basin, were both annexed in 1903.

Sewers in the North Shore suburbs were connected to the eight-mile long North Shore Channel, a small channel constructed with a 1907 War Department permit, and completed in 1911. The channel diverted Lake Michigan water through works erected in Wilmette to the North Branch. From there the sewage and water mixture flowed to the South Branch and the Main Channel. Little objection was raised to the North Shore Channel, since it emptied into the Chicago River and, therefore, did not require an additional diversion. The only requirement was that the original diversion be divided so that part of it came through the Chicago River's Main Branch, and the other part through the North Shore Channel; the two parts were united where the diverted water entered the South Branch. As a matter of practice, the Sanitary District did increase the total diversion over time toward the 10,000 c.f.s. maximum, as increased demands on the system warranted it.

The Calumet region (the Calumet River basin's urban district) posed a much more serious problem.[1] To begin with, the region is situated in both Illinois and Indiana (see map 10). The Illinois portion of approximately 94.5 square miles lies south of Eighty-seventh Street, Chicago; the Indiana portion of approximately 47.5 square miles extends 10.7 miles eastward from the Illinois state line. The region was interspersed with sand ridges, intermediate marshes, and lakes. It was quite low: one-third of the Illinois area was below the ten-foot contour, and one-fourth was below the five-foot contour. The Indiana portion was similarly low. The principal obstacle, therefore, was drainage.

The annexation of the Illinois portion, which "included the Calumet River from its mouth, a short way up the Grand Calumet, and a long way up the Little Calumet, the total distance by way of the winding streams being not much short of 25 miles," created a great deal of controversy.[2] Some argued that the Calumet (and the North Shore) annexations were neither necessary nor justified as a part of the sew-

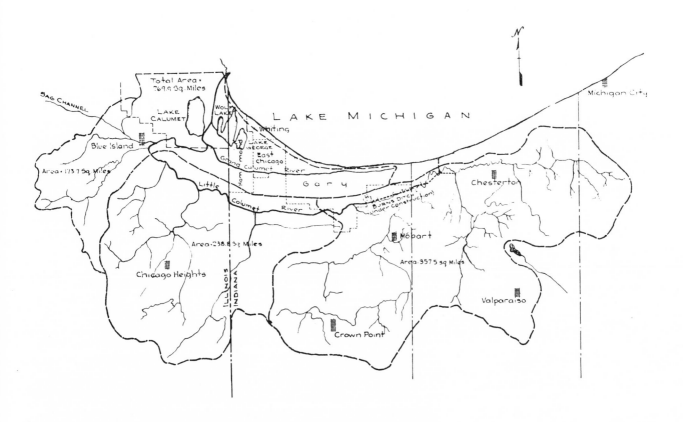

The watershed of the Grand Calumet and Little Calumet rivers indicating the drainage areas of main stream and principal tributaries. From Bulletin no. 23, *The Disposal of the Sewage of the Sanitary District of Chicago: A Report to the District Engineer*. Chicago: U.S. Engineer Office, 1927.

Map 10.

age disposal scheme for the city's central and densely populated areas. Others argued that the metropolitan area should be treated as an aggregate, the long-run interests considered, and no provision made for disposing of the sewage of any part without reference to the needs of the whole. Nevertheless, the fact remained that the Sanitary District now was responsible for the Calumet region's sewage disposal, and, whatever strategy was adopted, the purpose of that strategy would be to protect the Lake Michigan water supply.

The Sanitary District's attempt to extend the dilution method to the Calumet region was the event that brought about a legal confrontation of all the parties having an interest in the amount of the Sanitary District's Lake Michigan diversion.[3] In the main, the interested parties were other Great Lakes states and Canada, who had filed suit against the district; their interest was in the effect of the district's diversion on lake levels. As noted earlier, the natural cycle of lake levels appears to be a more significant factor than the district's diversion. Simultaneously, the population-equivalent of the Main Channel was being reached, and the Sanitary District began to investigate sewage treatment methods for both industrial wastes and domestic sewage. The district's decision to construct the Calumet-Sag Channel was made during this period of experimentation, a period in which a great deal of information was available about the relative worth of alternative methods.

THE BACKGROUND

The possibility of constructing a canal through the Sag Valley was first projected by the 1887 Drainage and Water Supply Commission report. Their proposed Sag Valley Canal was to have a 1,000 c.f.s. capacity, 10 percent of their recommendation for the Main Channel. The Calumet region, however, was not included within the Sanitary District's original boundaries. It had been omitted because its problems were distinctive, and its area encompassed two states. The Sanitary District Enabling Act did make provision for auxiliary districts and branch channels, upon terms agreeable to the parent district. An auxiliary district comprising the Calumet region's Illinois portion was considered, but the resources of such a district would have been inadequate, and the idea was dropped. The alternative was annexation to the Sanitary District, in which case the resource burden would fall upon the parent district.

The Drainage and Water Supply Commission evidently contemplated diverting as much storm water as possible. "A glance at the map and an examination of the ground" caused the commission to believe that this was a practical proposition. Their idea about how this diversion could be effected was contained in their report:

> Both branches of the Calumet river can be diverted west of the Indiana state line into Wolf Lake and thence into Lake Michigan. the Desplaines river can have its flood waters diverted into the North Branch . . . and the contained waters can be led . . . directly into the lake. Salt Creek, a branch of the Desplaines river, can readily be turned southwardly . . . discharging into the Desplaines opposite Sag, and thus reducing the necessary storm water capacity in the new channel between Sag and Summit.[4]

It was estimated that a channel between Calumet and Sag would cost $2.5 to $3.0 million; the Calumet flood waters diversion was estimated to cost between $0.35 and $0.40 million.[5] It should be recalled that the southern section of the Main Channel had proved capable of handling 4,000 c.f.s. more than the northern sections. Thus it was entirely practicable to consider a 4,000 c.f.s. capacity channel through the Calumet region, which would join the Main Channel at its southern end and would utilize the full constructed capacity of the Main Channel.

A second proposal developed out of the Pure Water Commission of 1896–1897. It was this group that projected the Calumet region's intercepting sewer system. Its report, in February 1897, recommended the exclusion of all flood waters from the urban district. It also recommended changing the Illinois and Michigan Canal to a route through the Sag Valley, with a terminus at the Calumet River. The canal was to be fed by pumps, with an ordinary capacity of 1,000 c.f.s., and an

Table 11. *Percentage Purification in Seven Alternative Sewage Treatment Methods*

Method	Percentage Purification		
	Suspended Matter	Organic Matter	Bacteria
Fine screen (30 mesh or finer)	15	10	15
Sedimentation	65	30	65
Septic treatment	65	30	65
Chemical precipitation	85	50	85
Contact filters*	85–90	65–70	80–85
Sprinkling filters*	85–90	65–70	90–95
Intermittent sand filters*	95–99	90–98	98–99

*The figures for the last three forms of treatment are based on the assumption that the sewage is given some form of preparatory treatment before it is applied to the filters, and that with the sprinkling filters, the effluent is allowed to settle.

Source: Rudolph Hering and George W. Fuller, "Report made to the International Waterways Commission on the Disposal of the Sewage of Chicago and the Calumet Region," 18 December 1906, p. 17.

emergency capacity of 1,500 c.f.s. The ordinary capacity would provide legal dilution for a 300,000 tributary population. The report claimed that ordinary floods from the restricted area would be handled more efficiently than those in the Chicago district, but it aroused little attention and less action.[6]

The Sanitary District, confronting the Calumet region's problems, adopted the same methodology which it had used in its previous works, a channel which received the discharge from the sewer system and diverted it from the Lake Michigan water supply. The district's decision to construct the Calumet-Sag Channel was made so routinely that it is apparent the district was not prepared for the controversy that the decision aroused. The North Shore Channel was constructed without controversy, and the lack of an early start on the Calumet-Sag Channel resulted in increasing opposition as time passed.

THE CONTROVERSY

When the Sanitary District decided to construct the Calumet-Sag Channel, a considerable controversy arose as to whether they should be allowed to do so. The district's principal opponents were the other Great Lakes states, Canada, and the federal government. Their argument was predicated on the assumption that the district's diversion reduced the levels of the Great Lakes and created dangerous harbor conditions. In fact, natural forces were a more significant determinant of lake levels, but neither side seemed to comprehend this. The simplest way to approach the developing controversy is through an examination of a series of reports which established the facts. Both sides appeared to agree on the facts; the controversy was nurtured by their interpretation.

The Hering-Fuller Report

U.S. participation in the second International Waterways Commission (IWC), a joint American and Canadian body, was authorized by Congress in 1902. Commission members were appointed the same year, but the commission was not organized until 1904, when the Canadian members were appointed. Specifically, the commission was charged with investigating the control of the level of Lake Erie and the diversion of Great Lakes water from its natural outlet. In this latter connection the commission was to investigate the Chicago diversion, in general, and the proposed Calumet-Sag Channel, in particular. In 1906 the IWC requested two sanitary engineers, Rudolph Hering and George Fuller, to report on several questions connected with the proposed extension of the dilution method in the Chicago area. The questions that the IWC referred to Hering and Fuller included the following:

a. Is the extension of the dilution method to the outlying territory the only way to preserve the lives and health of the people of Chicago?

b. For the Calumet area, are there not other methods of sewage disposal which may be applied at a cost not exceeding much, if at all, the cost of the method of dilution proposed, and which will be equally effective in preventing the pollution of the lake waters?

c. Description of the various systems of sewage disposal which are available for the Calumet area, with a statement of their relative efficiencies.

d. Statement of the approximate relative costs of the last mentioned so far as they can be given without the preparation of detailed plans.[7]

The IWC accepted the Main Channel and the 10,000 c.f.s. diversion as given, and they instructed Hering and Fuller to do likewise. The questions they raised revolved around increasing the district's total diversion by 4,000 c.f.s.

The Hering-Fuller report, issued in December 1906 and reprinted as part of the IWC report of January 1907, summarized what was well known about the proposed channel and river reversal. It would extend from the Little Calumet River near Blue Island, through the Sag Valley, and become confluent with the Main Channel near Sag Station. With respect to reversing the flow of the Calumet River, the report said:

The natural flow of the Calumet River exceeds 12,500 cubic feet per second. It is proposed, if suitable legislation can be secured, to construct a dam below Thorn Creek at the southern boundary of the Sanitary District and divert into Lake Michigan, through a channel to be built about seventeen and one-half miles east of the State Line, the flow of this stream with a drainage area of about 587 square miles. The size of the proposed Calumet Canal is too small to secure at all times a reversal of flow of the remaining portion of the area, which is about 240 square miles. It is proposed to put a controlling lock on the canal east of Blue Island to prevent flood waters from this lower area entering the canal, at which times sewage entering the river on the lake side of the lock would go into the lake.

The proposed canal is insufficient to carry in the future all the storm flows of the Sag Valley itself. These would at least in part require diversion through present or other channels.[8]

The population of the Illinois portion of the Calumet region was approximately 50,000 in 1894, and 100,000 in 1900. The expectation was that population growth would continue to be quite rapid; one million was anticipated within a short time, because the region was a desirable location for manufacturing development.

With the legal dilution ratio set at 3 1/3 c.f.s. per 1,000 population, the proposed 4,000 c.f.s. channel could handle the sewage of a 1.2 million tributary population, exclusive of industrial wastes. The proposed channel's estimated cost was $12 million. This meant that sewage disposal would cost a minimum of $10 per person with the maximum expected population, or $120 per person with the 1900 population. Maintenance costs would be relatively low, since most of the sewage could reach the channel by gravity (through the Calumet River). Hering and Fuller, however, stressed their belief that the Calumet region's population would eventually far exceed 1.2 million.

The experts did not regard the proposed channel as a potential threat to the Lake Michigan water supply. If that water supply were treated with a germicide and/or filtered, methods in keeping with the best contemporary water purification practices, it would be kept relatively bacteria free. The only purification required by the Calumet region's sewage was that it be kept "fairly clear and non-putrescible." The experts felt the district's proposed channel accomplished that objective.

Hering and Fuller's most significant contribution to the controversy was the section of their report that dealt with alternative sewage disposal methods. Their cost considerations put the Sanitary District's decision to pursue the open sewer technology into the perspective of the technologies available to the district at the turn of the century. Seven methods other than dilution were considered. Table 11 displays the approximate degree of purification for each method. From the table it can be observed that the first four methods could not produce, by themselves, a nonputrescible effluent; they could do so only in combination with a filtering technique. The prominent, contemporary filtration methods comprise the last three entries. Hering and Fuller argued that they only needed to consider further these three alternative filtration methods.[9]

Of the three, the most widely known was the intermittent sand filter, which was usually referred to as "land treatment." The Drainage and Water Supply Commission (1887) considered this alternative for the entire Chicago area, but they rejected it because of its greater expense. The Chicago area experience with land treatment had been poor, but Hering and Fuller dismissed this and considered intermittent sand filters anew. They found that only by disregarding the Illinois state line could a sufficiently large tract of suitable sand be found in the Calumet region. This area was situated between the Little Calumet and Grand Calumet rivers, extending eastward from Hammond, Indiana, for several miles. The most promising site within the Sanitary District lay in Thornton Township. This site was rejected, however, because there was an insufficient area for projected needs, and, furthermore, this ground was too shallow.

The other two filtration schemes became prominent at the turn of the century, and both made considerable progress in a short time. Sewage purification works of "artificial construction" utilized filters of a coarse, firm material, such as broken stone or slag. As such, they were referred to as "coarse-grained" filters, as opposed to the "fine-grained" sand filters. These newer techniques were called "contact" or "sprinkling" filters, depending on how the sewage was applied to the filters. These filters produced an effluent which would not putrefy, even when they were operated at a rate far in excess of that possible for sand filters.

Hering and Fuller described each method, described a suitable Calumet region site for constructing each type of plant, and estimated the approximate construction costs of each. These estimates were "based upon unit prices in accordance with experience elsewhere." It is interesting to note that in their report, Hering and Fuller recommended that if sewage filters were adopted for the Calumet region, then a system of separate, as opposed to combined, sewers was most appropriate. Existing sewers could be utilized for storm and surface water only. New sewers then could be constructed for the purpose of handling domestic sewage only, or vice versa. Industrial wastes were considered to be a separate problem, and, as such, were to be kept out of all sewers. This, however, was only a recommendation and was independent of cost considerations. Consequently, although Hering and Fuller deemed it advisable to construct a duplicate sewer system to separate sewer functions, their cost estimates abstracted from this idea. The cost estimates, therefore, implicitly assumed the continuation of the combined sewer approach, which they felt was consistent with the dilution method.

Table 12. *Summary Table of Estimated Costs of the Three Filtration Methods*

| | Filtration Method | | |
| | Intermittent | | |
Estimate	Sand	Contact	Sprinkling
Construction Cost	$11,063,000	$11,787,500	$ 9,257,500
Annual Operating Cost	866,000	551,000	419,000
—Capitalized at 5%	17,320,000	11,020,000	8,380,000
Total Cost	$28,383,000	$22,807,500	$17,637,500

Source: Rudolph Hering and George W. Fuller, "Report made to the International Waterways Commission on the Disposal of the Sewage of Chicago and the Calumet Region," 18 December 1906, p. 35.

The estimated costs for the three alternative methods are summarized in table 12. In each case, Hering and Fuller made what they considered to be liberal estimates. They then capitalized the estimated annual operating costs at 5 percent per annum, by use of the formula $V = N/r$, where V is the present capitalized value, N is the permanent annual receipts, and r is the discount rate.[10] By using this formula, the assumption was made that the estimated annual operating costs would remain approximately the same for an indefinitely long time-period. There was no mention of how long such a plant was expected to remain operative. Likewise, there was no mention of why 5 percent was chosen as the interest rate, but this did not prove to be crucial to the argument, for the filtration method with the lowest estimated construction cost also had the lowest annual operating cost.

There appear to be three reasons why the sprinkling filter alternative had the lowest estimated total cost. First, sprinkling filters could be installed on a smaller filter acreage than was necessary for contact filters. Second, they involved a smaller cost for intercepting sewers, pumping stations, and other appurtenances than was necessary for intermittent sand filters. Third, they would have a smaller annual filter upkeep cost than was necessary for either intermittent sand filters or contact filters.

Hering and Fuller stated their conclusions with respect to the cost estimates as follows:

> The present population (1906) on the Calumet area of the Sanitary District being less than 200,000 would naturally require but a portion of the cost of the estimated works and of their operation to be expended at the outset.

> Of the available methods of disposing of the sewage of the Calumet area, *other than by dilution,* the sprinkling filter method, being the cheapest both in cost of construction and of operation, and accomplishing an adequate degree of purification, is clearly, the most advantageous one. (Emphasis added)[11]

This report was significant, because it effectively reduced the controversy to the dilution method versus sprinkling filters. In their comprehensive approach to the task requested by the IWC, Hering and Fuller gave the opponents of the dilution method an alternative, around which they rallied, and some persuasive arguments, upon which the case for sprinkling filters ultimately rested. These opponents were principally other Great Lakes states and Canada, who believed Chicago's diversion reduced the level of the Great Lakes in general and reduced the waters in their harbors in particular. Although it specifically excluded the dilution method from consideration, the report gave the Sanitary District some food for thought with respect to its future sewage disposal strategy.

There is one troublesome feature in Hering and Fuller's conclusion. The assumption was made, implicitly, that each of the three alternatives had the same growth facility. The estimates were based on a 1.2 million population, but, as Hering and Fuller noted, the region's population at that time was less than 200,000. Hering and Fuller had argued that only a plant large enough to handle the current population was necessary; the works could be increased as population warranted. Since sprinkling filtration had proven least costly for a given population of 1.2 million, they inferred that it would also prove least costly for a population of 200,000. This, however, need not have been the case.

A more relevant cost estimation procedure would have been to assume a population growth pattern and to estimate the cost of each alternative constructed, as the growing population required. The present value of this capital outlay could then have been compared to the present value of the estimated costs of the Calumet-Sag Channel. Perhaps the reason this was not done was that the majority of the proposed channel's costs would be incurred at once. Dredging operations were not feasible for more than relatively minor increases in channel capacity. Consequently, construction costs were estimated for all three filtration methods on an "all-at-once" basis, and the argument that they could be built as needed was then invoked in their favor. Since the estimated channel cost was only $12 million, compared with $17.6 million for sprinkling filters, this argument favoring sprinkling filters was not presented as effectively as would have been the case had present value calculations been utilized.

There is little doubt that present value calculations would have lessened the estimated costs of each alternative. The question is whether they would have lessened them by the same proportion. If it were the case that sprinkling filters required larger initial works, less frequent additions, and larger additions than was true for, say, contact filters, the cost differential between the two would be diminished. If this were the case, the almost exclusive use of sprinkling filtration as the dilution method's alternative would not have been warranted.

Nevertheless, such hypothetical circumstances were not considered, and sprinkling filtration was *the* alternative. The dilution method's opponents found as many arguments favoring sprinkling filtration and as many converts as was possible. Hering and Fuller provided the estimates; the recipients of their report, the International Waterways Commission, gave both new significance.

The IWC Report on the Chicago Drainage Canal

The IWC issued its report in May 1906, recommending limitations on Canadian and United States diversion. Its recommendation was that Canada limit Great Lakes diversions to 36,000 c.f.s.; the United States, to 18,500 c.f.s. In addition, a diversion not to exceed 10,000 c.f.s. was authorized for Chicago's sanitary needs. The commission recommended further that legislation be enacted, or a treaty be formulated, to make these diversions official.

The United States Congress passed such an act in June 1906, which limited the diversion from the Niagara River and called for a treaty to the same effect with Great Britain-Canada. Such a treaty was negotiated in 1910. This treaty acknowledged both countries' rights to the water of the Great Lakes, but both the act and the treaty were silent on Chicago's diversion of Great Lakes water. Comments taken from contemporaries indicate that this silence should in no way be taken as an attempt to deny Chicago's diversion. Senator Henry Cabot Lodge of Massachusetts, in discussing the act before its passage, said that "the report of this bill in its present condition would not in any way endanger the rights of Chicago to have water from the lake. The first section of the bill protects the rights of Chicago. No treaty would be made by our commissioners which would impair or infringe these rights." Elihu Root, then secretary of state, in hearings on the treaty conducted by the Senate Committee on Foreign Relations, commented: "We are now taking 10,000 cubic feet per second out of Lake Michigan at Chicago, and I refused to permit them to say anything in the treaty about it. I would not permit them to say anything about Lake Michigan. I would not have anything in the treaty about it, and under the circumstances I thought it better not to kick about this 36,000. They consented to leave out of this treaty any reference to the drainage canal." At the same time, the legal adviser to the State Department, Chandler P. Anderson, prepared a memorandum for this committee which said in part: "Attention is called to the express provision in this article that it shall not apply to cases already existing which would seem to cover, and was certainly intended to cover, the canal system of Chicago."[12]

In January 1907 the IWC issued a report on the Main Channel in which the Lake Michigan diversion, for both the Main Channel and the proposed Calumet-Sag Channel, was questioned. The body of the report was devoted to promoting an alternative means for disposing the Calumet region's wastes. First, the report attacked the method whereby the 4,000 c.f.s. capacity had been decided:

> The amount which it is proposed to divert . . . is fixed by accident rather than by design, being the excess which the Chicago Drainage Canal is found capable of carrying after providing for the 10,000 cubic feet from the Chicago River, for which it was originally constructed. It is certain that no greater amount than 4,000 cubic feet can be diverted from the Calumet without checking the flow from the Chicago River, and thus giving relief to a suburban portion of the city at the expense of the richest and most populous centers.[13]

Also, the report quoted Sanitary District official proceedings to the effect that the 4,000 c.f.s. figure was adopted as a result of the fortuitous circumstance of excess capacity in the Main Channel's southern section.

Formally, the IWC report recommended "that the government of the United States prohibit the diversion of more than 10,000 cubic feet per second for the Chicago Drainage Canal."[14] They found that the 4,000 c.f.s. figure was insufficient to accommodate Calumet River floods, which meant that the proposed canal would be ineffective at times. The main attack on the Calumet diversion, however, was based on the Hering and Fuller report.

The IWC report introduced Hering and Fuller as engineers who were considered among the country's top sanitary experts.

> One of them, Mr. Hering, was chairman of the commission of 1887, whose report . . . was the foundation . . . of the drainage canal. The conclusions reached are those of friends of Chicago and not of her enemies or rivals.[15]

The Hering-Fuller report's estimates and conclusions were quoted in the IWC report, and their entire report was included in the IWC report as an appendix:

> A method of sewage disposal for the Calumet region is proposed which for a population of 1,200,000 is estimated to cost $17,637,500. For the present population of about 200,000 only a part of the expense need be incurred, and the works can be developed as the population increases. It can, when the necessity arises, be applied with a population much exceeding 1,200,000. The cost of diverting the Calumet River into the Chicago Drainage Canal is estimated at $12,000,000. The greater efficiency at present and in the future of the method now proposed (sprinkling filters) would justify a considerable increase of cost, but in

view of the fact that the entire expense of the diversion must be incurred at the outset, while by the new method the expenditures will be regulated by the growth of population, the difference in cost may be considered unimportant.[16]

After this careful reworking of the Hering-Fuller report, the IWC concluded that the dilution method should not be extended into the Calumet region. The commission regarded a 4,000 c.f.s. canal as inefficient compared to the available alternatives, but what comes through most clearly was their opposition to increasing the Lake Michigan diversion. The commission accepted the 10,000 c.f.s. diversion as a fact and concluded that the Main Channel was effective in handling the sewage for which it was originally intended. This, evidently, was meant to eliminate the possibility that some portion of the 10,000 c.f.s. diversion might be utilized for the Calumet-Sag Channel.

The IWC concluded, in words strongly reminiscent of the Hering-Fuller report, that

> The extension to the Calumet region of the method of sewage disposal already applied to the Chicago River is not necessary to preserve the health of Chicago, there being other and better methods available for the Calumet region. The final cost of these methods is somewhat greater than that of the one proposed, but the works can be developed as the population increases, and only a part of their cost need be incurred at present, while their greater efficiency justifies the incease of final cost.[17]

Having found in favor of an alternative method, the commission concluded:

> A careful consideration of all the circumstances leads us to the conclusion that the diversion of 10,000 cubic feet per second through the Chicago River will, with proper treatment of the sewage from areas now sparsely occupied (Calumet), provide for all the population which will ever be tributary to that river, and that the amount named will therefore suffice for the sanitary purposes of the city for all time.[18]

Thus, the IWC report officially sanctioned the position of the proposed channel's opponents. It should not be forgotten, however, that this position was based on the Hering-Fuller report, and that that report specifically excluded the proposed channel from consideration.

Langdon Pearse's Reply

In 1914, Langdon Pearse, one of the Sanitary District's leading engineers, commented that the "excellent work" of the International Waterways Commission had been "twisted."

> The International Waterways Commission did so [make recommendations adverse to dilution] only on the best of expert advice . . . that the Calumet region could be cared for both suitably and economically by method of sewage purification, but both gentlemen [Hering and Fuller] were asked to report on methods other than dilution, and both have time and again . . . reiterated the fact that the best and most economical method of all for the entire territory of the Sanitary District was sewage diversion and dilution.[19]

Pearse offered no explanation as to how the IWC reached the conclusion it did, but Pearse's position was consistent with the Hering-Fuller report's conclusions. The argument that treatment plants could be built as needed appeared in the Hering-Fuller report as a comment on the cost estimates; it was not a part of an argument that the Calumet-Sag Channel could not be expanded as needed. What Pearse appears to have argued was that dilution could be as flexible as treatment, and, since the IWC specifically excluded dilution as an alternative, the IWC's favored alternative still needed to be compared to dilution before a final decision could be reached. Where the "twisting" occurred is unclear.

What is clear, however, is that the IWC recommended to the United States secretary of war that the Sanitary District be limited to a 10,000 c.f.s. diversion. Consequently, it must have not been a great surprise when Secretary of War William Howard Taft denied the district's 1907 permit application to divert an additional 4,000 c.f.s. Secretary Taft, however, did agree to a lawsuit to establish whether or not the Sanitary District had the right to divert the additional water without a War Department permit. In the autumn of 1907, the Sanitary District started construction on the Calumet-Sag Channel, and in March 1908 the federal government instituted suit to enjoin the district from constructing the channel and diverting through the channel any lake water other than that which the secretary of war authorized.[20] This suit, joined later by a companion suit and the suits of the other Great Lakes states and Canada, dragged on in the court until 1930.

The Sanitary District never admitted that the federal government had any jurisdiction other than that with respect to the Chicago River. They were determined to fight this suit which would have prevented them from fulfilling their state charter requirements. If they were to become restricted to a total diversion of 4,167 c.f.s., a large portion of the expenditures which the Sanitary District had already made for the Main Channel and appurtenances would have been wasted.

Langdon Pearse estimated that if the federal government's position were upheld in court, an additional expenditure of approximately $100 million would have to be made over the next ten years to reach a point with another technology which, with dilution, they already enjoyed. Including the additional operating costs, the total damages were estimated to be more than $200 million.[21]

Rudolph Hering's Report
The Sanitary District felt it had a great deal at stake, and, in August 1907, they hired Rudolph Hering, of Hering and Fuller, "in connection with the anticipated litigation between the United States government and the Sanitary District of Chicago."[22] Much of Hering's October 1907 report duplicated the earlier Hering-Fuller report. Hering's report referred to the "discovery" of the "additional carrying capacity" in the lower Main Channel, and the decision to utilize this excess capacity in the proposed Calumet-Sag Channel. Hering stated that the Main Channel had been designed for a 10,000 c.f.s. capacity up to Summit, but he was criticized by the Sanitary District for his failure to note that provisions had been made also for expanding the

capacity in the northern section between Summit and the Chicago River. The Sanitary District evidently had envisioned progressive enlargements of the Main Channel. After a lengthy argument, Hering reached the conclusion that the 4,000 c.f.s. could be more cheaply provided through the Calumet-Sag Channel than by enlarging the Main Channel. Against this argument was the notion that, since the population tributary to the Main Channel was more than sixteen times that which would be tributary to the Calumet-Sag Channel, absolute cost comparisons were less valid than per capita cost comparisons.

The most interesting feature of Hering's report was the cost estimates he made comparing sprinkling filters with dilution. In addition to all the assumptions made in his earlier report with Fuller, Hering acknowledged that intercepting sewers would be needed for the Calumet region's low-lying sections, regardless which method were selected. The comparison was made for two given populations, "1,200,000 in the distant and 300,000 in the early future." This comparison is given in table 13.

Table 13. *Rudolph Hering's Calumet Region Cost Estimates*

Estimate	300,000 Population	
	Sprinkling Filters	Dilution
Construction Cost	$ 4,761,000	$15,533,000
Operation, Maintenance, and Renewals	169,000	35,600
—Capitalized at 5%	3,380,000	712,000
Total Cost	$ 8,141,000	$16,245,000

Estimate	1,200,000 Population	
	Sprinkling Filters	Dilution
Construction Cost	$ 9,257,000	$15,705,500
Operation, Maintenance, and Renewals	530,000	135,500
—Capitalized at 5%	10,600,000	2,710,000
Total Cost	$19,857,500	$18,415,500

Source: *Proceedings of the Sanitary District of Chicago*, 28 August 1907, p. 789.

Lyman Cooley, "The Calumet District," June 1913, p. 18.

Hering's figures were then adjusted to take into account an ordinance of January 1908, which extended the proposed Calumet-Sag Channel east from Blue Island; this added $1.5 million to the dilution method. Offsetting this increase was the fact that the channel developed waterpower at both Lockport and Joliet; the capitalized value of the former was estimated to be $5.5 million. The value of the waterpower was estimated to be $25 per horsepower per year. This meant an additional $272,800 in Lockport revenues, which, when capitalized at 5 percent, translated as a deduction of $5,456,000 from the dilution method estimates. Although the additional Joliet revenues were excluded by a 1908 constitutional amendment, they were estimated to be $255,300, which, when capitalized at 5 percent, translated as a deduction of $5,106,000.[23]

These same estimates were reported elsewhere on a total annual cost basis (operating expenses plus fixed interest) net of Lockport waterpower revenues. The alternative estimates did not allow for Joliet waterpower sales, and the estimates did not credit the treatment works with any return.[24] The comparison is given in table 14. Once allowance was made for waterpower, the comparison was the same in either form. Sprinkling filters were relatively less expensive in the "early future," whereas the channel was a great deal less expensive in the "distant future." Since the Lockport waterpower facilities had already been developed, it was consistent to reason with the waterpower revenues deducted from the estimated costs. As such, the estimated costs did not provide an unequivocal argument in favor of either approach, and there was no basis for decision.

Table 14. "C.R.E.B." Calumet Region Cost Estimates

Population	Sprinkling Filters	Dilution
300,000	$360,240	$384,000
1,200,000	900,300	490,000

Source: Soper, Watson and Martin, A Report to the Chicago Real Estate Board on the Disposal of the Sewage and Protection of the Water Supply of Chicago, Illinois, p. 137.

Hering's report argued in favor of the channel because, other things being equal, dilution was an older, better understood, and less odoriferous approach. He remarked, concerning artificial treatment in general, that "It is necessary to surround the works with sufficient lands, so that odors which do sometimes arise, will not become a nuisance to residents." Hering concluded his basic argument for dilution thusly:

> A final disposition of sewage by at once diluting it with a sufficient quantity of running water had the advantage of simplicity in operation and is, therefore, always preferable to any method of treatment, because it requires less attention, care and labor, and, from a sanitary point of view is quite as satisfactory, if the sewage is properly mixed with the diluting water and not used as a potable supply until actual oxidation has made it safe. . . . As yet, the least expensive method of sewage treatment has not been developed to a final state. No municipal plant of sprinkling filters has yet been operated in America, although several are now under construction. . . . On the other hand, the dilution method of sewage purification being the prevailing one and the oldest one in use, is thoroughly known as to what it can do and what it cannot do. We may, therefore, consider its works to be more permanent.[25]

Other arguments were presented for dilution, but these were the most significant. The rebuttal of the opponents of dilution was predictable: sprinkling filtration was less expensive in the "early future" and could be expanded at a rate commensurate with population growth.

The Sanitary District Engineering Department's Report

The Hering report accomplished little in the way of direct action, because the secretary of war refused the Sanitary District a permit to divert the additional 4,000 c.f.s. Simultaneously, conditions in the Calumet region were quickly becoming intolerable. The sewers south of Eighty-seventh Street discharged into the Calumet River, and the population was growing at a rapid rate. The sewage settled in the Calumet River and was flushed into Lake Michigan, contaminating Chicago's water supply. Sanitary District engineers were faced with the problem of developing alternatives to the contested 4,000 c.f.s. channel.

Their problem was to consider the sewage-handling alternatives for both Chicago and Calumet: first, with a 10,000 c.f.s. diversion, and, second, with a 14,000 c.f.s. diversion. This was constrained by the objective that all the sewage should be diluted locally, which was to say that all sewage entering either the Chicago River and its branches or the Calumet River should have sufficient lake water to dilute it, so that at no point within the Sanitary District's jurisdiction would these rivers become objectionable.

The consensus of the consulted engineers was that a channel of some capacity should be constructed between the Calumet River and the Main Channel at the Sag, even if sewage treatment plants also were constructed. Such a channel would prevent the river from becoming polluted during the dry season. This was also the opinion of the Sanitary District's engineering department, which argued that the stagnant Calumet River, passing through a growing manufacturing district, would become polluted even if sewage were diverted from it. They felt that an artificial current was a necessity during the dry season—it would take the polluted Calumet River away from Chicago's water supply. An artificial current would reduce the water-supply pollution threat at all times, but it was conceded that heavy rains and freshets would still cause the Calumet region to drain into Lake Michigan.[26]

Having reached the conclusion that a channel was desirable, regardless of the pending litigation's outcome or any decision affecting sprinkling filters, the problem was to determine the optimal channel's capacity. The engineering department's report made cost estimates of channels with varying capacities. The number of days a channel of given size would discharge into the lake or lie stagnant was also estimated. These estimates are given in table 15.

Table 15. *Chicago Sanitary District's Engineering Department's Cost Estimates of Various Capacity Channels for the Calumet Region*

Capacity (c.f.s.)	Cost	Days into Lake	Stagnant	Total
1,000	$ 4,516,000	101.5	83	184.5
2,000	6,228,000	22.3	8	30.4
3,000	8,178,000	9.8	6	15.8
4,000	11,073,000	5.5	1.3	6.8

Source: George Wisner, "Sewage Disposal of the Calumet District," 9 June 1909, p. 6.

One of the arguments favorable to the 4,000 c.f.s. canal was that it would be a navigable channel for large lake-steamers. The engineering department, however, now claimed that this had never been asserted by any authority, and the best that could be hoped was that vessels of ten- to fourteen-feet draught would find such a channel navigable. The larger lake-steamers could possibly be towed through the channel, but it would be too small for the free navigation of such ships. Therefore, the engineering department argued in favor of the 2,000 c.f.s. channel, on a sanitary and cost basis. If, in the future, a navigable channel were desired, the recommended channel's capacity could be increased by dredging. The Sanitary District was advised to plan ahead by purchasing a right-of-way sufficient to accommodate the larger channel, although initially a smaller channel would be constructed. The enlargement of the Calumet-Sag Channel, and the improvement to the Little Calumet River in order to make the route available for larger barge tows was authorized in 1946. Work did not begin until 1955, and it was nearly complete in 1975.[27]

This decision was consistent with that reached by the Commission on Calumet Sewage, which made its report in February 1909.[28] That group concluded that it would be practically impossible to keep Calumet River tributaries unpolluted, no matter what steps were taken toward justifying the Calumet region sewage outside the Chicago Sanitary District's jurisdiction. Therefore, it was desirable to divert the Calumet's daily flow. Secondly, they concluded that it would be unwise to discharge raw sewage into the Calumet River. They proposed constructing an intercepting sewer system on either bank of the river, beginning near the river's mouth. This would require the construction of pumping works. Finally, the commission recommended that experimental stations be developed to study different sewage treatment processes as a hedge against future growth.

The Committee on Engineering's Report

In May 1910, the Committee on Engineering of the Chicago Sanitary District recommended the immediate construction of the Calumet-Sag Channel.[29] The secretary of war had prohibited the district from using any part of the 10,000 c.f.s. for the proposed channel, saying that it required an act of Congress. The Committee on Engineering's report focused on three schemes they felt could be instituted under the federal government restrictions, and they estimated the cost of each. Navigation features were specifically excluded from consideration, but no mention was made whether water power potential was included in the channel estimates. The estimates from this report are given in table 16. The conclusion of the Committee on Engineering was that, given these figures, a 2,000 c.f.s. channel should be constructed because it was superior to the others from the standpoint of sanitation, economy, and practicability.

The task of protecting Chicago's water supply by reducing lake pollution was a problem that extended beyond the Sanitary District's geographical boundaries. This was particularly true of the Calumet region's Indiana cities. Two of Chicago's water intakes were within one-third mile of the Illinois-Indiana boundary projected into Lake Michigan. While the state lines provided a limit on Sanitary District authority, it placed no limit on the sewage and waste flow. It was estimated that the sewage from a 163,000 population eventually reached Lake Michigan from the Calumet region, and this excluded millions of gallons of industrial wastes which daily entered the lake from the Calumet region's industry.

Table 16. *Cost Estimates for Alternative Calumet Region Projects*

Project	Cost
525 c.f.s. sewer	$4,240,000
1,000 c.f.s. channel	4,300,000
2,000 c.f.s. channel	5,640,000

Source: *Calumet-Sag Channel — A Vital Necessity*, 25 May 1910, p. 10.

It is interesting to note that it was not until late 1927 that the Indiana State Board of Health finally offered some help; they required sewage treatment by the northern Indiana towns. Pressure from such sources as the Sanitary District, the city of Chicago, and the Chicago Regional Planning Association induced some corporations to adopt sewage treatment before discharging their wastes. Nevertheless, as late as 1930 most of the communities bordering Lake Michigan discharged untreated sewage directly into the lake. These included Michigan City, Indiana; Kenosha, Wisconsin; and the cities and villages of Lake County, Illinois, immediately north of the Chicago Sanitary District's jurisdiction. In Lake County, however, the North Shore Sanitary District was investigating means of sewage treatment.

It appeared to those considering the construction of a channel in 1910 that any diversion of Calumet region sewage would be desirable. The proposed channel would be a source of occasional pollution, but considerable pollution would still reach Lake Michigan from the Calumet region's Indiana section. Sewage from the Indiana Harbor Ship Canal and the Upper Grand Calumet, which included nearly all of Gary and East Chicago's sewage, would flow constantly into the lake. A small portion of the Little Calumet's flow would reach Lake Michigan through Burns Ditch. Lake pollution, primarily from these sources, would be greater if the Chicago Sanitary District did not adopt some diversionary method, either dilution or sprinkling filtration.[30]

THE CALUMET-SAG CHANNEL AND THE EXISTING LITIGATION

The Committee on Engineering's report came at the same time that Sanitary District engineers were developing specifications and plans for such a channel. Three years of controversy had reduced the proposed capacity of this channel from 4,000 c.f.s. to 2,000 c.f.s. On 30 June 1910, a new secretary of war accepted the Sanitary District's application and issued the necessary permit to construct the Calumet-Sag Channel and to reverse the Calumet River's flow. The permit carried with it several conditions, the most important being that the Sanitary District could not divert any water in addition to that already authorized by the secretary of war.[31] It must be emphasized that this permit was issued in the face of a 1908 War Department suit which would prohibit the district from constructing the channel.

In September 1911, work began on the sixteen-mile Calumet-Sag

Channel. It extended from Stony Creek on the North Calumet River, along the route of the Illinois and Michigan Canal's Calumet feeder, to Sag, approximately thirteen miles above Lockport. It reversed the ordinary flow of the Calumet River and diverted all the sewage away from Lake Michigan.[32] The channel had controlling works at its eastern end to control the flow. The appurtenances, such as bridges, were all designed to provide for navigation, when and if the channel were enlarged. Under the law, the initial 2,000 c.f.s. capacity would provide for sewage disposal by dilution of a 600,000 population. This was only half the Calumet region's predicted population, and it was expected that the channel would be enlarged to accommodate the larger population.

Early in 1912 the Sanitary District applied to the secretary of war for a permit to divert a minimum 10,000 c.f.s. from Lake Michigan, for both its completed works and those in the process of completion. This included the Calumet-Sag Channel. This request was denied in January 1913, after a public hearing. By 1915 the Sanitary District had expended approximately $3.2 million of an estimated $8.2 million to construct a 2,000 c.f.s. channel, and had obligated itself for approximately $5.4 million of the total.[33] Ceasing constructing until such time as the existing litigation was resolved would have meant the continued pollution of Lake Michigan by Calumet region sewage. If the litigation were resolved against the Sanitary District, the channel might prove superfluous. Yet construction had begun on a 2,000 c.f.s. channel—construction that wasn't completed until 1922.

After five years, testimony had begun to be heard in the 1908 injunction suit, which involved the district's right to reverse the Calumet River's flow and divert additional Lake Michigan water to operate the Calumet-Sag Channel. In October 1913 the federal government instituted a second blanket injunction suit designed to cover all questions relating to the district's diversion of any Lake Michigan water in excess of the amount permitted by the secretary of war. Both suits were prosecuted continuously, and expert testimony was obtained from the country's best informed hydraulic and sanitary engineers.

The existence of the first federal suit, and the possibility of the second, raises the question of why the 1910 permit was issued in the first place. Initially, the permit application had been rejected, when it requested a 4,000 c.f.s. additional diversion. Later, the secretary of war prohibited the Sanitary District from using any part of the already permitted diversion for the Calumet-Sag Channel, saying that it required an act of Congress. The 1910 Calumet permit contradicted this last prohibition. The first injunction suit challenged the Sanitary District's right to divert any Lake Michigan water through the Calumet-Sag Channel. The issued permit could have been construed as its right to operate the channel, but the War Department continued to press the injunction suit after the permit was issued. This would seem to exclude the usual contention that the permit was issued because of the change in administrators.

The contradiction between enjoining construction and then issuing an operating permit should have been a signal to the Sanitary District that its permit request might be refused, but, officially, it claimed ignorance. George Wisner, the district's chief engineer, stated in April 1915 that

> Up to the time that the request was made of the Secretary of War that a permit be granted for a diversion of 10,000 cubic feet per second of water from Lake Michigan, the officials of the Sanitary District had no reason to suppose that there would be any opposition to the withdrawal of this amount of water from Lake Michigan. It was also believed that a permit for the withdrawal of this amount would be granted, up to January 8, 1913, when the permit was refused by the Secretary of War.[34]

As noted, the secretary of war never officially acknowledged any diversion greater than 4,167 c.f.s., and the Sanitary District had no official reason to believe that he looked favorably upon a diversion in excess of that figure. The War Department's failure to press for this diversion and the general assumption elsewhere of a 10,000 c.f.s. diversion were evidently what the Sanitary District took as "no opposition." It was not until the initiation of the second injunction suit that the district addressed itself to the alternatives. The first suit challenged the construction of the Calumet-Sag Channel, a channel that was fast becoming a reality. The second suit challenged the efficacy of the district's technology.

THE SANITARY DISTRICT'S DECISION

In early 1915 the Sanitary District's Committee on Engineering passed an order requesting George Wisner, the chief engineer, to report to the district's board of trustees on ". . . the uses to which the Calumet-Sag Channel could be put in case the decision in the Government suit was adverse to the contentions of The Sanitary District of Chicago."[35] Such an event would have forced the Sanitary District to supplement its existing works with some form of sewage treatment. Wisner's report assumed that whatever future steps might be taken, they would prove faithful to the original Sanitary District Enabling Act's basic principles. If it proved impossible to divert sufficient water to oxidize the sewage, then some other process would be used to render the sewage innocuous and nonputrescible. This would have to be some form of sewage treatment works, and

> . . . the sewage or effluent from purification works constructed to take care of the sewage in the Calumet region should be in some manner conducted to the Main Channel. The most practicable and cheapest way to do so is by open channel from Blue Island to . . . Sag. The channel under construction will accomplish that purpose.[36]

This contention was consistent with Wisner's premise that the revised scheme should utilize to as great an extent as possible the works existing under the old scheme. He appeared to argue that some part of the permitted diversion·would be used to flush the effluent from the purification works down the Calumet-Sag Channel to the Main Channel.

In the following lengthy quotation, Wisner summarized the situation facing the Sanitary District in 1915. He emphasized the "predicament" which the secretary of war's "unexpected" refusal had caused.

Since the filing of the injunction suit in March, 1908, and even prior thereto, the officials of the Sanitary District have had the choice of two alternatives—one to stand still and do nothing for the relief of the Calumet district and await the result of long litigation with the United States Government, and the second, to go ahead on some construction work to remove the danger of a typhoid epidemic in the Southern part of this city. If the right of the District to divert a given quantity of water had been determined, the solution of this problem both from a physical and financial standpoint, would have been a comparatively simple engineering problem. In 1913, a further uncertainty developed which had not been anticipated by the officials of the District, namely that the United States Government would deny the right of the District to abstract 10,000 cubic feet per second of water from Lake Michigan, holding the District to its permit to abstract only 4,167 cubic feet per second. This was not known until January, 1913, when the permit was denied by the Secretary of War. In the meantime, the right of way for the construction of a channel for 2,000 cubic feet per second, capable of development to 4,000 cubic feet per second had been largely obtained. The District then adopted a policy for the disposal of the sewage through a canal to connect with the Main Drainage Channel at the Sag, and a vast amount of money had been expended on the furtherance of this plant. Hence, the District found itself in the embarrassing position, of either having to continue the work with the uncertainty of the outcome of the litigation with the United States Government or abandoning the project and do nothing pending the outcome of a long run and protracted litigation. In the one case the officials of the District would be criticized for not going ahead on work of a constructive character to preserve the health of the people, and on the other hand they would be criticized for taking a chance on doing something that might prove, when the final outcome of the litigation had been determined, somewhat more expensive than if they had selected an alternative scheme.[37]

Consequently, and somewhat unbelievably, Wisner generated a new set of cost estimates to help determine the Sanitary District's course. Three alternatives were considered. The first was the 2,000 c.f.s. Calumet-Sag Channel already under construction. The second contemplated installing purification works and a sewer to carry the resulting effluent to the Main Channel. Cost estimates for this second project were based on the assumption that the existing channel project would be completely abandoned as of 1 January 1915, and the money theretofore expended would be lost. The estimate did not include any saving that might accrue from contracts which had been let but not completed. Like the existing channel project, this scheme provided only for the dry-weather flow. The storm flow was to be sterilized, and then discharged into Lake Michigan through the Calumet River.

The third project contemplated completing the Calumet-Sag Channel as planned, and then, under the assumption that the flow was limited to 4,167 c.f.s., installing treatment works. Under this scheme, all storm water and sewage was to discharge into the channel following treatment. None was to be allowed to pass into Lake Michigan, except when freshets or heavy floods placed too great a burden on the channel's capacities.

Table 17. *Wisner's Calumet Region Project Cost Estimates*

Project	First Cost	Annual Cost
Completing Proposed Channel	$12,583,677.00	$ 769,387.00
Covered Conduit, Purification Works	15,831,253.78	1,182,511.00
Channel Built, Plus Treatment Works	16,079,332.00	1,193,220.00

Source: George Wisner, "Sewage Disposal of the Calumet District," 9 June 1909, pp. 242–45.

Table 17 summarizes Wisner's estimates of construction and annual cost for each scheme. The estimates were based on an assumed population of 300,000. The estimated costs of the latter two projects were within 1 percent and could be considered identical for all practical purposes. The open channel had additional benefits which did not accrue to the covered conduit, and, therefore, Wisner's recommendation was to complete the channel, regardless of the litigation's outcome. Wisner supported this conclusion in this manner:

> It would seem to me that the general policy of preventing sewage or the effluent coming from sewage disposal stations from entering Lake Michigan should be continued, and especially is this so when it can be accomplished at comparatively small expense. . . . The construction and operation of this canal will be the last step in the general scheme to prevent sewage from entering Lake Michigan between the Lake County line, north of Glencoe, and the Indiana state line, thus guaranteeing the effectiveness of any purification works that may have to be installed. . . . In case this policy is to be continued, there is no choice as between the method of building an open conduit or canal such as is being constructed or a sewer to carry the effluent of sewage disposal station. The advantages of the former are: first, its better effectiveness in handling not only the dry weather flow but also the storm flow coming from the Calumet district; its value for barge canal purposes; its value for drainage of property, thus creating values; and lastly, in case the District obtains some 10,000 cubic feet per second diversion from Lake Michigan it is much the cheaper and will handle twice the population the other projects would be capable of doing, as estimated.[38]

SUMMARY

Armed with new estimates and faced with the possibility of an unfavorable litigation outcome, the Sanitary District proceeded to complete the Calumet-Sag Channel. If the district considered this to be a crucial juncture, as it evidently did, one wonders why Wisner did not base his estimates on a population which was consistent with previous estimates. Instead, he used a population base that was half the 600,000 maximum population a 2,000 c.f.s. channel could service under the legal restrictions. Perhaps increasing a completed channel from 2,000 to 4,000 c.f.s. was less costly than any alternative, but this needed to be demonstrated.

Although these estimates, as well as the others, showed that the costs were relatively close, the decision was always in favor of the dilution method. In Wisner's estimates, the complete channel plus treatment works were slightly more expensive than a covered conduit plus purification works; yet the decision was to complete the channel.

It was clear that the dilution method's days were numbered; nevertheless the decision was to pursue the dilution method. It appears that cost was not the decisive factor, particularly if expected costs were considered. If the total diversion were limited to either 10,000 c.f.s. or 4,167 c.f.s., then the waterpower potential was not relevant. What appeared time and again as the persuasive argument in favor of the dilution method was an open channel's navigation potential. This appears to be the one factor that consistently swung the decision to the dilution method, although at this late date, in the face of the very minor roles of the Illinois and Michigan Canal and the Main Channel as transportation routes, it is quite surprising that the navigation potential of these channels was taken seriously. In the light of what the Sanitary District could reasonably expect the future to bring, it is somewhat surprising that the Calumet-Sag Channel was completed. Yet it should not be forgotten that the reports discussed in this chapter stretch over three decades and that Wisner's 1915 report was issued twelve years after the Illinois portion of the Calumet region was annexed to the district. This twelve-year period was one of continuing controversy concurrent with rapid advances in sewage treatment technology and population. The Sanitary District of Chicago's conservative engineering decision to pursue the dilution method in the Calumet region evidently was predicated on that method's *known* capabilities, the necessity of implementing some method in the Calumet region, and a lack of awareness of the controversy such a decision would engender. New constraints were entering the district's decision process, but the district did not incorporate them as quickly as interested parties outside Chicago desired. The Calumet-Sag Channel decision was based on the same objectives and constraints as the decision that led to the Sanitary District's creation.

NOTES

1. Lyman E. Cooley, *Supplement to the Brief—The Calumet District* (Chicago: Sanitary District of Chicago, June 1913), p. 1.

2. Lake Calumet and the Illinois portion of Wolf Lake are also in this area. George A. Soper, John D. Watson, and Arthur J. Martin, *A Report to the Chicago Real Estate Board on the Disposal of the Sewage and Protection of the Water Supply of Chicago, Illinois* (hereafter the *CREB Report*), 1915, p. 130.

3. See Louis P. Cain, "Unfouling the Public's Nest: Chicago's Sanitary Diversion of Lake Michigan Water," *Technology and Culture,* October 1974, pp. 594–613.

4. Quoted in *CREB Report,* p. 130, from the "Report of the International Waterways Commission," 1 January 1907, Appendix A, p. 24.

5. *CREB Report,* p. 130.

6. Cooley, *The Calumet District,* p. 5.

7. Rudolph Hering and George W. Fuller, *Report Made to the International Waterways Commission on the Disposal of the Sewage of Chicago and the Calumet Region,* New York, 18 December 1906, p. 1.

8. Ibid., pp. 15, 16.

9. For large installations, filtration was felt to be more economical if the sewage were first "clarified" by septic tanks, or some other appropriate method. Septic tanks are large sedimentation basins in which accumulated sludge undergoes bacterial action.

10. Although the formula was not explicit in their report, it is implied by the fact that Hering and Fuller multiplied the estimated annual operating costs by a factor of twenty.

11. Hering and Fuller, *Report to the IWC,* p. 36.

12. All quotations are from George W. Fuller, "The Sewage Disposal Problem of Chicago," 19 February 1925, pp. 7–8.

13. Lyman E. Cooley, *The Calumet District,* p. 10. The same theme was repeated many times throughout the IWC Report.

14. Sanitary District of Chicago, *Copy of the International Waterways Commission Report Issued by the Board of Trustees of the Sanitary District of Chicago,* March 1924, p. 17.

15. Ibid., p. 14.

16. Ibid.

17. Ibid., p. 16. See also, Cooley, *The Calumet District,* p. 12.

18. Ibid., p. 16. See also *CREB Report,* p. 132.

19. Langdon Pearse, *The Sanitary Situation of Chicago, Water Supply and Sewage Disposal,* 29 January 1914, p. 4. The occasion was Pearse commenting on the *CREB Report.*

20. See George M. Wisner, *Sewage Disposal of the Calumet District* (Chicago: Sanitary District of Chicago, 9 June 1909), p. 1. See also George M. Wisner, *Report on the Advisability of Building Calumet-Sag Channel* (Chicago: Sanitary District of Chicago, 1915), p. 235. Also Fuller, "The Sewage Disposal Problem of Chicago," p. 6.

21. Pearse, *The Sanitary Situation of Chicago,* p. 4. Total damages were the sum of total expenditures, past, present, and future, plus operating costs.

22. Quoted in Cooley, *The Calumet District,* p. 17.

23. See Cooley, *The Calumet District,* p. 18.

24. *CREB Report,* p. 137.

25. Cooley, *The Calumet District,* p. 19.

26. Wisner, *Sewage Disposal of the Calumet District,* p. 2.

27. For a discussion of barge traffic on the channels in the late 1930s, see Carl W. Condit, *Chicago, 1910–29,* p. 247.

28. Sanitary District of Chicago, *Sewage Disposal of the Calumet District* (Report of the Commission on Calumet Sewerage), 8 February 1909.

29. Sanitary District of Chicago, *Calumet-Sag Channel: A Vital Necessity,* 25 May 1910. See also *CREB Report,* p. 129.

30. See Max R. White, *Water Supply Organization in the Chicago Region,* p. 607.

31. Wisner, *Report on the Advisability of Building Calumet-Sag Channel,* pp. 235, 236.

32. Sanitary District of Chicago, *Engineering Works,* August 1928, p. 31. Also *CREB Report,* p. 131. Also R. Isham Randolph, "The History of Sanitation in Chicago," *Journal of the Western Society of Engineers,* October 1939, p. 236.

33. Wisner, *Report on the Advisability of Building Calumet-Sag Channel,* p. 238.

34. Ibid., p. 237.

35. Ibid., p. 235.

36. Ibid., p. 237.

37. Ibid., pp. 240–41.

38. Ibid., p. 245.

6
The Advent of
Sewage Treatment

While the courts wrestled with the case against the Sanitary District's 10,000 c.f.s. diversion, continued population growth and increasing industrial wastes also worked against sole reliance on the dilution method. Once Chicago's population-equivalent reached 3 million, the Main Channel could not support a lake diversion sufficient to dilute the sewage in the legally prescribed proportion.[1] Some method that could supplement dilution had to be found. While the Sanitary District maintained a steadfast advocacy of dilution, it was not deluded in the belief that the dilution method alone could provide adequate handling of the ever-increasing sewage volumes.

Industrial wastes contributed significantly to Chicago's population-equivalent. The problem was most acute in the South Branch's South Fork, more commonly known as "Bubbly Creek," adjacent to the Stockyards area (see map 7). The Sanitary District noted the problem as early as 1890. In January 1915, it issued a report concerning sewage treatment for the Stockyards-Packingtown district.[2] This report was devoted to the sanitary conditions within the square-mile area containing the slaughter and packing houses. While the area drained into Bubbly Creek, the drainage pattern was decidedly random. None of the streets had been "dedicated," and sewers were laid in every direction. No limitations had been placed on the quantity or composition of the liquids and semi-liquids which were allowed to discharge into the sewers.[3]

The amount of wastes diminished somewhat, as the larger firms expanded vertically and processed the by-products of the slaughtered animals. The smaller firms, however, continued to discharge "blood, offal, tankage and other objectionable material" directly into the sewers in considerable amounts. It was estimated that, by 1917, the pollution originating in the Stockyards district was equivalent to that from one million people, and none of this was included in calculations regarding the capacity of the Main Channel.[4]

THE BACKGROUND

In 1908 the Sanitary District began experimenting with various sewage treatment methods.[5] It appears that the Sanitary District wasted little time covering itself against possible defeat in the legal proceedings that began the same year. By 1909, it had become evident to the district's chief engineer, George Wisner, that the dilution method was inadequate as constructed, that the tributary population exceeded the constructed maximum of the Main Channel, and that nothing had been initiated with respect to the industrial wastes problem. Consequently, Wisner felt that, at a minimum, means had to be implemented which would supplement dilution with sewage treatment.[6]

The Thirty-ninth Street Pumping Station, which had been constructed originally to provide a flushing current for the South Branch, and later served as a pump for the South Side sewers which had once discharged into Lake Michigan, was a ready-made site for a sewage treatment laboratory. Experimental work began there in March 1909, under Langdon Pearse's direction.[7] These experiments continued at Thirty-ninth Street until 1911. In October of that year, Wisner publicized and emphasized the need for sewage treatment facilities in his annual report.

Wisner's 1911 report was the first to ascertain the extent of industrial pollution and the first to recommend solutions. Although Wisner's report was only preliminary, it had two principal consequences with respect to the Stockyards district. First, in 1911 the packers contributed almost $27,000 to dredge Bubbly Creek. This was done in 1913, at a total cost of $24,500. Second, in 1912 the packers contributed $2,600 to construct the Packingtown testing station, which commenced operations in October of that year. Wisner's investigation had shown that the "wastes were of such magnitude and such strength that special tests were required to determine the best methods of treatment."[8] In January 1916 the activated sludge method was added and tested extensively until September 1918, when the facility was closed. The district was convinced that the activated sludge technique would produce a high-grade effluent requiring little or no dilution.

The Stockyards sewage was unusually endowed with suspended and dissolved materials and was considerably warmer than the city's domestic sewage. This meant that the oxygen requirement was significantly greater; the district's biological tests fixed this as six to ten times that of domestic sewage. Previous tests had demonstrated that all known sewage treatment methods could be utilized in the Stockyards-Packingtown district, and it had been the purpose of the Packingtown testing station to ascertain the most efficient method. It was found practicable to remove the solids, and, by utilizing the activated sludge process, to place them into a form within which they would acquire commercial value as a fertilizer.

It is interesting to note the fact that the packers contributed to the search for a solution to the problems their operations created for the district. While the district had never given serious consideration to the problem of industrial pollution prior to 1911, their works had to cope with industrial sewage because it was deposited into the city's sewer system. Inasmuch as industries paid property taxes to both the city and the Sanitary District, it was expected that sewage disposal services would be received. This raises questions of economic equity. The Stockyards were producing wastes equivalent to that from one million people, but it is doubtful that their property taxes were equivalent to that generated from the residences of an equal population. If this is true, the greater than proportionate share of the tax bill for sewage disposal borne by individuals was a transfer to industrial polluters, of which the Stockyards were among the worst offenders. In brief, the

Stockyards were being subsidized by the general populace. Yet that can be a desirable situation. The packers generated jobs and tax revenues for Chicago and might have located elsewhere in the absence of such a subsidy. Economic equity may require an answer to the question of how large a subsidy is desirable rather than the simpler question of whether any subsidy is desirable. This is not the place to confront these questions; they involve value judgments which are of such a nature that no single correct answer may result from the analysis. Suffice it to note that it appears the packers were receiving a subsidy.

Why then did the packers contribute money for the establishment of a testing station? The written record provides few clues, but this much is clear: Bubbly Creek was noxious and the odor had become unbearable. The Sanitary District did not have ready funds to invest in the necessary works, and it was the Stockyards who stood to gain the most from any improvement in the handling of their wastes. To say that they gladly received the benefit it not the same thing as saying they willingly bore the cost. How much coercion was required to obtain the packers' funds is a subject for further study.

THE RESEARCH

George Wisner's 1911 report outlined the approach he felt most advisable, but he added that these were only his opinions and that more detailed studies were necessary. Wisner proposed that almost all the district's sewage be treated by sprinkling filters, settling basins, or both. He predicted that settling basins would remove 25 percent of the organic matter and that the resulting effluent from either approach would not add to the water's organic pollution. The report made allowance for the gradual construction of the works; only the most necessary would be constructed immediately.

The year 1930 was chosen as the terminal year, and all facilities were designed to handle effectively that year's estimated population. Wisner's report contained only a very crude estimate of 1930's population; ward and precinct populations were extrapolated by extending their growth rates between 1900 and 1910 to the period between 1910 and 1930.[9] The choice of 1930 was less arbitrary than were the population estimates. Wisner gave the following as his reason for choosing 1930:

> The year 1930 has been selected as a suitable year to design to, since whatever goes into service around 1920 should be capable of serving for ten years thereafter. It will be entirely possible to extend the design to a date beyond 1930, but it is not thought advisable to do so at this time, for the reason that improved methods may be discovered for the artificial purification of sewage that are unknown at this time.[10]

The motivation to limit planning to a twenty-year interval reflected the tremendous advances that had taken place in sewage disposal knowledge over the last decade of the nineteenth century and the first decade of the twentieth century. New methods had been invented; cost-reducing innovations had been made in older methods. Even if this had not been the case, the uncertainties that existed with regard to extending the dilution method dictated that Wisner consider some sewage treatment technology.

Wisner's proposals embraced the entire Sanitary District, were complete with cost estimates and suggested completion dates, and probably were somewhat more than the "skeletons upon which to start detailed studies" which he considered them to be. Table 18 summarizes Wisner's proposals and, for each project, gives Wisner's estimates of total cost, annual cost, and tributary 1930 population.

Table 18. *Wisner's Sewage Treatment Project—Estimates*

	Population Estimated in 1930	First Cost	Annual Cost in 1930
Settling Projects:			
Calumet	301,100	$ 695,750	$ 69,850
39th Street	518,000	1,302,000	123,130
Lawrence Avenue	218,200	746,000	66,900
North Branch	606,410	1,552,300	155,600
West Side	513,800	1,204,000	124,600
West 22nd Street	475,100	1,202,000	116,930
Stockyards	324,900	618,800	67,000
Intercepting Sewers:			
Calumet	301,100	2,242,500	160,000
Settling and Sprinkling Filter Projects:			
Calumet	301,100	2,761,700	261,800
North Branch	606,410	5,943,700	548,900
West Side	513,800	4,985,000	447,800

Source: George Wisner, "Report on Sewage Disposal," 12 October 1911, pp. 65, 66.

Wisner's suggested timetable was that the intercepting sewers, pumping stations, and settling basins for the Calumet region be started first, so that they could be completed with the Calumet-Sag Channel. A settling plant was to be constructed at a sharp bend in the Calumet River, east of the channel. This was done to remove a significant amount of solid matter prior to discharging the sewage into the channel. Two settling plants in the Stockyards district were to be completed by 1915, reflecting their urgency. Eight settling plants were to be constructed on the North Branch. These were to be started by 1922 and in operation by 1930. Other cities' experience and the Sanitary District's experiments suggested that each plant would require between one and nine and one-half acres. The resulting effluent would be immediately discharged into the North Branch. On the West Side, the sewers were to be extended and five settling plants constructed on the Main Channel by 1925. The two pumping stations at Thirty-ninth Street and Lawrence Avenue were to be converted, and settling tanks were to be constructed adjacent to the existing works. The sewage effluent from the Thirty-ninth Street station was to be discharged without further treatment. In like manner, the effluent resulting from the Lawrence Avenue stations was to be discharged into the North Branch. The settling basins at the Thirty-ninth Street Pumping Station were to be in operation by 1930, if necessary. The West Twenty-second Street installation, on the Main Channel, would not be needed until 1930, and no date was set for the Lawrence Avenue settling plant. As can be seen, the existing channel system still played a major role in Wisner's scheme. He also advocated that sprinkling filters be added later to the Calumet, North Branch, and West Side settling plants. Intercepting sewers would be necessary to divert the sewage to the treatment works. The sprinkling filter installations would treat completely the sewage of these three major sites.[11]

For his cost analysis, Wisner operated on the assumption that intercepting sewers and a pumping station would be constructed in the Calumet region, regardless of whether the sewage was treated or not.[12] Under this assumption, the Calumet settling project proved to be the cheapest project that contemplated complete sewage treatment, on both a first and an annual cost basis. Altogether, Wisner's proposal called for a total expenditure of approximately $10 million, allocated over a twenty-year period. The annual costs, including interest and depreciation, given Wisner's timetable, were estimated quinquenially. These estimates are given in table 19.

Table 19. *Estimated Quinquennial Annual Costs of Wisner's Project*

1915	$ 80,000
1920	213,000
1925	386,000
1930	710,000

Source: Soper, Watson, and Martin, *A Report to the Chicago Real Estate Board on the Disposal of the Sewage and Protection of the Water Supply of Chicago, Illinois*, p. 201.

The 1914 Industrial Wastes Report made public the findings of the Packingtown testing station's first two years. The report recommended that Bubbly Creek be filled and that a sewage treatment plant be constructed to purify the wastes sufficiently for discharge into the Main Channel. Fine screens were to be placed in the individual companies, or in groups of companies, and the grease skimmed. This would relieve the sewage of its more coarse ingredients. The sewage would then pass to a district sedimentation plant where it would be unified with that coming from other companies and discharged into the Main Channel. The sedimentation plant was to be located at the west end of Bubbly Creek. An intercepting sewer was to be constructed to carry the sewage to that point.

Eventually, some form of biological treatment would prove necessary, and, in 1914, this meant sprinkling filters. Land of suitable area and price would have to be found, and sewers would have to be laid to carry the sewage westward from the settling plant. The cost of this project was estimated to be $985,000 initially, and $3,000,000 complete, exclusive of land, legal, and engineering expenses. The report did not give the volume of the sewage to be treated, nor did it give any details of the proposed works.[13]

By 1916 experiments with newer sewage treatment techniques

caused the Sanitary District to arrive at slightly different conclusions. On the basis of continuing research, Dr. W. D. Richardson, representing the packers, and Langdon Pearse, representing the Sanitary District, issued a "preliminary statement" in which both agreed that the activated sludge process was probably the best sewage treatment method to employ on the Stockyards-Packingtown district's wastes.[14] The activated sludge process was developed between 1910 and 1915. It consisted of mixing the sewage with an "activated" sludge, within which there was a highly developed microbe life. The mix was then oxygenated and clarified by sedimentation. The fine screening proposed (in 1914) as preliminary treatment could have been included prior to aeration, but there was little evidence from which to argue either for or against. The activated sludge could be settled out of the mix in the final sedimentation tanks, and then remixed with incoming sewage. The system could be arranged so that there was a more or less continuous flow of activated sludge, although this was but one of several possible arrangements. Well-operated sludge plants could remove approximately 90 percent of the suspended solids and between 90 and 95 percent of the five-day biochemical oxygen demand.

In April 1917 a report was issued that developed a sewage collection and treatment scheme at considerable length, complete with cost estimates, but only in a "preliminary way." This was supplemented later the same year by a comprehensive survey of each slaughter and packing house, which attempted to estimate the flow and amount of pollution for which each was liable.[15]

World War I diverted both men and materials to the war effort, to the detriment of the industrial wastes testing projects. Efforts on the Stockyards problem were suspended, and others were postponed until after the war. In 1919, negotiations between the packers and the Sanitary District resumed, and the packers offered to pay 60 percent of the treatment and the net operating costs, if the Sanitary District would pay the other 40 percent. A suggested form of contract was drafted and put into proof in the autumn of 1919, but the matter laid dormant for several years thereafter.

Little had changed by 1923; the engineers were waiting for the packers and the district's trustees to agree on a definite site for the treatment works. The ensuing years had strengthened their belief in the efficacy of the activated sludge method, and, by 1923, the Sanitary District had over a year's experience in operating such plants. The 1917 recommendations were altered only in the respect that it was now felt desirable to treat the entire flow with activated sludge as soon as possible rather than develop the plant progressively through screening and later enlarge it to include activated sludge.

Arguing for the immediate commencement of the Packingtown project, Langdon Pearse, the Sanitary District's sanitary engineer, wrote the following to E. J. Kelly, the Sanitary District's chief engineer and later mayor of Chicago, in 1923:

> The investigations of 1917 indicated that the pollution coming from Packingtown and the Union Stock Yards was equivalent to that from one million people. The removal of this load of organic matter from the

Main Channel and the Illinois River would make an enormous difference in the condition of the Illinois River and the Canal. By treating the sewage close to its point of origin, as recommended by Richardson and Pearse in 1917, the prompt construction of works is furthered which will produce a greater effect upon our sewage treatment scheme than any other project under consideration, for less money, largely because of the small amount of intercepting sewers to be built. . . . There is no question but what the treatment of the industrial waste from Packingtown and the Union Stock Yards would make the biggest improvement for the least outlay of any work the District has in contemplation, and could be put in operation in the quickest time.[16]

A testing station, constructed along the North Branch to investigate tannery wastes, was operational from December 1919 to 1922. Manufacturing wastes were investigated at the Corn Products Company, resulting in methods by which over 90 percent of the plant's wastes were reduced. This plant had the capability of adding to the Main Channel a sewage load equivalent to that from a 404,000 population. While these test stations and other Sanitary District projects did not entirely eliminate the industrial wastes problem, they gave promise that sewage treatment could significantly improve existing conditions.

When these Sanitary District studies and tests were beginning, the two-story Imhoff tank and the trickling filter were just coming into use.[17] The Imhoff tank, named for its designer, Karl Imhoff, was introduced into the United States from Germany and England. The process involved dropping solids through slots in the bottom of a sedimentation chamber into a sludge compartment. The sludge was permitted to digest until the majority of the organic material had turned to a gas or a liquid. The remaining material was stabilized, then dried, and either dumped or sold as fertilizer. Trickling filters were also introduced into the United States from England. Untreated effluent was intermittently sprinkled over filters composed of a bed of coarse rocks covered with biological growths. As the sewage was sprayed into the air and over the rocks, it absorbed oxygen from the atmosphere which increased the rate at which the organic material underwent biological oxidation and mineralization.

The district's first projects were aimed at testing these two methods, and when the first treatment plant was opened in 1914, it was a full-scale experimental Imhoff-trickler plant, designed to handle the village of Morton Grove's 1,200 people. The sedimentation plant was opened in December 1914, and a trickling filter was added in May 1920.[18] The station was of considerable experimental value but did little to relieve the entire district's sanitary situation.

THE ADOPTED PLAN

In August 1919 the Sanitary District's Board of Trustees adopted an ordinance which

. . . required the construction each year of sufficient plants so that at the end of twenty-five years only half the amount of sewage and waste passing through the Drainage Canal at the date of the passage of said ordinance would be discharged into the Des Plaines River.[19]

Thus, the district instituted Wisner's 1911 program to locate and construct sewage treatment plants to supplement the dilution method. In 1921 the Illinois legislature authorized the Sanitary District to execute its construction plans at a stipulated installation rate.

The district's experience with the activated sludge method at the Stockyards-Packingtown treatment plant confirmed experiments in Massachusetts and Great Britain, which were given as testimony earlier as to the efficacy of the method. The district began construction of the Des Plaines River activated sludge plant in May 1919 and put it into operation in August 1922. For the location of the various sewage treatment works, see map 9. The plant was designed to treat the sewage, almost exclusively domestic, from a group of lower Des Plaines River villages.[20] This represents the first activated sludge plant built by the Sanitary District, excluding the experimental units the district had used to test various types of activated-sludge installations. Initially, the Des Plaines River plant was designed for a 45,000 tributary population and an average daily sewage flow of 4.5 million gallons, with a constructed daily maximum flow of 6.75 million gallons. Six years after these works opened, the tributary population had grown to 66,400. Including work completed through 31 December 1927, the total construction costs of the Des Plaines River works were $1,950,000.

In October 1920 the Sanitary District began constructing the Calumet sewage treatment works. Consisting of a battery of Imhoff tanks and sludge drying beds, it was placed in operation in September 1922. Additionally, activated sludge tanks and trickling filters were installed on an experimental basis. The works were designed to handle industrial as well as domestic wastes. The Calumet region's tributary area had great potential for industrial growth, and some paint manufacturers were located there by 1920. The works were designed for an average daily sewage flow of 56 million gallons, a figure which it was estimated the works would reach after ten years of operation. The initial installation was designed for a 225,000 population. The total construction costs of the works, as of 31 December 1927, were $6,970,000.[21]

In 1923 and 1924 two smaller plants were installed in the villages of Glenview and Northbrook, north of Chicago. This alternative was preferred to connecting these villages to the overtaxed North Shore Channel. The Glenview works were started in June 1923, and operations began in October 1924. They were designed for a 1,200 tributary population and an average daily sewage flow of 180,000 gallons. Total construction costs were $103,400.[22] Construction on the Northbrook works began in April 1924, and in April 1925 they were opened. They were designed for a 1,500 tributary population and a 180,000-gallon average daily sewage flow. Total construction costs were $91,000.[23] Both works were the Imhoff tank-trickling filter type and were required to handle domestic sewage almost exclusively.

The most pressing problem that the district faced in the early 1920s was the heavily polluted North Shore Channel.[24] The North Side and the northern suburbs had grown rapidly in the post-World War I years, and the North Shore Channel was unable to handle the sewage effectively. Consequently, the polluted channel, emptying into the North Branch, contributed to the Chicago River's befouling in the "Loop" area. It was apparent that some form of sewage treatment was necessary, and, to that end, the district appointed a committee to investigate whether trickling filters or the activated sludge method would be preferable for the final treatment of the North Side's sewage, so that, on the average, approximately 85 percent of the organic matter would be removed. The committee recommended the activated sludge method,

> . . . because of the importance of guarding against the possibility of objectionable conditions arising in the immediate vicinity of Imhoff tanks and trickling filters large enough to serve a population of 800,000 people. It was further concluded that in view of the uncertainty of securing a market for the dried sludge, it would not be wise for the Sanitary District to undertake to convert the activated sludge into commercial fertilizer. . . . In the case of trickling filters at the particular site in question a much larger area of land than usual was provided for in the estimates in order to secure the isolation needed for such a large plant.[25]

Concurrent with this committee's work, the controversy regarding the Sanitary District's lake diversion had been intensified, in 1922, by the initiation of injunction proceedings by the state of Wisconsin before the United States Supreme Court. Also, the district's original War Department permit was to expire in 1925. Therefore, in 1924, the district formed an Engineering Board of Review, which consisted of twenty-eight leading hydraulic and sanitary engineers, whose purpose was to investigate the district's problems and then report. Their report, issued early in 1925, encompassed a comprehensive plan which the district subsequently adopted.[26]

Pursuant to the review board's recommendations, the Sanitary District filed an application with the War Department "for permission to divert from Lake Michigan an annual average of 10,000 cubic feet per second of water as measured at Lockport." This request was granted essentially because, on 3 March 1925, the War Department issued the Sanitary District a five-year permit which allowed them to divert an annual average of 8,500 c.f.s., in addition to that diverted for Chicago's water supply.

The review board proposed that seven large sewage treatment plants be located throughout the district. This plan required a greater investment in a larger number of sewage treatment facilities than Wisner's plan of the preceding decade, the plan the district was then implementing. This reflects little more than the continued growth of Chicago's population-equivalent and the fixed capacity of the Main Channel. The report made estimates of each proposed plant's character and efficiency, so that the entire scheme would prove adequate to preserve sanitary conditions in the Main Channel and Illinois River through 1945. Population estimates for 1945 were also included. The scheme and its predicted results are summarized in table 20.

The review board's seven proposed plants were predicted to be 56 percent efficient in treating the sewage of a 6,787,000 population-equivalent. This meant that the Main Channel would still carry 44 per-

Table 20. *Engineering Board of Review's Sewage Treatment Project—Estimates*

Plant	Type of Treatment	Tributary Population Plus the Population Equivalent of Industrial Wastes		Percentage Efficiency of Treatment
North Side	Activated Sludge	1,171,000		85
Calumet	Imhoff Tanks	354,000		33 1/3
Des Plaines	Activated Sludge	105,000		85
Stockyards	Activated Sludge	1,250,000		85
Corn Products	Trickling Filters	475,000		75
West Side	Imhoff Tanks	2,075,000		33 1/3
Southwest	Imhoff Tanks	1,357,000		33 1/3
	TOTAL	6,787,000*	AVERAGE	56%

*Omits a "miscellaneous" item of 298,000.

Source: Sanitary District of Chicago, "Report on the Commission Appointed by Federal Emergency Administration of Public Works Reviewing Plans of West-Southwest Sewage Treatment Project of the Sanitary District of Chicago," May 1934, p. 51.

cent of the sewage load, equivalent to the total load from a 3,022,000 population, very close to the legal maximum. The report also estimated the total 1945 flows, measured at Lockport, which would be necessary to maintain the dilution method's sanitary condition up to that year. These flows are given in table 21a. Dividing these figures by the 3,022,000 population-equivalent of the Main Channel, then multiplying by 1,000 gives the total flow per 1,000 population of the residual sewage load. These figures are given in table 21b.

Table 21a. *Estimated 1945 Main Channel Flows*

Maximum	10,000 c.f.s.
Average	5,900 c.f.s.
Minimum	3,000 c.f.s.

Table 21b. *Estimated 1945 Main Channel Flows Per 1,000 Population*

Maximum	3.30 c.f.s.
Average	1.95 c.f.s.
Minimum	0.99 c.f.s.

Source: Sanitary District of Chicago, "Report on the Commission Appointed by Federal Emergency Administration of Public Works Reviewing Plans of West-Southwest Sewage Treatment Project of the Sanitary District of Chicago," May 1934, p. 51.

These figures appear to represent the minimum requirements set up by the 1925 Board of Review. The plan contemplated that in the year 1945 the residual pollution load would be reduced by the addition of trickling filters at the Calumet Plant, to be followed by the same improvements at the West Side and Southwest Plants in 1955.[27]

It should be noted that the 3 1/3 c.f.s. per 10,000 population maximum estimated by the review board was the same as the maximum prescribed by the Sanitary District Enabling Act of 1889. This should not be too surprising, because the 10,000 c.f.s. maximum flow equaled the Main Channel's designed flow, and the approximately 3 million population-equivalent equaled the Main Channel's maximum population. Therefore, any flow less than 10,000 c.f.s., or any population-equivalent greater than 3 million, or both, would result in a total flow less than the prescribed minimum. Yet it should not be forgotten that these figures were estimated for 1945 and were not averages for the twenty-year period. Until that time, it was anticipated that the dilution system would remain sanitary. Consequently, additional sewage treatment works were planned for 1945, in order to return the Main Channel's load to a manageable, and prescribed, level. Further additions were anticipated so that the residual sewage load would remain within the legal limitations of the Main Channel.

The picture that emerged from the review board's report was one where the dilution method remained the principal feature in Chicago's sewage disposal scheme, even though the sewage load which the Main Channel was expected to handle was defined to be a "residual." It was clear that the review board realized that the district's population-equivalent was too large for the Main Channel to handle in toto. Consequently, sewage treatment would be necessary to handle the excess demand placed on the Main Channel's purifying capabilities. The residual population-equivalent could never exceed 3 million for very long, nor was the review board in a position to advocate a diversion in excess of 10,000 c.f.s. Treatment works were necessary for all the sewage that the Main Channel could not handle efficiently. Furthermore, the channels constructed for the implementation of the dilution method could be used to receive the effluent discharged from the treatment plants.

Even though there had been millions of dollars devoted to conducting sewage treatment experiments and to constructing sewage treatment plants, the basis of the Sanitary District's sewage disposal strategy was rooted firmly in the dilution method. What appeared in the review board's report was the logical evolution of the original strategy. The city had grown to be so large that there was some question whether the dilution method could be extended sufficiently to handle the city's sewage. When the legal difficulties that the Sanitary District encountered in attempting to fulfill its charter obligations were added to the tremendous growth of the population equivalent, the case against extending the dilution method was persuasive. In the early 1920s, however, the execution of the sewage treatment scheme was not intended to supplant the dilution method, but rather to complement it, handling the excess over the maximum legal capability of the Main Channel.

THE SANITARY DISTRICT AND THE SUPREME COURT

The lawsuits brought by all interested parties against the Sanitary District, including the War Department and several Great Lakes states, were consolidated and heard as one.[28] The controversy over the Main Channel's effect on lake levels climaxed with injunction proceedings which the state of Wisconsin brought before the Supreme Court early in 1922.[29] The Sanitary District's concern in this matter was clear. If the injunction were enforced, it would effectively remove the efficiency of discharging diluted, untreated sewage into the Illinois River valley.

At stake was the dilution method, which had cost more than $125 million.

By 1909 the district began to make moves in the direction of waste treatment, in the realization that the area they served had mushroomed, and they might lose the court case.[30] Testing stations had been built to study various treatment methods for domestic sewage and for packinghouse, tannery, and corn products wastes. By 1922 the district had planned and was constructing sewage treatment plants. Unquestionably, the district's expectations about how these suits would be settled played an important role in strategy considerations.

Hearings were held before Charles Evans Hughes, acting as a special master for the Supreme Court. They began in June 1926 and lasted over a year.[31] Hughes reported that the Sanitary District's new, 1925 War Department permit was valid, for it had been issued by the secretary of war under authority conferred by Congress. Hughes recommended that the suits be dismissed.[32] Nevertheless, Chief Justice William Howard Taft, secretary of war between 1904 and 1908, held that the lake states were entitled to a decree and sent the case back to Hughes, who was to determine how much time the district required to complete its sewage treatment works.[33]

On 21 April 1930 the Supreme Court issued its decree, which limited the volume of lake water the Sanitary District could divert for the Main Channel to successively lower flow levels over a period of eight years.[34] The court's motivation for issuing this kind of decree was the Sanitary District's comprehensive sewage treatment program. The reason for extending the reduction over an eight-year period was to give the district time to complete its program and time to make necessary adjustments. Unfortunately, no consideration was given to those situations where it might prove desirable to increase the diversion for, say, dangerously high lake levels. The decree set a precedent for court-ordered limitation rather than governmental regulation. The limits and the timetable which the Supreme Court decreed are given in table 22. The explicit flow restrictions resulted from a rehearing of the case before a new master.[35]

Table 22. *Supreme Court Decree Flow Restriction*

Effective Date	Limit of Annual Average Net Diversion
1 July 1930	6,500 c.f.s.
31 December 1935	5,000 c.f.s.
31 December 1938	1,500 c.f.s.

Source: Sanitary District of Chicago, "Report on the Commission Appointed by Federal Emergency Administration of Public Works Reviewing Plans of West-Southwest Sewage Treatment Project of the Sanitary District of Chicago," May 1934, p. 52.

The Supreme Court's decision created the need for a floodgate, or two-way lock, in the Chicago River's mouth to prevent any outflow during flood periods. This was constructed in 1936–1938. The careful water-flow budgeting, which the court decree required, removed the ability of the Lockport control gates to handle the entire tributary area's storm-water flow, and removed their ability to prevent polluted storm-water discharge into Lake Michigan.

The order removed all doubt that some form of treatment was necessary. Open sewers had proven incapable of handling both domestic and industrial wastes, anyway. The district was aware that the Main Channel's maximum tributary population-equivalent would soon be reached, and sewage treatment was contemplated to supplement dilution. The first 3 million population-equivalent, including the effluent from the treatment plants, was to be handled by dilution, and the remainder was to be handled by sewage treatment. What the order accomplished was to reverse these priorities; treatment handled the initial sewage collection, while dilution handled the effluent.

The transition went smoothly. A large part of the $125 million which the Sanitary District had expended on the dilution method was incorporated, at least partially, into the revised approach. The introduction of sewage treatment, as a supplement to dilution, was accomplished while the district was testing alternative treatment methods. The ascendancy of sewage treatment was one that required only minor adjustments in projected plants and resulted in relatively minor losses at existing sewage treatment installations. There is a question whether the Sanitary District's continued advocacy of the dilution method throughout the litigation was premised on a fixed dedication to dilution, or whether dilution became an unofficial proxy for the Sanitary District's independence from federal government intervention on matters concerning the Lake Michigan diversion. Whatever the case, the district clearly was ready for almost any contingency which the Supreme Court decision might have created, and it appeared to have achieved this preparedness at minimum cost. The existence of this long legal dispute undoubtedly caused the district to consider alternatives to the dilution method earlier than might have been the case otherwise.

The available evidence does not provide any insight into the War Department's true motivation in this long affair. At the outset, the department seems to have been concerned solely with navigational dangers in the Chicago River. Over time, the emphasis turned to the department's right to regulate the total Lake Michigan diversion. Officially, this shift was justified in terms of the navigational danger posed by decreasing Great Lakes levels. Injunction suits were filed, but the War Department did not push its suits vigorously. The Sanitary District's actions give the impression that it received the War Department's entreaties as idle threats. There are three hypotheses that appear consistent with the evidence. First, the War Department earnestly pursued what it considered the wisest course with respect to the lake-levels controversy, while the Sanitary District considered the pollution problem more important. This is the most plausible hypothesis. Second, the War Department was apathetic in this matter and prosecuted the Sanitary District only to appease the other Great Lakes states and Canada. Third, the War Department was interested only in establishing its bureaucratic supremacy over the Sanitary District, in seeing its position legally vindicated regardless of the consequences. Whatever the case—and the printed record does not afford sufficient grounds to select among these alternatives—the War Department appears to have felt that its job was completed when the Supreme Court decree was issued.

The Sanitary District's conservative approach to technological change had paid off, from an economic viewpoint. By waiting as long as it did, the district was able to make its investment in the sewage treatment method which it considered to be the most efficient and economical. This was the activated sludge method, the last major sewage treatment method to be developed.[36]

THE SEWAGE TREATMENT WORKS

With the review board's plan and the 1922 committee's report as guides, the Sanitary District began constructing large sewage treatment works. The North Side works were begun in 1923, and formally opened on 3 October 1928. The Des Plaines River works strongly influenced the design.[37] The tributary area was approximately seventy-eight square miles and was sewered on the combined system. The North Side works employed the activated sludge method, with preliminary settling. The excess sludge was shipped via a seventeen-mile main to the West Side sewage treatment works. Those sections which were capable of relatively easy extension were designed for an 800,000 tributary population, the estimated 1930 human population. This translated as an average daily sewage flow of 175 million gallons, with a constructed maximum 50 percent greater than that amount. Those sections which were not capable of easy extension were designed for the estimated 1960 population requirements.

The North Side project, as was true of all the projects, made as much use of existing structures as was possible. The existing North Side intercepting sewer divided into two branches. One went north to Glencoe; the other, south to Fullerton Avenue, Chicago. Because the local sewers had been constructed to discharge into the North Shore Channel, the new intercepting sewers were placed parallel to the channel, and in close proximity to it, beneath the local sewers. Special drop connections were constructed to connect the local to the intercepting sewers. A "hydraulic jump" was built into the drop connection in order to "dissipate the energy of the oncoming sewage, thus preventing a disturbance of flow in the interceptor." Additionally, a controlling device was included in the drop connection which enabled the local sewers to discharge directly into the channel whenever the sewage flow or storm water run-off flow exceeded the maximum capacity of the treatment works. In other words, the dilution method's collection system was utilized until the point at which the sewage discharged into the channel. At that point, the sewage dropped into newly constructed intercepting sewers to complete the trip to the treatment works. When the sewage flow was greater than the treatment works could handle, the collection sewers discharged directly into the North Shore Channel, as they had done previously.

The West Side sewage treatment works were begun in 1927. This installation provided only for primary treatment, which is to say that it provided for "Imhoff-tank sedimentation and digestion of the sludge without further treatment of the clarified effluent."[38] The initial installation consisted of Imhoff tanks for settling and digesting the West Side sewage and for digesting the waste sludge from the North Side Sewage Treatment Works; sludge drying beds; and a railroad system, with complete rolling stock for collecting and conveying the dried sludge to the dumping grounds.

The Sanitary District's long-term plan for the West Side works contemplated trickling filters for final treatment, and, to that end, the district acquired a nearby site to accommodate both an extension of the Imhoff tanks and the construction of a trickling filter, or possibly an activated sludge plant. The total tributary area, sewered principally on the combined system, comprised approximately 100 square miles which were heavily endowed with industry. The clarified effluent was discharged into the Main Channel.

The district planned to install three Imhoff tank batteries to handle the sewage from a 1,850,000 population-equivalent with an average daily sewage flow of 400 million gallons. By 1930, however, only two batteries had been completed; but the figures quoted above were the district's projections for 1940. The constructed maximum flow was 50 percent larger than the projected 1940 average. As was the case at the North Side Works, those sections of the works not easily enlarged were constructed to handle the projected 1960 demands.

The last project proposed by the review board was the Southwest Sewage Treatment works. These works were to treat the sewage from an area which included Chicago's South Side, from the "Loop" to Eighty-seventh Street. This was a tributary area of approximately 60 square miles, with a 1925 population of approximately 900,000. The effluent was to be discharged through the Calumet-Sag Channel. Construction on these works did not begin until 1935, but the preliminary engineering work had begun during the Supreme Court hearings.

Prior to 1930, the Sanitary District expended $80 million to implement the Engineering Board of Review's sewage treatment program (see Appendix 2). An estimated $120 million additional expenditure was necessary to complete the program. This meant that the district had committed itself to spending an estimated $200 million in order to complement the dilution system and its appurtenances.

As a result of the Supreme Court decree the district was forced to revise its plans for implementing the review board's program. The reduction in the available volume of diluting water meant that the Sanitary District had to increase individual treatment plant efficiency, if pollution levels were to be minimized within the Main Channel, Des Plaines and Illinois rivers, and all other affected waterways.[39] Accordingly, the district adopted the activated sludge method to treat all the sewage and adjusted individual plant capacities. These adjustments are given in table 23.

This revised program involved little change in the North Side works. Although designed for a 175 million-gallon daily capacity, the works were found, once operations began, to be more efficient. In 1936 final settling basins were added, which increased the works' nominal daily capacity from 180 to 250 million gallons.

Table 23. *Chicago Sewage Treatment Plant Adjustments*

Plant	Daily Capacity
North Side	220 m.g.d.
Calumet	136 m.g.d.
West-Southwest	1,000 m.g.d.

Source: Sanitary District of Chicago, "Report on the Commission Appointed by Federal Emergency Administration of Public Works Reviewing Plans on West-Southwest Sewage Treatment Project of the Sanitary District of Chicago," May 1934, p. 53.

The Calumet activated sludge plant opened on 15 December 1935. By studying similar situations, district engineers were convinced that there were few economies obtained by incorporating the existing Imhoff tanks and the proposed activated sludge mechanisms in a comprehensive sewage treatment program. Accordingly, the district abandoned the existing Imhoff tank installation, which had cost almost $7 million. Considerable attention was given to designing the aeration works for the Calumet and West-Southwest Sewage Treatment Works. Prior investigation justified the district's use of the flow type of aeration, and it emphasized the need for clean air. Consequently, diffuser plates of greater porosity were used in the newer activated sludge plants. In general, the original layout was maintained, and the newer works differed from the older plants only with respect to such details as diffuser plates.[40] Construction of the new works began in 1931, but it had to be halted in 1932 because of insufficient funds. The works were completed under financing arranged through the Public Works Administration.[41]

Construction of the Southwest works began in 1935; it was opened in the autumn of 1939.[42] The Sanitary District decided to locate the Southwest works adjacent to the existing West Side works. This decision, and innovations in sludge incineration, enabled the district to treat the Imhoff tank effluent from the West Side works in some way other than by the trickling filters, which originally had been contemplated for final treatment. As noted, the first two Imhoff tank batteries at the West Side works were in operation by 1930, but construction on the third battery had to be suspended for lack of funds. In 1932 the Sanitary District made application to the Public Works Administration to finance the entire West-Southwest project.

The district's plan was to concentrate at the West Side works the entire West and Southwest district's flow, including the Stockyards and Corn Products wastes and the sewage which had been handled at the Des Plaines River works.[43] All this sewage was to be treated by a 1,000 million gallon daily capacity activated sludge installation, into which the existing Imhoff tanks would be incorporated. Public Works Administration funds were insufficient to complete everything which the district's application outlined. Therefore, the district established priorities and completed the project in the late 1930s, when funds were more plentiful.

Concurrent with developing these sewage treatment works, the Sanitary District emphasized the need to enlarge the sewer network to collect sewage from the tributary area and deliver it to the treatment works. Consequently, by World War II, almost every sewered area within the district connected to an intercepting sewer, which led to a sewage pumping station, and then to one of the three major treatment works. Again, the federal government assisted the Sanitary District financially. Without the federal loan and grant, it would have been difficult for the district to have reached the high percentage of sewage purified as early as it did. Moreover, it should be added that many of the district's financial difficulties stemmed directly from the fact that the construction of all these works required the district to make large capital expenditures during the middle of the Great Depression.[44]

The Sanitary District of Chicago has removed practically all of Chicago's pollution from Lake Michigan—the exception occurs when an occasional severe storm is of sufficient force to require opening the locks, permitting discharge directly into the lake. Such is the continuing legacy of sewer outfalls and dilution. It is quite doubtful that the district will meet foreseeable problems by significantly changing its sewage disposal strategy. At present, the district is moving in the direction of 100 percent sewage treatment, but even when that is achieved, the resulting pure effluent will still be discharged into the Illinois River valley, thus following a century-old tradition.

NOTES

1. Population-equivalent is the total human population plus the population that would be necessary to produce domestic wastes equivalent to the area's industrial wastes. A 3 million population, exclusive of industrial wastes, was estimated by 1922, and 4 million was estimated by 1940. R. Isham Randolph, "The History of Sanitation in Chicago," *Journal of the Western Society of Engineers,* October 1939, p. 238.

2. George A. Soper, John D. Watson, and Arthur J. Martin, *A Report to the Chicago Real Estate Board on the Disposal of the Sewage and Protection of the Water Supply of Chicago, Illinois* (hereafter the *CREB Report*), 1915, p. 197.

3. Industries present in the area included: livestock handling and storage, slaughtering and packing, margarine works, rendering establishments, soap factories, glue factories, casing works, sausage making, garbage rendering, fruit canning, pickle manufacturing, brewing, and fertilizer works.

4. *CREB Report,* pp. 196, 197. See also Sanitary District of Chicago, *Summary of Packingtown Treatment Situation,* prepared 1919, issued November 1923, p. 6, and Randolph, "Sanitation in Chicago," p. 238.

5. George W. Fuller, "The Sewage Disposal Problem of Chicago," 19 February 1925, p. 6.

6. Langdon Pearse, "Chicago's Quest for Potable Water," *Water and Sewage Works,* May 1955, reprinted, p. 7. Also Sanitary District of Chicago, "Memorandum Concerning the Drainage and Sewerage Conditions in Chicago," p. 15.

7. Full-scale experiments were carried on with screens, settling tanks, septic tanks, biolytic tanks, Imhoff tanks, trickling filters, Dunbar filters, and the separate digestion of sludge.

8. Sanitary District of Chicago, *Summary of Packingtown Treatment Situation,* p. 4. Fine screens, settling and Imhoff tanks, trickling filters, chemical precipitation, and sludge pressing were all tested in full-scale experiments.

9. See George M. Wisner, *Report on Sewage Disposal* (Chicago: Sanitary District

of Chicago, 12 October 1911), p. 32.

10. Ibid.

11. See Wisner, *Report on Sewage Disposal*, p. 46ff.; see also *CREB Report*, p. 200.

12. Wisner, *Report on Sewage Disposal*, p. 65.

13. *CREB Report*, p. 198.

14. Sanitary District of Chicago, *Summary of Packingtown Treatment Situation*, p. 5.

15. This was published as a report of the Sanitary District's chief engineer to the board of trustees in November 1917 and was financed by the packers.

16. Sanitary District of Chicago, *Summary of Packingtown Treatment Situation*, p. 6. See also Randolph, "Sanitation in Chicago," p. 238.

17. Sanitary District of Chicago, *Report of Commission Appointed by Federal Emergency Administration of Public Works Reviewing Plans of West-Southwest Sewage Treatment Project of the Sanitary District of Chicago*, May 1934, p. 49.

18. Randolph, "Sanitation in Chicago," p. 238. The works were designed for an average daily sewage flow of 180,000 gallons. The station was built at a cost of $66,000 to test the Imhoff tank-trickling filter method, but it was shortly thereafter that the activated sludge method's potential began to be realized.

19. George F. Barrett, *The Waterway from the Great Lakes to the Gulf of Mexico: America's Greatest Need* (Chicago: Sanitary District of Chicago, 1926), p. 79.

20. Randolph, "Sanitation in Chicago," p. 239, and Sanitary District of Chicago, *Engineering Works*, August 1928, pp. 63–67. The villages included Elmwood Park, Melrose Park, Forest Park, River Forest, Maywood, Bellwood, and a portion of Oak Park. The tributary drainage area encompassed approximately 12.5 square miles, which were drained by combined sewers.

21. Sanitary District, *Report of Commission Appointed by Federal Emergency Administration*, p. 50. See also Randolph, "Sanitation in Chicago," p. 238, and Sanitary District of Chicago, *Engineering Works*, p. 67. The tributary area was approximately 53 square miles. A later enlargement enabled these works to handle sewage from the neighboring towns of Riverdale, Dolton, Harvey, South Holland, and Phoenix, as well as an area of Chicago east of Jeffrey Avenue and north of Eighty-seventh Street, along Lake Michigan to Seventy-fifth Street.

22. Randolph, "Sanitation in Chicago," p. 238, and Sanitary District of Chicago, *Engineering Works*, pp. 59, 61.

23. Randolph, "Sanitation in Chicago," p. 238. See also Sanitary District of Chicago, *Engineering Works*, pp. 61, 63.

24. Sanitary District, *Report of Commission Appointed by Federal Emergency Administration*, p. 50.

25. Fuller, "The Sewage Disposal Problem of Chicago," p. 12. Fuller was a member of the committee, along with Harrison P. Eddy and T. Chalkley Hatton.

26. Sanitary District, *Report of Commission Appointed by Federal Emergency Administration*, p. 50.

27. Ibid., p. 51.

28. Randolph, "Sanitation in Chicago," p. 237.

29. Sanitary District, *Report of Commission Appointed by Federal Emergency Administration*, p. 50.

30. Pearse, "Chicago's Quest," p. 7.

31. Randolph, "Sanitation in Chicago," p. 237. See also Sanitary District, *Report of Commission Appointed by Federal Emergency Administration*, p. 52.

32. 278 U.S. 367; 49 S. Ct. 163; 73 L. Ed. 426 (1928). Hughes's recommendations are part of the official record only to the extent that they are discussed in this opinion.

33. Ibid. Taft felt that the threat to navigation represented by the lower lake levels upheld the position of the lake states. Therefore, the War Department legally could dictate the district's total diversion.

34. 281 U.S. 179; 50 S. Ct. 266; 74 L. Ed. 799 (1930). The district's diversion was to be measured by the total flow at Lockport, minus the amount which Chicago pumped through its waterworks, and minus that amount which private parties, usually industry, pumped.

35. 289 U.S. 710; 53 S. Ct. 671; 77 L. Ed. 1465 (1932). The final decree is enumer-

ated in 289 U.S. 395; 53 S. Ct. 409; 77 L. Ed. 703 (1932).

36. See Nathan Rosenberg, "Factors Affecting the Diffusion of Technology," *Explorations in Economic History,* Fall 1972, pp. 3–33, especially section 3, for a discussion of the costs and benefits of the conservative approach to adopting technological change. For more on the activated sludge method in Chicago, see Carl W. Condit, *Chicago, 1910–29,* pp. 244–46.

37. Randolph, "Sanitation in Chicago," p. 238. See also Sanitary District of Chicago, *Formal Opening Program: The North Side Sewage Treatment Project,* 3 October 1928. The plant was constructed to treat the sewage, principally domestic, from Chicago, north of Fullerton Avenue, and from the North Shore suburbs of Evanston, Wilmette, Kenilworth, Winnetka, Glencoe, Niles Center (Skokie), Niles, and Tessville. See Sanitary District of Chicago, *Engineering Works,* p. 71.

38. Randolph, "Sanitation in Chicago," p. 238. The works were designed to treat the sewage of Chicago, between Fullerton Avenue, the Chicago River, and the Main Channel; the "Loop" district; and "certain limited areas" south of the South Branch, as well as the towns along Salt Creek and the Lower Des Plaines River. See Sanitary District of Chicago, *Engineering Works,* p. 81.

39. Sanitary District, *Report of Commission Appointed by Federal Emergency Administration,* p. 52.

40. Pearse, "Chicago's Quest," p. 8. See also Randolph, "Sanitation in Chicago," p. 238.

41. Sanitary District, *Report of Commission Appointed by Federal Emergency Administration,* p. 53.

42. Randolph, "Sanitation in Chicago," p. 238.

43. The district closed these works in 1931.

44. Discussed in Randolph, "Sanitation in Chicago," p. 238.

7

Problems and Research: A Look to the Future

The adoption of sewage treatment was the last major decision affecting Chicago's sanitation strategy. By World War II, Chicago's water supply and sewage disposal methodology closely resembled that in use today. Almost all the necessary works had been erected. The development of Chicago's sewage treatment works has been discussed in the last few chapters; the development of the waterworks has been discussed to the 1870s, when the basic strategy was implemented. In the late nineteenth and early twentieth centuries, modifications were made in the water supply strategy, and they are discussed in the first section of this chapter. The second section presents some research topics suggested by this study. The final section examines three contemporary problems, with antecedents in this study, that must be resolved.

WATER SUPPLY MODIFICATIONS

Beginning in the late nineteenth century, with continued urban growth and the annexation of suburban areas, Chicago constructed additional pumping stations, dug new lake tunnels with intakes protected by cribs, and finally, in 1898, began the task of combining the several tunnel and pumping station systems into an integrated whole. (A chronology is presented in Appendix 3.) As early as the mid-1880s it was clear that the two tunnels emanating from the original Two-Mile water intake crib, off Chicago Avenue, could not provide all the water demanded by Chicagoans. Therefore, expansion was necessary. Three new cribs (Four-Mile, Sixty-eighth Street, and Carter H. Harrison) were opened between 1892 and 1900 (see maps 6 and 11). Prior to 1910 the city operated the four cribs plus eight water tunnels, seven pumping stations, and the Lake View crib and tunnel which became part of the system when Chicago annexed the city of Lake View in 1889. In the period between 1910 and World War II three new cribs (Edward F. Dunne, Wilson Avenue, and William E. Dever), four water tunnels, and four pumping stations were added to Chicago's water supply system. Since World War II the system has been expanded by the addition of three tunnels, one pumping station, and two filtration plants.

In 1894 the Chicago Department of Health began bacterial water analysis. These studies convinced city officials of two things: first, water intake cribs located two to four miles from shore were not sufficient to guarantee pure water; second, the Main Channel, while keeping Lake Michigan free of Chicago's sewage, could not keep all impurities out of the lake. At the turn of the century there were two prominent techniques for improving the quality of water: chlorination and filtration. Chicago began to experiment with chlorination in 1912, and four years later adopted the practice for the whole water supply system—chlorine was added to the water supply at the pumping stations. This enabled the typhoid death rate to be reduced for the second time within a generation. The rate, which had been 67 per 100,000 population in the 1890s, fell to 14 per 100,000 by 1910, after the Main Channel was completed. It fell again to 1 per 100,000 by 1919, after the introduction of chlorination. At that time, this was the lowest rate in the nation.[1]

As early as 1910, the Commission on Calumet Sewerage recommended that filtration be adopted because of the pollution from ships, because of the potential pollution from Calumet River flooding if the Calumet-Sag Channel was not approved, and because the normal condition of the lake was turbid.[2] The water department, however, did not adopt filtration on the basis that the lake water, under "normal" conditions, was sufficiently clear to make it unnecessary. By 1928, the continued turbidity of the lake water was such that an experimental filtration plant was introduced into the system. Two years later, Chicagoans voted to construct a major filtration plant on the South Side at Seventy-ninth Street and the lakeshore. Construction of the South District Filtration Plant began in 1938 and continued until 1942, when the war diverted resources elsewhere. Construction resumed in 1945 and was completed in 1947. The engineering of a filtration plant was well established by the time Chicago elected to filter its water supply, but the size and capacity of this plant still afforded a challenge. Upon completion, it was the largest water processing facility in the world.[3] The capacity of this plant, which gets its water from the Edward F. Dunne intake crib, is 840 million gallons per day, approximately 75 percent of the city's average daily consumption in 1947, but little more than half the maximum consumption of the summer months. Filtered water was then available to all Chicagoans living south of Pershing Road and to approximately thirty suburban areas to the south and southwest of the center of the city.

Filtration for the rest of the city was to be accomplished via the Central District Filtration Plant at Ohio Street and the lakeshore. Construction began in 1952 and was completed in 1964. Its operation essentially is identical to that of the South plant. The capacity of the Central plant, which gets its water from the William E. Dever intake crib, is 1.7 billion gallons per day. On an average day this plant processes 960 million gallons. It has supplanted the South plant as the world's largest water processing facility.

The two filtration plants were the two major additions to Chicago's water system in the postwar years. The filtration plants placed many of the intake cribs in a standby role; others were simply taken out of service (see map 12). By the mid-1960s Chicago had the largest water supply system of any urban area in the world. It served the city and sixty-six of its suburbs. It had the capability of delivering almost three billion gallons of water daily through seventy-five miles of water tunnels and four thousand miles of water pipes. The city's per capita daily consumption of more than 200 gallons, which has remained relatively

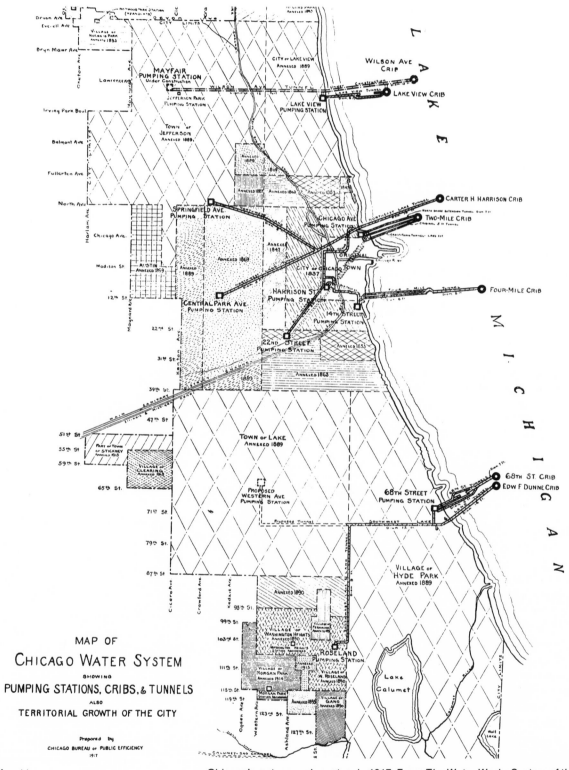

MAP OF
CHICAGO WATER SYSTEM
SHOWING
PUMPING STATIONS, CRIBS, & TUNNELS
ALSO
TERRITORIAL GROWTH OF THE CITY

Prepared by
CHICAGO BUREAU OF PUBLIC EFFICIENCY
1917

Map 11.   Chicago's water supply system in 1917. From *The Water Works System of the City of Chicago.* Chicago: Chicago Bureau of Public Efficiency, 1917.

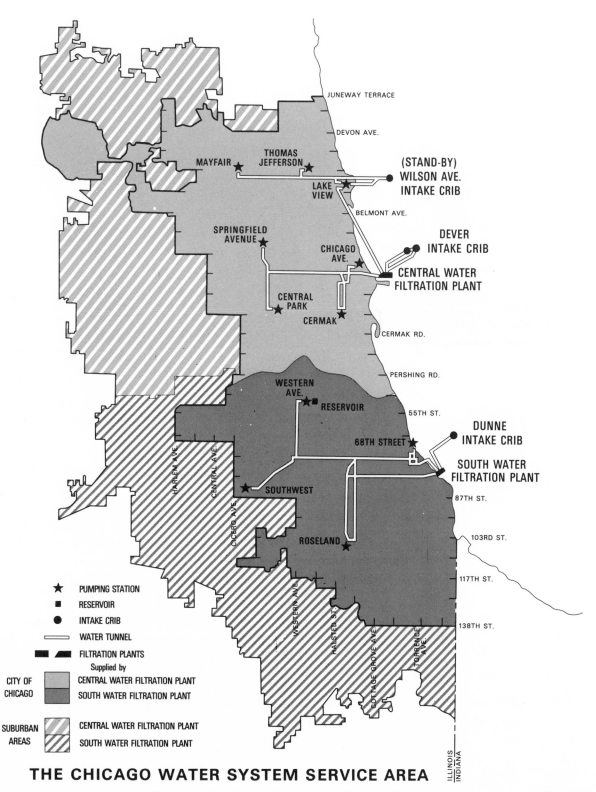

THE CHICAGO WATER SYSTEM SERVICE AREA

Chicago's water supply system today. Courtesy of the Chicago Department of Water and Sewers.   Map 12.

The South District Water Filtration Plant. Chicago Historical Society.

stable for several years at a rate below that of the 1920s and 1930s, is reputedly the highest in the world. Lake Michigan offers an unlimited water supply, yet the city has invested a large amount in maintaining and improving the quality of that water. This effort is manifest in the size and complexity of Chicago's water treatment works.[4]

SUGGESTIONS FOR FURTHER RESEARCH

Prior to the availability of public works funds in the 1930s, Chicago had spent more on sewage disposal-drainage than any other city. Today Chicago's sewage treatment works, like the waterworks, are the largest in the world.[5] This is not surprising, because Chicago is the largest city in the world located on a freshwater lake. Historically, such cities utilized the lake as both water supplier and sewage depository. Chicago's sanitation strategy, as it evolved in the nineteenth century, separated these two functions, but it did not require these treatment works. The separation depended in the first instance on the conjoining of three natural factors: a junction of lake and river, a flat topography, and a proximate divide between the lake's drainage area and the contiguous drainage area. Continued human and industrial population growth, plus external forces, necessitated treatment works. While many lakefront cities are located at the mouth of a river, so that the alternative of reversing the river's flow and connecting it to a contiguous drainage area is technologically available to them, only Chicago has found this alternative economically feasible. The reasons underlying Chicago's uniqueness in this respect should be explored.

Most students of intergovernmental affairs favor interstate cooperation in pollution control matters. There have been a few studies that

The Central District Water Filtration Plant, the world's largest water treatment facility.
Chicago Historical Society.

have attempted to estimate the scale economies, but more work is
necessary before the facts will be established. The desirability of interstate cooperation is clear in the interaction between the War Department and the Sanitary District of Chicago and the impact on Chicago's
water supply of pollutants from areas outside the Sanitary District that
dump their wastes into Lake Michigan. Effective regional water quality
management requires unified administration over natural drainage areas rather than autonomous administration within political areas. The
boundary lines of the natural drainage areas are the various geological
divides, and these do not conform to national boundaries, much less
state boundaries.

One specific question that could be addressed is, would Chicago's sanitation strategy have been more efficient had the Sanitary
District of Chicago, the major institution emerging from the evolution of
that strategy, been more responsible for all sanitary decisions within
the metropolis? In 1900 the Chicago metropolitan area was confined
generally to Cook County, and the Sanitary District of Chicago contained the most populated areas of the county. Thus, in 1900, by grant-

The West-Southwest Sewage Treatment Works, the world's largest sewage treatment facility. Courtesy of the Metropolitan Sanitary District of Greater Chicago.

ing the Sanitary District authority over all sanitation problems, a de facto metropolitan solution would have been reached. In recent years the Sanitary District, now the Metropolitan Sanitary District of Greater Chicago, has been legally constrained to Cook County, while the Chicago metropolitan area extends over seven counties in two states.

If, as is alleged, the scale economies inherent in sanitation works argue for metropolitan decision-making, then granting the Sanitary District responsibility for all sanitary decisions would have been a constructive step.[6] The increase in the district's work load would have been minor; it was already charged with surveilling Lake Michigan water to ascertain that sewage pollution was absent; the enlarged district would have had the responsibility for preventing all forms of water pollution. Such a multipurpose special district would have set the pattern for metropolitan cooperation in this and other areas of concern.

The alternative to a single comprehensive district would be an alliance of smaller jurisdictions or municipal governments. History suggests that in such a situation, where municipalities are physically as well as externally linked, an alliance becomes a catalyst for annexation rather than cooperation. Where municipalities give priority to maintaining their separate identities, metropolitan area cooperation often faces implicit opposition.[7] The single-purpose Sanitary District was a separate supragovernment, and only in a limited way was it required to cooperate with smaller local governments. The failure to encourage

132

lasting metropolitan cooperation was a serious oversight in the Sanitary District Enabling Act, in spite of the fact that the metropolitan area grew beyond the Chicago Sanitary District. If a multipurpose metropolitan district had been created for preventing water pollution, it would have been a simple, logical step to extend it to include other forms of pollution.

Although to create such a metropolitan district would have been constructive, it would have evolved from Chicago's sanitation strategy only in the last generation. Extrapolating from Chicago's sanitary history, one can only speculate that a combined sanitation district could affect some efficiencies in operation; but it is doubtful that Chicago's strategy could be altered. In its time, the Sanitary District was, theoretically, the most efficient alternative; but the efficiency of any institution, whether it is a single or a combined district, is diminished if its reach does not extend to include the affected area. With industrial growth, the areas affected by water pollution have grown faster than the areas of dense population; but in the past this increased pollution brought reactions from urban areas. In the mid-nineteenth century, the area with the responsibility for action was extended from the individual's property to that of the municipality. By the turn of the century, this area was enlarged to the metropolis, most of which was contained within a single county. Present metropolitan areas may extend over several counties, in several states, but the area has been limited by legislation. This rigidity means that the Sanitary District is less efficient than it might be.

This book's focus on the economic and technological decisions affecting the utilization and conservation of Lake Michigan has minimized the contribution of other disciplines to this subject. Clearly, there are possibilities for further research suggested from the perspective of these disciplines. For example, the role of engineers in the political decision-making process surrounding the development of sanitation works is well known.[8] The technologies advocated by engineers have to be accepted by city officials and often by the electorate as well. This means that before a comprehensive, meaningful history can be written the economic and technological problems also must be considered from an interdisciplinary viewpoint which comprises law, politics, science, sociology, and others in addition to economics and history. There is a great deal of research to be done, and it has only just begun.

The technological advice of engineers was accepted in almost every case concerning Chicago's sanitation strategy, although that advice became somewhat confused during the debate over the Calumet-Sag Channel. The few exceptions raise interesting questions. Consider the case where Chicago's city council reduced the grade recommended by Chesbrough's sewerage-drainage proposal from twelve to ten feet. What kind of expertise did the city council appeal to in justifying such a change? Did Chesbrough ignore their enlightened input in forming his proposal? Or did the council interject its ignorance after the fact? What was the role of the city government's elected officials vis-a-vis its professional staff? In the water supply decision of 1863 Chesbrough was instructed to consider alternatives suggested by the city council. In the 1890s three chief engineers on the construction of the Main Channel were fired because they could not work harmoniously with the district's trustees. In Chicago the end product was consistent with the engineering plans, but such consistency may be the exception and not the rule. If so, it would be interesting to know why.

It does not appear that the potential for graft played any role in deciding among alternatives, but only the most naive would argue that graft did not accompany the construction and operation of the works. Is the assumption that graft can be ignored in the evolution of Chicago's sanitation strategy correct? What was the role of graft in city government? Was it simply a transfer from taxpayers to corrupt city officials as the evidence suggests, or was it something more complex? Certainly graft attended other services provided by city government. Substantive evidence may be difficult to find. There have been few convictions, and fewer memoirs of graft-takers. The circumstantial evidence and unproved accusations establish a clear picture of how graft operated, but more needs to be done to establish proof of how it was done, its role within the city government, and its effect on the citizenry. This needs to be done for both the specific cases of Chicago's city council and the Sanitary District of Chicago and for the general case of urban government.

Two topics that would provide fruitful research are suggested by the two historical "accidents" that form the basis of Chicago's sanitation strategy. The first accident was the failure to finish the Illinois and Michigan Canal as a deep-cut canal; and the second was the discovery of the canal's sewage-handling potential. What would have been the effect of completing the Illinois and Michigan Canal according to the original deep-cut plan? It was argued that the state lacked the financial wherewithal to proceed according to the original plan but that additional locks and pumping stations were consistent with the state's finances. The decision to proceed with the shallow-cut canal was based on cost considerations which extended into the future, to the time when the canal would be completed. Yet it appears that the decision-makers foresaw that the canal would be enlarged at some future date to conform to the deep-cut plan to provide a through route for ships. The question becomes one of how the history of the canal might have changed had all the future costs been anticipated correctly at the time of the decision to adopt the shallow-cut canal. Would the state still have proceeded as it did? Would it have adopted a deep-cut canal? Or would it have adopted an intermediate solution? A deep-cut canal would not have required pumps at the Chicago end to maintain its summit level. Would the solution of "reversing" the Chicago River have been discovered if river water did not have to be pumped into the canal?

The circumstances under which the canal's sewage-handling potential was discovered need to be established. In particular, when was the Chicago River *first* reversed? As noted earlier, it is only supposition that the discovery that sewage could be flushed down the canal was made by a canal worker, and it is clear that pumping sewage-laden water into the canal is not the same thing as reversing the river. There is evidence that the canal's potential was realized in the mid-1850s, but there is no evidence that the river was reversed prior to the installation of larger pumps in 1871. Yet the reversal came as no surprise. Whether the river had been reversed or not earlier was of no consequence, because the engineers understood the consequences of increasing the amount of river water pumped into the canal. In any event, the fact remains that the Chicago River was reversed approximately thirty years before the Sanitary District began to operate its Main Channel; it was not the Sanitary District that first reversed the river. This whole episode needs the attention of a careful historical sleuth.

The Chicago Hydraulic Company provides another area for further research. In many cities the merits of private versus public ownership were debated, and Chicago was no exception. The traditional explanation for the shift from private to public water companies is that the private companies did not provide water to all citizens: "The actual and prospective profits of the companies were rarely great enough to induce the directors to build systems adequate to provide all needs. The companies laid their pipes through the districts that promised the largest returns and left the poorer or more remote districts without a supply."[9] Not only were the poor areas without a supply, but the city gained only a limited amount of water for fire hydrants and less for other purposes. How accurate is this traditional explanation for Chicago? Given that the Lake Michigan Hydraulic Company had been chartered to supply the north division of the city—but it never did—it would seem fair to conclude that much of the traditional explanation is germane. This, too, is an episode that would benefit from further research; the quotation above provides a hypothesis capable of empirical testing. Because cities viewed the provision of sanitation services as natural monopolies, and typically extended some monopoly power to the private companies they chartered, it would be interesting to know what restrictions on prices and/or quantities would have been necessary to procure water for the poorer sections of the city, fire prevention, and other civic purposes. Were these potential restrictions manifest when the Chicago City Hydraulic Company replaced its private predecessor? Were these potential restrictions economically and/or politically viable? Quite simply, what were the politics behind chartering a private company and then taking over its franchise?

The argument that private companies supplied water to "the districts that promised the largest return" suggests questions about the distributive effects of sanitation works and the way they were financed. The usual method of financing waterworks was to issue bonds and to meet the principal and interest out of water sales and property taxes; the bonds issued for sewage works were paid solely out of tax revenue. The operating costs for both sets of works were also paid out of these revenues. How seriously did the business cycle affect financing efforts? The effect of the Panic of 1837 on the Illinois and Michigan Canal is clear; the effect of the Great Depression on the construction of sewage treatment works is less clear. The cessation of construction on the South District Filtration Plant during World War II is a similar effect from a different cause. Since the Great Depression, federal government funds have been available for sanitation works. Has this been an effective improvement in finance? In the case of Chicago the answer would appear to be yes, in that these funds helped acquire large sewage and water treatment plants which were extensions of the city's sanitation strategy. In other cities these federal programs have been adjudged failures.[10]

Water resources are an important factor in the location decision of some industries which use water as an input in their production processes. Is this also true of industries that produce large quantities of wastes? The large quantities of wastes produced by the Stockyards and other industries would suggest that an inexpensive waste disposal system might be an important consideration in their location decision. Most of Chicago's initial planning considered only domestic wastes. By the turn of the century, Chicago was confronted with factories which daily produced wastes equivalent to that of several thousand people. An analogous situation developed when suburban areas were annexed to the Sanitary District, or for that matter to Chicago. Industries paid property taxes for their public services, just as private homes did. But if a large industry produced wastes equivalent to 1,000 homes but didn't pay 1,000 times as much in taxes, then industry was being subsidized by homeowners. The equity of this situation needs to be carefully researched.

An analogous question is present with respect to water, with one complicating factor: the water meter. Water services were financed by a user charge in addition to property taxes. User charges may have been flat-rate charges such as those imposed by the Chicago Hydraulic Company on all users and the city of Chicago on homes today, or metered charges such as those imposed on large consumers today.[11] How were these rates set? What was the rationale for regressive quantity discounts being included in both metered and nonmetered rates? If the rates were lower for large users, then large industrial users were being subsidized by home consumers. Whether or not this is equitable depends on the size of the subsidy and the extent to which the industry may benefit the home consumer. In both the water and the sewage cases, there is nothing necessarily evil about such subsidies, for if inexpensive water and/or sewage service is needed to attract industry, then a subsidy may prove to be a net benefit to homeowners. Whether Chicago's financial arrangements subsidized industry, how much they subsidized industry, and the equity of these arrangements are topics for further research.

The whole question of water meters is an interesting one in which there is too little information. Did the public readily accept the idea of metering its consumption? The introduction of a new water system often led to an increase in the system's per capita daily pumpage, but the introduction of water meters checked this tendency. Meters provide several identifiable benefits to a city, but they cost that city something for installation, upkeep, and reading. A comparison of the benefits and costs of water meters may explain why Chicago elected to meter only the large consumers. It might also suggest additional ways to economize on the use of water.

Throughout this book the demand for sanitation works has been treated in impressionistic terms. That Chicagoans wanted improvements to these public works as a result of, say, a cholera epidemic is not the same thing as knowing what quantity of service they demanded at each price. In many cases they had the opportunity to vote on a particular project, a particular price-quantity combination. A more thorough study of demand should reveal whether there were projects, say, 100 percent sewage treatment, that had a minimum price so expensive Chicagoans did not demand them at that price. Also, such a study should disclose if the interdependencies between water supply and sewage inherent in Chicago's freshwater lakefront site are revealed in the public's demand for these services; does the public perceive sanitation services as two separable commodities or as a single interdependent one? The obvious importance of such a study is that it would help to determine the acceptable level of pollution control. One common allegation is that the public will not, or cannot, pay the bill for a 100 percent clean environment. The demand side must be investigated in order to determine the level for which Chicagoans can and will pay.

The downstream effects of Chicago's strategy need to be developed more carefully. Why did Joliet and Peoria legislators attempt to get the Sanitary District Enabling Act repealed? Why did the State Board of Health argue that the Main Channel posed little threat to downstream communities? Does the same hold true today? Would it hold true today had the diversion remained at 10,000 c.f.s. and the extent of sewage treatment been reduced correspondingly? Answers to these questions about the continued efficacy of polluting the Illinois River requires a study of conditions not only in Chicago but in downstream communities as well. One of its goals should be the discovery of an acceptable pollution level in the Illinois River valley.

Finally, more research is needed on the external factors that have shaped Chicago's strategy—in particular, the role of the courts and the role of Canada. The Supreme Court limited the district's diversion as a result of suits brought by other Great Lakes states, Canada, and the War Department. The court also made decisions with respect to the sanitation strategies of other cities. Are the court's decisions consistent, or is the court simply a stochastic element in the decision process? If the latter, then how attuned is the court to the political environment? Beginning in 1954, the Sanitary District attempted to obtain federal legislation increasing its diversion above the court-ordered 1,500 c.f.s. Several bills were submitted which either failed to pass or were vetoed by President Eisenhower because of Canadian objections.[12] In the 1950s, Canada's interests were involved with the construction of the Saint Lawrence Seaway. Since that waterway was not opened until 1959, Canada's interest was that nothing artificial, such as increasing Chicago's diversion, be done to lower the lake levels. Would Canada's objections have been so persistent after the seaway opened? Perhaps, but by that time the focus of concern had changed to the other plaintiffs of the original lake-level suit.

In 1958 six Great Lakes states brought suit against the Sanitary District. If it had been successful, this suit would have required the district to return all treated waste water to the lake, raising lake levels. It also would have required a large investment in treatment works so that the introduction of waste water would not jeopardize the Lake Michigan water supply. The most likely alternative was improvements to the sewage treatment works so that the recycled water would be as pure as the lake water. The whole question of the possibilities for recycled water needs careful study. Less likely were improvements to the water treatment works or some combination of the two. Fortunately for the city this suit was settled in its favor in 1966; but this left the district in the same position in which it had been after the first Supreme Court decision in 1930.[13] The city, however, was limited to a 1,700 c.f.s. diversion for its water supply. Thus Chicago could divert a total of 3,200 c.f.s. from the lake. While this has not constrained the city, the district has not stopped its attempt to increase its diversion through passage of an act in Congress. Curiously, the bill being considered at the time this book is being written is sponsored by Representative James G. O'Hara of Michigan, a state that was party to both suits and which has had a serious erosion problem in the past few years because of high lake levels.

WHAT OF THE FUTURE?

There are three problem areas suggested by this study. First, pollution control and the lake-levels controversy need to be confronted as interdependent circumstances. This is, perhaps, the most critical methodological problem. The federal government has been involved from the beginning with the lake-levels controversy, and this often has been in conflict with pollution and sanitation objectives. As noted, the question of Chicago's diversion still was not resolved in the late 1960s.[14] The Sanitary District's limited diversion necessitated inflexible solutions to several problems. It required a greater investment in sewage treatment by the Sanitary District whenever the population-equivalent increased or the diversion decreased. It rendered unlikely an increase in the diversion when the flood or erosion threat posed by high lake levels, such as those of the early 1970s, could be lessened thereby. Officials of the Army Corps of Engineers have estimated that, if water were diverted through the Main Channel, the level of Lakes Michigan and Huron could be reduced by four inches.[15] It also should be noted that a larger diversion would increase the amount of electrical power that the Sanitary District could generate when the Main Channel empties into the Des Plaines River, an important consideration during the "energy crisis." Finally, the Supreme Court's limitations on the district's diversion led to a situation where the federal government controlled the Sanitary District indirectly via its maximum diversion decree. Although wisdom is increasingly brought to bear on this matter, the Sanitary District is still subject to indirect pollution control. Curiously, the pollution issue is not particularly prominent in the discussion, nor is cost. The dominant theme continues to be the effect on lake levels, in spite of the fact that it should now be clear to all that in determining such things as harbor conditions, the natural cycle is more important in lake levels than Chicago's diversion.

Second, the district's works are insufficient to handle the volume of drainage created by a major storm. There are two dimensions to this problem. As noted earlier, the channel system is used for any overflow during storms, and the overflow is composed of both street runoff and sewage. On occasion, the floodgates of the channel system have been opened, and sewage has entered Lake Michigan. Furthermore, the system does not drain rapidly enough in some neighborhoods, and they become flooded. One obvious solution to the first part of this problem would be to replace Chicago's combined sewers by constructing a separate set of storm sewers to collect the street runoff and deposit it either in the treatment plant or the channel system. The old sewers would still be used to carry sewage to the treatment plants. In this way, any overflow deposited in the channel system would be street runoff, and not sewage. Unfortunately, such a system is tremendously expensive. With respect to the second part, the Sanitary District has proposed to construct underground storm tanks in flood-threatened neighborhoods. In this way, the flood water can be collected and held until the demand on the treatment system decreases. Such a scheme would not only resolve the neighborhood flooding problem; it would also reduce the probability of opening the floodgates. So far, the district has only begun to construct the works that will bring this plan to fruition.

Third, increasing human and industrial populations, as well as environmental concerns, make complete sewage treatment a desirable goal for the metropolitan area. Since the opening of the Main Channel, the Sanitary District has had the authority to keep all wastes within its jurisdiction out of Lake Michigan. Despite this, Chicago's Lake Michigan water supply has not been pollution-free.

Today, three neighboring areas are the primary polluters of Lake Michigan. First, the North Shore Sanitary District (which extends along the Lake Michigan shore from Highland Park to the Illinois-Wisconsin state line) discharges chlorinated effluent from a number of primary treatment plants directly into the lake. Beginning in the late 1960s, the North Shore Sanitary District instituted a search for an economic method that will completely treat their sewage prior to discharge.

Second, the wastes of the cities and industries of Kenosha and Racine, Wisconsin, drain into the lake and add to the pollution load. They, too, have taken steps to improve the situation.

Third, the cities and industries of northern Indiana have been, and probably still are, the worst offenders. Their windblown, lake-deposited sewage reaches Chicago's southern water-supply intakes. In 1943 the state of Illinois brought suit in the Supreme Court against the state of Indiana, four northern Indiana cities, and twenty industries to prevent their polluting of Lake Michigan.[16] No testimony was ever heard, but some improvements were made. In total, $15 million was expended to reduce industrial wastes. The Standard Oil Company of Indiana, the largest single offender, alone invested $6 million for oil separators, collecting this more sanitary sewage in its plant, and discharging it into the sewers of Whiting, Indiana (where it eventually was transported to the Hammond, Indiana, sewage treatment works). The only municipal project required by the suit was a $90,000 sewer revision program in Whiting. These projects were completed in 1950, and they reduced the pollution in the southern end of Lake Michigan. In general, those improvements proved ineffective, as human and industrial populations continued to grow. Continued legal action in the federal courts appears to be the only workable solution.

Furthermore, pollution problems internal to Chicago have not been solved. At the present time, approximately 95 percent of the sewage is treated. The effluent from the treatment plants is discharged into the channel system where the remaining wastes are treated. The days of the open sewer are not entirely a thing of the past. The Supreme Court could have forced complete treatment in 1930, but the rationalization for such an action would have had to have been couched in terms of pollution control. The court was concerned with lake levels. The War Department did not have that power explicitly; whether any federal body had the interest is a moot point. Yet, even with complete treatment, it is likely that the channel system still would be used as a depository for some of the effluent. The solid-waste-handling capacity of the channel system is a function of the diversion from Lake Michigan. Since the latter has been set by the Supreme Court, a fixed percent of treatment, combined with an increasing volume of human and industrial wastes, will lead to a greater volume of effluent than the channel system can handle. Increasing the percent of treatment, or the diversion, will enable the channel system to handle a larger volume of effluent. Nevertheless, even if both these events were to occur, it is still likely that the volume of wastes will exceed the capacity of the channel system. Some effluent will have to be diverted from the channel system and an alternative depository found. This is, perhaps, the most critical practical problem facing the Sanitary District today. The district has filled several large lagoons near its treatment plants. Some sludge has been barged to reclaim land in Fulton County, Illinois, which had been strip-mined; and some is available within the district for use as a fertilizer. Complete treatment will not eliminate this problem, and increasing the percent of treatment now will merely postpone it.

Judge Cardozo once wrote that history is a seamless web. This is true of Chicago's experience. The problems were inherent in Chicago's freshwater lakeshore site. Sanitation decisions were generated internally out of Chicago's history. The city's sanitation strategy today can be traced back to the discovery that the Illinois and Michigan Canal's pumps were relieving the polluted Chicago River. The Sanitary District today still operates on a mandate which Chicago has enforced since the water supply decision of 1863: the city's water supply is to be conserved. Since the Chicago Sanitary District's contribution to Lake Michigan pollution has been small, the conclusion is that they have successfully fulfilled their mandate to the present. Whatever the future holds, one suspects that it, too, will be consistent with Chicago's site and history.

NOTES

1. James C. O'Connell, "Chicago's Quest for Pure Water," Public Works Historical Society, Essay No. 1, June 1976, p. 18.

2. Carl W. Condit, *Chicago, 1910–29,* (Chicago: University of Chicago Press, 1973), pp. 248–49.

3. Carl W. Condit, *Chicago, 1930–70* (Chicago: University of Chicago Press, 1974), pp. 26–27.

4. Ellis L. Armstrong, ed., *History of Public Works in the United States, 1776–1976* (Chicago: American Public Works Association, 1976), pp. 240–41.

5. Chicago's works should be compared with the new plant in New York City, scheduled for completion in 1982. See Armstrong, *History of Public Works,* p. 427.

6. See Louis P. Cain, "The Search for an Optimal Environmental Jurisdiction; Sanitation Districts in Illinois, 1889," Department of Economics, University of British Columbia, Discussion paper 76–08.

7. See Louis P. Cain, "Annexation, A Panacea for the Urban Crisis? The Case of Chicago," Department of Economics, University of British Columbia, Discussion paper 76–09.

8. See, for example, Daniel H. Calhoun, *American Civil Engineer: Origins and Conflict* (Cambridge, Mass.: MIT Press, 1960), and Forest Hill, *Roads, Rails, and Waterways* (Norman: University of Oklahoma Press, 1957).

9. Nelson M. Blake, *Water for the Cities* (Syracuse, N.Y.: Syracuse University Press, 1956), p. 77.

10. See A. M. Freeman, R. H. Haveman, and A. V. Kneese, *The Economics of Environmental Policy* (New York: John Wiley & Sons, 1973), pp. 6, 118.

11. The city of Chicago places water meters in buildings described as "three flats and over." Single family homes and duplexes are subject to a flat-rate fee; meters will be installed only if they are specifically requested by the owner.

12. Condit, *Chicago, 1930–70,* p. 254.

13. See, for example, the report of the special master, *Wisconsin et al. v. Illinois et al.,* Supreme Court of the United States, October term, 1966, Albert B. Maris, special master. See also Condit, *Chicago, 1930–70,* pp. 254, 268.

14. See Condit, *Chicago, 1930–70,* pp. 254–57, 268, for an excellent description of the Sanitary District during the Vinton Bacon years, 1963–1970.

15. *Chicago Sun Times,* 29 November 1972, p. 18.

16. The four cities were Hammond, East Chicago, Gary, and Whiting. See Langdon Pearse, "Chicago's Quest for Potable Water," *Water and Sewage Works,* May 1955, reprinted, p. 9.

APPENDIX 1
Financial Data from the Sewer and Water Departments of Chicago

Prior to the Chicago Fire, financial data for both the water and sewer departments are scarce, but they are generally available after 1871. The data should answer two major questions: (1) Who paid the construction and operating costs? and (2) Was "good financial management" the rule? Data capable of yielding a clear answer to the first question are presented through 1894 for the sewer department, and through 1901 for the water department. Data capable of answering the second question are presented through 1894 for the sewer department, and through 1915 for the water department. The format of the Department of Public Works accountants' report underwent several changes through these years, and cutoff dates were established at points where major format changes raised serious questions about the data's comparability over time.

In general, both water and sewer receipts were greater than expenses, permitting either bonded indebtedness to be retired or a contribution to be made to the relevant department's construction costs (see table 24). Expense data for both departments include operating costs, construction costs, and interest payments. Receipt data for the sewer department include the department's share of the city's property tax revenue and miscellaneous sources. The sewer department data reflect receipts and expenses from the "Sewer Fund." In the late 1870s, this account evidently was split in half, with the new account entitled the "Sewer Tax Fund." The differences between these two accounts were never fully explained. To be consistent, only the "Sewer Fund" data are reported in table 24. An approximate rule of thumb is that the receipts and expenses of the combined funds are twice the reported figures.

Receipt data for the water department include the proceeds from the sale of metered and unmetered water. This understates the water department's revenues which include, in addition to water collections, water service cock permits, plumbers' licenses, water meter installation, interest from investments, rent from owned property, and advances to lay water pipes. These latter categories are excluded because they were a relatively small fraction of total revenue and were

Table 24. *Annual Financial Statement (in thousand dollars)*

| Date | Waterworks | | Sewerage Works | |
	Receipts	Expenses	Receipts	Expenses
4–1–1864	192	129	107	101
4–1–1869	421	111	505	212
4–1–1872	446	437	978	711
6–2–1873	544	303	546	599
6–1–1874	709	622	936	717
6–1–1875	706	617	1,059	1,068
12–31–1875	638	628	1,126	915
12–31–1876	834	673	887	1,133
1877	909	440	1,089	874
1878	944	892	483	286
1879	922	547	175	235
1880	866	760	103	90
1881	937	840	121	117
1882	1,050	1,371	113	108
1883	1,143	1,068	109	106
1884	1,204	1,152	130	128
1885	1,422	1,091	401	382
1886	1,375	1,364	365	355
1887	1,490	1,803	376	351
1888	1,557	2,421	421	414
1889	1,622	2,282	551	567
1890	2,110	3,324	740	615
1891	2,272	3,543	420	532
1892	2,570	3,403	530	547
1893	2,799	3,859	386	536
1894	2,964	3,460	515	487
1895	3,076	3,146		
1896	3,129	3,342		
1897	3,327	2,861		
1898	3,424	5,701		
1899	3,203	4,725		
1900	3,225	3,420		
1901	3,372	3,098		

Source: City of Chicago, Department of Public Works, *Annual Report*.

sporadically reported. In 1891, for example, when water rates collected were almost $2.3 million, these other sources amounted to less than $0.4 million, and 1891 was a year in which these sources contributed a larger share than usual. The larger users were metered; the smaller ones, unmetered. The available evidence suggests that these user charges were established on an average cost basis.

The original cost of the works was financed by bonds and, as noted, by surplus revenue allocated to construction expenses. Sewer loan bonds were first issued in 1855; water loan bonds, in 1863. During the years 1871–1876, $2 million in tax assessments were made to help finance waterworks construction. For example, in 1887, the total original cost of the waterworks was $11.4 million, of which $2.7 million came from taxes, $3.9 million from surplus revenue, and $4.8 million from bonds, both outstanding and cancelled (see table 25).

For the first several years, the data reported in table 25 had to be adjusted. In 1872, $953,000 had to be subtracted, $887,000 for cash-

Table 25. *How the Waterworks Were Paid For (in thousand dollars)*

Date	Water Loan Bonds	WLB Cancelled	Surplus Revenue	Taxes	Misc[a]	Total Original Cost of Works
4-1-1872[b]	4,820		556	290	-953	4,713
6-2-1873	-239	239	55	258	187	500
6-1-1874			179	400	412	991
6-1-1875			163	531	354	1,048
12-31-1875			182	217	270	669
12-31-1876			136	392	-270	258
1877			164			164
1878	-294	294	88			88
1879			n.a.	n.a.		119
1880	-332	+326	n.a.	n.a.		253
1881			n.a.	n.a.		177
1882			n.a.	n.a.		373
1883			(645)[c]	(626)[c]		343
1884			404			404
1885			259			259
1886			572			572
1887			462			462
1888			997			997
1889			1,382			1,382
1890	984		2,146			3,130
1891			724		1,435	2,159
1892	-30	711[d]	1,737[d]		-1,101	1,317
1893	-45	365[d]	433		666	1,418
1894	-226	-441[d]	2,097[d]		-333	1,098
1895	-389	412	1,486[d]		-469	1,040
1896	-47	47	1,632[d]		-197	1,435
1897	-147	147	1,628[d]			1,628
1898	-15	15	1,526[d]		1,699	3,224
1899	-15	3,524[d]	-2,299		600 + 197	2,008
1900	-20	-3,346	635		3,866	1,135
1901	-15	15	697			697
Total	3,990	2,308	18,686	2,714	6,166 + 197	34,061

Notes:

[a] See description of miscellaneous items in the text.

[b] These figures represent the totals to 1872.

[c] These figures summarize the total of the yearly additions to surplus revenue and taxes during the years in which this information was not reported.

[d] These figures appear to, or, in fact, do, contain an additional amount equal to the water certificates cancelled or expired water fund investments.

Source: City of Chicago, Department of Public Works, *Annual Report.*

on-hand, and $66,000 for the discount on 6 percent water loan bonds outstanding. These bonds generally had been sold at a 7 percent par value. In 1873 and 1874, $776,000 and $354,000, respectively, had to be subtracted for cash-on-hand. In December 1875, $270,000 had to be added, because the account was overdrawn.

Between 1879 and 1883, the water department did not report how the works were paid for. Total bonds outstanding (by inference, the bonds cancelled) and the total original cost of the works were reported elsewhere. Further, sometime between these two years, taxes contributed an additional $626,000 to total original cost, but the exact year(s) was not reported. Likewise, the surplus revenue was not reported. Therefore, all that can be inferred is the sum of surplus revenue and taxes. Since these omissions occur in the middle of the series, the relevant entries are reported as not available.

In 1889, Chicago annexed the towns of Lake, Hyde Park, and Lake View. These towns had $984,000 in bonds outstanding for the construction of waterworks. Chicago absorbed both this indebtedness and the constructed works. Evidently, there were no sewage works to absorb.[1] The water loan bonds of the annexed towns were paid as they came due, and the outstanding principal was reported on these bonds specifically. The value of the annexed works, however, was lumped into the figure for the total original cost of the city's works, making it impossible to separate the total original cost of the annexed works from the 1890 additions to Chicago's existing works. Thus, the records include the remaining principal that Chicago was to pay, the cancelled debt that these towns had already paid, and the total original cost of all the works the city operated. After 1890, other towns annexed themselves to Chicago, but the only record indicating that the city absorbed other waterworks is an entry "from annexed territories" of $197,000. This entry first appeared in 1899, and then every year thereafter. No explanatory comments were included in the Department of Public Works' *Annual Report.*

In 1891, an item labeled "water fund investment" appears in the tabulation that explains how the works were paid for. Again, no explanatory comments were included. The following year this item appears for the last time. In 1893 the water department began to issue water certificates, and these certificates appear in the tabulation for each year thereafter. The first year, $1 million was issued at 5 percent interest; one-third of this sum was due on 1 June 1894, on 1 December 1894, and on 1 June 1895. The method of reporting water certificates was haphazard; some years the water department reported the amount outstanding and its composition; some years they reported only the amount outstanding; and finally they reported the amount outstanding and the amount cancelled without reference to its composition. In some years the amount of water certificates cancelled is included, evidently, in the surplus revenue figure; in others, in the total bonds cancelled figure. It is unfortunate that water certificates were so poorly tabulated. By 1901, over $6 million in certificates had been issued, and most of this debt had been cancelled. In the eight years that the water department reported this short-term indebtedness, its sum was almost equal to the long-term indebtedness represented by the water loan bonds. Although the water department did not stop reporting the composition of the funds used to finance its works until 1903, it stopped reporting receipt and expense information in 1901.

The sewer department never reported the composition of the funds used to finance its works; it reported only the composition of its bonded indebtedness and the total original cost of its works. Further, the sewer department stopped reporting the composition of its bonded indebtedness in 1895. Since patterns similar to those of the water department are visible for the sewer department in the receipt-expense data of table 24, and the bonded indebtedness outstanding data of table 27, the inference is that the sewer system was financed in an analogous manner to the waterworks.

The waterworks were financed through bonds, both outstanding and cancelled, which were relatively constant; surplus revenues, which increased through time; short-term indebtedness, which was particularly significant around the turn of the century; and tax assessments,

Table 26. *Structure of Bonded Indebtedness*

	Issued	Due	Principal (in thousand dollars)	Interest Rate
Sewer Loan Bonds	1855		87	6%
	1855		765	7%
	1860–64		212	7%
	1864–69		778	7%
	1869–72		840	7%
	as of 12-31-1882:	7-1-1884	458	7%
		7-1-1888	343	7%
		7-1-1889	44	7%
		7-1-1892	490	7%
		7-1-1894	785	7%
		7-1-1895	13	7%
	1880	7-1-1890	490	4 1/2%
	1884	7-1-1904	458	4%
	1888	7-1-1908	387	4%
	1892	7-1-1912	490	4%
	1894	7-1-1914	782	4%
Water Loan Bonds	1863		1,030	6%
	1863		103	7%
	1864–69		1,587	7%
	1869–72		2,100	7%
	as of 12-31-1882:	7-1-1897	50	6%
		7-1-1898	82	6%
		7-1-1888	150	7%
		7-1-1889	225	7%
		7-1-1890	294	7%
		7-1-1892	795	7%
		7-1-1894	541	7%
		7-1-1895	1,485	7%
	1882	7-1-1902	333	3.65%
	1888	7-1-1908	150	4%
	1889	7-1-1909	225	3 1/2%
	1891	7-1-1910	333	4%
	1892	7-1-1910	108	3 1/2%
	1892	7-1-1912	821	4%
	1893	7-1-1914	130	4%
	1895	7-1-1915	1,485	4%
	1910	7-1-1913	500	4 1/2%
	1912	11-1-1913	.4	5%
General Corp. Bonds	1908		1,000	4 1/2%
	1908		400	4%
Water Loan Refunding Bonds	1915	due serially	1,340	4%

Source: City of Chicago, Board of Public Works, *Annual Report.*

which were particularly significant in the 1870s when the second lake
tunnel and the tunnel under the "Loop" were being constructed.

Table 27. *Bonded Indebtedness*

Date	Water Loan Bonds Principal (in thousand $)	Avg. r	Sewer Loan Bonds Principal (in thousand $)	Avg. r	Comb Avg. r	Yields on Am RR Bonds
1855			$ 850	6.90		
6-30-1860			850	6.90		8.59
4-1-1864	$1,133	6.09	1,062	6.92	6.49	6.27
4-1-1869	2,720	6.62	1,840	6.95	6.77	8.13
4-1-1872	4,820	6.78	2,680	6.96	6.84	7.60
6-2-1873	4,581	6.77	2,637	6.97	6.84	7.76
6-1-1874	4,581	6.77	2,637	6.97	6.84	7.53
6-1-1875	4,581	6.79	2,637	6.97	6.86	
12-31-1875	4,581	6.79	2,637	6.97	6.86	7.06
12-31-1876	4,581	6.79	2,637	6.97	6.86	6.68
1877	4,581	6.79	2,637	6.97	6.86	6.62
1878	4,287	6.84	2,623	6.97	6.89	6.45
1879	4,287	6.84	2,623	n.a.	n.a.	5.98
1880	3,955	6.91	2,623	6.53	6.76	5.60
1881	3,955	6.91	2,623	6.53	6.76	5.19
1882	3,955	6.68	2,623	6.53	6.62	5.24
1883	3,955	6.68	2,622	6.53	6.62	5.23
1884	3,955	6.68	2,622	6.01	6.41	5.15
1885	3,955	6.68	2,622	6.01	6.41	4.89
1886	3,955	6.68	2,622	6.01	6.41	4.55
1887	3,955	6.68	2,622	6.01	6.41	4.65
1888	3,955	6.57	2,622	5.57	6.17	4.59
1889	3,955	6.37	2,622	5.57	6.05	4.43
1890	3,955	6.13	2,133	5.81	6.02	4.55
1891	3,955	6.17	2,133	5.12	5.80	4.71
1892	3,955	5.53	2,133	5.12	5.39	4.53
1893	4,084	5.48	2,133	5.12	5.36	4.65
1894	3,989	5.11	2,130	4.02	4.73	4.41
1895	3,989	4.00				4.27
1896	3,989	4.00				4.34
1897	3,857	3.92				4.11
1898	3,857	3.92				4.03
1899	3,852	3.93				3.85
1900	3,852	3.93				3.89
1901	3,852	3.93				3.83
1902	3,520	3.95				3.84
1903	3,520	3.95				4.03
1904	3,520	3.95				3.98
1905	3,520	3.95				3.89
1906	3,520	3.95				4.00
1907	3,520	3.95				4.27
1908	4,770	4.07				4.22
1909	4,545	4.10				4.07
1910	4,703	4.15				4.18
1911	4,516	4.15				4.19
1912	3,612	4.18				4.23
1913	2,904	4.13				4.44
1914	2,423	4.15				4.44
1915	2,269	4.15				4.62

Source: City of Chicago, Board of Public Works, *Annual Report. Historical Statistics of the United States*, series x–332, p. 656.

Lacking complete information, the analogous argument is that the sewer system was financed through bonds, both outstanding and cancelled, which were relatively constant, and surplus tax receipts, which grew with time; operating costs were financed through tax revenues. Since the bonded indebtedness of both the water and sewer departments was cancelled through funds generated by surplus revenues, the argument is that the users of both services ultimately paid for the construction and operation of the works.

Interest rates, in general, declined from the Civil War until the turn of the century, when they began to increase. Chicago's water and sewer loan bonds were issued, customarily, for twenty years (see table 26). After twenty years, if the department issuing the bonds lacked sufficient funds to retire the debt, a new bond issue was offered with an equal principal and, in the nineteenth century, a lower interest rate. The relative constancy, over time, of total water and sewer loan bonds outstanding reflects this policy (see table 27). The fact that these series did not grow with the increasing physical plants indicates that surplus revenue, or short-term indebtedness, was being used to retire the debt.

Table 27 gives the average interest rates on water loan bonds, sewer loan bonds, and, for the relevant interval, the weighted sum of these two. Additionally, Macauley's series of yields on American railroad bonds is included for comparative purposes. Since Macauley's series represents a much larger sample than the combined water and sewer loan bond series, and since Chicago was legally restrained from taking immediate advantage of falling interest rates, the expectation is that Macauley's series will lead the combined bond series, or either of the individual bond series. This is observable in table 27. The fact that the two sets of interest rates are close bears testimony to the high quality of the city's bonds. The indication is that Chicago did what it could to minimize the interest paid on funds borrowed to implement these important public works. Therefore, it seems fair to conclude that good financial management was the rule. It should be noted that financial feasibility is not necessarily the same as economic feasibility. This appendix is addressed to financial policies only; operating and management policies are additional factors which must be considered in answering the question of economic efficiency. Given that these departments were associated with a bureaucratic, and oftimes corrupt, city government, it would be difficult to argue that the entire operation was economically feasible.

NOTES

1. Of all the reasons put forward for annexation, sanitation appears to rest on the firmest ground. See Louis P. Cain, "Annexation, A Panacea for the Urban Crisis? The Case of Chicago," Department of Economics, University of British Columbia, Discussion paper 76–09. After 1889, a municipality could join the Sanitary District of Chicago and participate in a metropolitan sewerage scheme without annexing itself to Chicago. See Louis P. Cain, "The Search for an Optimal Environmental Jurisdiction: Sanitation Districts in Illinois, 1889," Department of Economics, University of British Columbia, Discussion paper 76–08.

APPENDIX 2
Financial Data from the
Sanitary District of Chicago

Financial data for the Metropolitan Sanitary District of Chicago are available to answer the same two questions asked of the water and sewer department data: (1) Who ultimately paid the construction and

Table 28. *Annual Financial Statement (in thousand dollars)*

	Bond Issues[1]	Gross Cash Receipts Bond Issues	Gross Cash Disbursements	Net Receipts[2]	Cash Balance
1890		75	68	7	7
1891		990	268	722	729
1892	2,000	77	962	1,115	1,844
1893		2,240	3,888	−1,648	196
1894	6,000	1,399	6,292	1,107	1,303
1895	4,000	2,538	7,401	−863	440
1896	800	7,376	8,493	−317	123
1897	800	5,826	6,457	169	292
1898	200	5,408	5,875	−267	25
1899	190	6,270	6,480	−20	5
1900	4,375	4,353	6,925	1,803	1,808
1901		1,340	2,993	−1,653	155
1902	3,500	1,379	3,644	1,236	1,391
1903	2,925	430	3,771	−416	952[3]
1904		4,314	3,942	372	1,325
1905	2,000	2,931	5,666	−735	520[3]
1906	500	3,119	3,694	−75	441[3]
1907	3,850	1,153	5,311	−308	130[3]
1908	1,000	5,487	5,884	603	733
1909	2,500	1,469	4,580	−611	122
1910	2,500	5,477	7,654	323	445
1911	1,000	4,687	5,123	564	1,009
1912		7,523	6,313	1,210	2,175
1913		5,878	6,736	−858	1,313
1914		6,581	7,316	−735	578
1915	2,000	6,382	7,614	768	1,346
1916		5,663	6,664	−1,001	343
1917	3,000	7,481	9,041	1,440	1,782
1918	2,000	7,482	10,111	−629	1,154
1919		8,821	9,675	−854	300
1920	2,000	6,314	8,042	272	28
1921	8,000	3,941	11,944	−3	25
1922	11,000	3,899	14,923	−24	1
1923	5,000	10,043	13,685	1,358	1,359
1924	10,000	8,908	18,896	−68	1,291
1925	19,000	9,455[4]	25,969[4]	2,486[4]	3,777[4]
		7,811[4]	24,305[4]	2,506[4]	3,826[4]
1926	15,000	11,414	24,918	1,496	5,322

Table 28. *(continued)*

	Bond Issues[1]	Gross Cash Receipts Bond Issues	Gross Cash Disbursements	Net Receipts[2]	Cash Balance
1927	21,000	11,109	31,026	1,083	6,406
1928	31,000	17,063	50,168	−2,105	4,301
1929	10,650	n.a.	n.a.	3,770	8,071
1930	16,000	22,985	39,847	−263	7,808
1931	1,841	30,882	40,265	−7,542	266
1932	57	n.a.	n.a.	−213	53
1933	41,938	24,725	24,026	42,673	42,726
1934		30,382	63,300	−32,918	9,808
1935		76,669	56,239	20,430	30,239
1936		33,440	45,000	−11,560	18,679
1937		39,249	46,760	−7,511	11,168[5] 20,367[5]
1938		38,021	47,128	−9,107	11,260
1939		35,069	37,030	−1,961	9,299
1940	9,000	36,059	42,628	2,431	11,730[5] 11,736[5]
1941	1,000	47,852	44,682	4,170	15,907
1942		41,563	45,037	−3,472	12,435
1943	1,000	40,935	41,394	541	12,976
1944	1,500	42,652	41,733	2,491	15,395
1945	2,000	80,111	78,685	3,325	18,720
1946	15,000	45,139	59,098	1,042	19,762
1947	12,000	79,006	89,353	1,652	21,414
1948	28,265	83,407	112,211	−536	20,878
1949	23,300	91,912	122,576	−7,364	13,514
1950	27,554	95,513	112,179	10,888	24,402
1951	2,000	173,054	178,997	−3,944	20,458
1952	15,400	127,865	144,596	−1,331	19,127
1953		134,858	133,262	1,595	20,722
1954		96,842	100,084	−3,241	17,481
1955		96,684	94,767	1,917	19,398
1956		161,525	161,964	−438	18,960
1957		190,118	183,118	6,999	25,959
1958		229,718	223,577	−3,859	22,100
1959		189,328	187,694	1,634	23,425
1960		151,153	156,370	−5,217	18,208
1961		217,071	214,217	2,854	21,062
1962		218,004	218,088	−84	20,978
1963		218,504	222,289	−3,784	17,194
1964		201,958	203,633	−1,674	15,519
1965		196,311	197,350	−1,039	14,480
1966		195,142	197,738	−2,596	11,884
1967		215,308	217,420	−2,113	9,909
1968		236,604	233,400	3,205	13,114

1. This is defined as the issued amount, exclusive of any discount.
2. This is defined as gross cash receipts (column 1 plus column 2) minus gross cash disbursements (column 3). In some cases, rounding creates a situation where the reported figure differs from the calculated figure.
3. In these years there were additions to the cash balance which did not appear as net reserves. In 1903, it was cash warrants in the hands of the clerk, and in 1905–1907, the difference is attributed to "due bills."
4. The first number reflects the clerk's annual report; the second, the auditor's annual report.
5. In these years a change in auditors created a redefinition of the cash balance, resulting in a revised figure.

Source: Metropolitan Sanitary District of Chicago, Board of Trustees, *Annual Proceedings*, the District Clerk's Annual Report, and the Annual Audit.

operating costs of the works discussed in chapters 4–6? and (2) Was "good financial management" the rule? Data are available from 1890, but they are generally only in the form of cash receipts, cash disbursements, and bond issues. Information relative to the aggregate value of the district's capital, and the yearly additions to it, is not available until 1925, the first year for which an annual audit report could be located.

The presence of a positive cash balance in 1968 (see table 28) indicates that aggregate cash receipts were greater than aggregate cash disbursements. On a year-by-year basis, gross cash receipts, including bond issues, were greater than gross disbursements in less than half the years (36 out of 79). Receipt data include bonds issued, taxes received, and miscellaneous sources such as electrical power and dried sludge sales. Disbursement data include bonds retired; interest, discounts, and premiums on bonds; improvements and betterments; maintenance and operation; and miscellaneous sources. Data for the years 1926 and 1927 are displayed in table 29. This table is included to emphasize the large proportion of gross cash receipts occupied by bond issues and taxes. In later years the district issued tax anticipation warrants, but these simply represent taxes in an altered form.

Table 29. *Sample Breakdown of Annual Financial Statistics (in million dollars)*

	1926	1927
Gross Cash Receipts	26.4	31.2
Bonds Issued	15.0	20.0
Taxes Received	11.2	11.9
Miscellaneous	0.2	0.2
Gross Cash Disbursements		
Bonds Retired	24.9	31.0
Interest, Discount and Premium on Bonds	4.34	4.92
Improvements and Betterments (Capital)	2.44	2.49
Maintenance and Operations	12.08	15.15
Departmental, Administrative, and Miscellaneous	3.24	3.26
Electrical Department Advances, etc.	2.55	4.84
Less Cash Collections From Customers, etc.	0.27	0.37
Accounts and Bills Received	−0.003	−0.003

Source: Sanitary District of Chicago, Annual Audit, 1926, 1927.

The data in table 28 are taken from the clerk of the district's annual report in the period 1890–1925, and from the annual audit in the period 1925–1968. The difference between these two sources is reflected by the fact that two numbers are reported for 1925. The auditor's report "corrected" the clerk's report in that it reduced cash receipts by $1.644 million and cash disbursements by $1.664 million. This increased net cash receipts by $20,000, and left unexplained the $49,000 increase in the district's cash balance. In 1937, and again in 1940, a change in auditors led to further revisions of the reported cash balance.

Table 30 reports the annual additions to the district's capital (improvements and betterments) and the total aggregated value of capital. The available financial reports do not indicate how the works were

Table 30. *Annual and Aggregate Capital Accumulation (in thousand dollars)*

	Yearly Addition	Aggregate Value
1924		103,394
1925	13,822	117,216
1926	12,077	129,294
1927	15,147	144,441
1928	25,523	169,963
1929	7,814	177,777
1930	7,810	185,587
1931	4,992	190,679
1932	2,837	193,516
1933	963	194,480
1934	9,031	203,510
1935	11,864	215,375
1936	17,042	232,417
1937	13,850	246,267
1938	-9,376[1]	236,891
1939	1,154	238,045
1940	2,397	240,442
1941	3,558	244,000
1942	848	244,848
1943	1,392	246,240
1944	1,436	247,676
1945	2,168	249,844
1946	5,786	255,630
1947	17,724	273,354
1948	23,777	297,131
1949	36,153	333,284
1950	10,039	343,323
1951	8,043	351,726
1952	14,388	366,114
1953	5,861	371,975
1954	3,712	375,687
1955	5,386	381,073
1956	8,594	389,667
1957	8,741	398,408
1958	12,590	410,998
1959	20,685	431,683
1960	19,097	450,780
1961	17,359	468,139
1962	20,261	488,400
1963	17,838	506,238
1964	21,528	527,766
1965	19,148	546,914
1966	18,497	565,411
1967	23,831	589,242
1968	29,583	618,825

[1] In 1938, the district dismantled, conveyed to other municipalities, or put out of service those parts of the dilution system which were not incorporated into the sewage treatment strategy.

Source: Metropolitan Sanitary District of Chicago, Annual Audit.

paid for, but it can be inferred that the vast majority of the funds were obtained through bond issues and taxes. In total, the district issued $381 million in bonds (see table 31), as compared to total capital of $619 million. If the assumption is made that all bond receipts were devoted to capital improvements, then the remaining funds came from

Table 31. *Structure of Bonded Indebtedness (in thousand dollars)*

Interest Rate (%)	Bond No.	Year of Issue	Amount
5%	1	1892	$ 2,000
5	2	1894	3,000
5	3	1894	3,000
4 1/2	4	1895	4,000
4 1/2	5	1896	800
4 1/2	6	1897	800
3 1/2	7	1898	200
3 1/2	8	1899	190
4	9	1900	1,000
4	10	1900	1,000
4	11	1900	2,375
4	12	1902	2,000
4	13	1902	1,500
4	14	1903	1,500
4	15	1903	1,425
4	16	1905	2,000
4	17	1906	500
4	18	1907	500
4	19	1907	500
4	20	1907	1,000
4 1/2	21	1907	850
4	22	1907	2,000
4	23	1908	1,000
4	24	1909	2,500
4	25	1910	500
4	26	1910	1,000
4	27	1910	1,000
4	28	1911	1,000
4	29	1915	2,000
4	30	1917	3,000
4 1/2	31	1918	2,000
5	32	1920	2,000
5	33	1921	3,000
5	34	1921	5,000
5	35	1922	5,000
4	36	1922	3,000
4	37	1922	3,000
4	38	1923	5,000
4	39	1924	5,000
4	40	1924	5,000
4	41	1925	3,000
4	42	1925	5,000
4	43	1925	5,000
4	44	1925	1,000
4	45	1925	5,000
4	46	1926	5,000
4 1/2	47	1926	5,000
4 1/2	48	1926	5,000
4 1/4	49	1927	1,000
4 1/4	50	1927	5,000
4 1/4	51	1927	5,000
4 1/4	52	1927	10,000
4 1/4	53	1928	10,000
4 1/4	54	1928	1,000

Table 31. *(continued)*

Interest Rate (%)	Bond No.	Year of Issue	Amount
4 1/4	55	1928	10,000
4 1/4	56	1928	10,000
4 1/2	57	1929	5,000
4 1/2	58	1929	2,500
4 1/2	59	1929	1,300
4 1/2	60	1929	700
4 1/2	61	1929	400
4 1/2	62	1929	500
4 1/2	63	1929	100
4 1/2	64	1929	100
4 1/2	65	1929	50
4 1/2	66	1930	180
4 1/2	67	1930	350
4 1/2	68	1930	5,050
4 1/2	69	1930	8,125
4 1/2	70	1930	530
4 1/2	71	1930	515
4 1/2	72	1930	10
4 1/2	73	1930	90
4 1/2	74	1930	1,000
4 1/2	75	1930	750
4 1/2	76	1931	475
4 1/2	77	1931	30
4 1/2	78	1931	1,175
4 1/2	80	1931	161
4 1/2	82A	1932	25
4 1/2	85	1932	32
4 1/2	78	1933	1,314
4 1/2	79	1933	3,060
4 1/2 A	82A	1933	4,690
4 1/2 B	82B	1933	1,820
4 1/2 A	83A	1933	5,792
4 1/2 B	83B	1933	3,616
4	87	1933	21,646
		TOTAL	$239,226

REFUNDING BONDS			
4%	A	1935	$ 20,719
4 to 5	B	1935	119,227
2 1/4	C	1939	4,661
2	D	1941	7,500
2	E	1942	3,000
2	F	1943	2,500
1 3/4	G	1944	2,000
1 3/4	H	1945	25,000
		TOTAL	$184,607

CONSTRUCTION BONDS			
2 1/2%	1	1940	$ 5,000
2 1/4	2	1940	4,000
2 1/4	3	1941	1,000
1 3/4	4	1943	1,000
1 3/4	5	1944	1,500

Table 31. *(continued)*

Interest Rate (%)	Bond No.	Year of Issue	Amount
1 3/8	6	1945	2,000
1 1/4	7	1946	5,000
2	8	1946	10,000
1 3/4	9	1947	2,000
2 1/4	10	1947	10,000
2 3/4	11	1948	15,000
2 3/8	12	1948	13,265
2 1/2	13	1949	15,000
2 1/4	14	1949	8,300
2 1/4	15	1950	8,554
2 1/8	16	1950	12,000
1 5/8	17	1950	7,000
2 1/8	18	1951	2,000
2 1/4	19	1952	15,000
2 1/2	20	1952	400
		TOTAL	$141,619

MISCELLANEOUS BONDS

3 1/8%	Cal-Sag Navigation	1957	$ 2,000
2.65	Office Building	1954	1,350
3 1/8	Corporate Working Cash	1958	10,000
3 1/8	Const. Working Cash	1958	5,000
4 1/2	Mt. Prospect Sewer Rev.	1958	2,000
		TOTAL	$ 20,350
		Total Bonds Issued	$585,802
		Less: Refunding Bonds	184,607
		TOTAL	$401,195

Source: Metropolitan Sanitary District of Chicago, Board of Trustees, *Annual Proceedings* and Mr. Gus G. Sciacqua, Clerk of The District.

tax receipts, the Public Works Administration, and miscellaneous sources. If, as suggested, the majority of total capital funds were generated by bond issues and taxes, and if tax receipts were employed to retire bonds, the conclusion is that the taxpayer ultimately paid for these public works.

The interest rate data also exhibit a pattern similar to that of the water and sewer department data. Between 1890 and 1933, Sanitary District bonds were issued at rates which varied between 3 1/2 and 5 percent (see table 31). The great majority of these bonds were issued at either 4 or 4 1/2 percent. Typically, these bonds became due sequentially over a period of nineteen or twenty years. Those issued for twenty years retired 5 percent of the principal each year; those issued for nineteen years retired 5.6 percent of the principal in the second through eighteenth years, and 4.8 percent in the nineteenth year.

In 1935 through 1945 a series of refunding bonds were issued. The Sanitary District has never forfeited on any bond, but these refunding bonds became necessary, as the district found itself obliged to make significant capital expenditures in the middle of the depression.

In fact, the usual depression pattern of decreases in the financial data is not present here.

Since 1953 the district has been on a pay as you go basis, but several specific bonds have been issued. The amounts of these bonds and the amounts of the refunding bonds were excluded from table 28, due to the fact that the latter extended existing debt, and the former were isolated issues for specific needs. Both types of bond issues carry interest which is compatible with construction bonds issued during the same period. Thus, the reason why the miscellaneous bond issues are separated from construction bonds is one of function. The specific purposes for which these miscellaneous bonds were issued were not for the direct "improvement betterment" of the district's capital. Since the taxpayer eventually generated the tax receipts that paid both the refunding and the miscellaneous bonds, for present purposes the inclusion or exclusion of these bonds in table 28 is a moot point. In either case, the burden of the debt fell on the user of the services the district provided.

Table 32. *Bonded Indebtedness (in thousand dollars)*

	Bonds Outstanding	Average Interest Rate	Yields on Am RR Bonds	Municipal High-Grade Bonds
1892	2,000	5.00	4.53	
1893	1,900	5.00	4.65	
1894	7,800	5.00	4.41	
1895	11,400	4.82	4.27	
1896	11,600	4.80	4.34	
1897	11,760	4.78	4.11	
1898	11,280	4.75	4.03	
1899	10,750	4.73	3.85	
1900	14,405	4.51	3.89	3.12
1901	13,506	4.50	3.83	3.13
1902	14,308	4.44	3.84	3.20
1903	16,249	4.35	4.03	3.38
1904	15,190	4.34	3.98	3.45
1905	16,056	4.29	3.89	3.40
1906	15,322	4.27	4.00	3.57
1907	18,927	4.21	3.27	3.86
1908	17,653	4.19	4.22	3.93
1909	18,805	4.14	4.07	3.78
1910	19,752	4.10	4.18	3.97
1911	19,058	4.07	4.19	3.98
1912	17,124	4.05	4.23	4.02

Source: Metropolitan Sanitary District of Chicago, Board of Trustees, *Annual Proceedings. Historical Statistics of the United States,* series x–331, 2, p. 656.

Table 32 presents the average interest rate on the district's bond portfolio for the years 1892 (when the first bonds were issued) to 1912. Since most of these bonds were issued at between 4 and 5 percent, and since such rates were consistent with those prevailing elsewhere, limiting the calculations to the initial twenty-year period provides insight without encountering significant diminishing returns. Once again, Macauley's series is included for comparative purposes. Like the water and sewer departments, the Sanitary District was legally constrained to a debt ceiling (5 percent of the assessed valuation) and, therefore, could not take immediate advantage of prevailing rates, which were lower than the rates at the time of issue. The expectation is, once again, that Macauley's series will lead the Sanitary District series, and this is what can be observed in table 32. The closeness of the two sets of rates bears testimony to the high quality of the district bonds.

Additional testimony comes from the series of high-grade municipal bonds. After 1912, this series averaged slightly more than 4 percent, rising to 4 1/2 percent in 1918. The district's bond issues in this period were at 4 percent, rising to 4 1/2 percent in 1918 (see table 31). Over the first decade of the twentieth century, the yield on municipal bonds increased, while the average interest rate on the district's bonds was declining. In 1912 they were almost equal, and had the district series been continued to 1913, it would have been less. Not only does this indicate that the district's bonds were high quality, but it further suggests that these bonds were acquiring a consistently improving reputation as time passed. The conclusion is that good financial management was the rule. As in the preceding appendix, a proviso must be made that this is relevant to financial feasibility only. The Sanitary District of Chicago was a bureaucratic organization whose operations could not be called economically feasible. All that can be said from these data is that it financed its operations in a feasible manner.

APPENDIX 3
Chronology

1673	Joliet reported to Father Dablon on the feasibility of a canal at Chicago
1795	Treaty of Greenville gave access to Indian land that became Chicago
1803	Construction of the first Fort Dearborn
1816	Construction of the second Fort Dearborn; Indians ceded land for the construction of the Illinois and Michigan Canal
1818	Illinois became a state
1822	Illinois received federal government permission and land to build the Illinois and Michigan Canal
1825	Illinois and Michigan Canal Company chartered and failed
1826	A second Illinois and Michigan Canal Company chartered
1827	Federal government donated land along the canal route
1832	Federal government constructed a lighthouse at Chicago
1833	State legislature terminated second canal company; Chicago incorporated as a village
1834	First attempt to solve sanitation problems: drainage ditch dug down State Street; public well dug for water supply
1835	A third Illinois and Michigan Canal Company chartered
1836	The Chicago Hydraulic Company chartered
1837	Chicago chartered as a city
1842	The Chicago Hydraulic Company began operations
1843	Construction work stopped on the Illinois and Michigan Canal
1845	Work resumed on the Illinois and Michigan Canal; the Lake Michigan Hydraulic company chartered (never became operative)
1848	Illinois and Michigan Canal opened
1850	First sewers installed
1851	The Chicago City Hydraulic Company incorporated, and the Board of Water Commissioners formed
1854	Completion of construction of municipal waterworks under the Chicago City Hydraulic Company and the Board of Water Commissioners
1855	Creation of the Board of Sewerage Commissioners; hiring of Ellis Sylvester Chesbrough; acceptance of Chesbrough's plan for sewage disposal and drainage
1858	First realization of Illinois and Michigan Canal's sewage-handling potentialities
1861	Creation of Board of Public Works incorporating earlier boards
1863	Acceptance of Chesbrough's lake-tunnel plan

1867	Two-mile Chicago Avenue lake tunnel and intake crib opened (now abandoned and destroyed)
1869	Construction of Water Tower and pumping plant completed
1871	Completion of the deepening of the Illinois and Michigan Canal; first recorded reversal of the Chicago River; the Chicago Fire
1874	Construction of the second Chicago Avenue water tunnel
1876	Construction of the Twenty-second Street Pumping Station (retired in 1959)
1885	Report of Citizens' Association of Chicago on sanitation
1886	Creation of Drainage and Water Supply Commission
1887	Report of Drainage and Water Supply Commission
1889	Sanitary District Enabling Act approved by Illinois legislature and ratified by a referendum of voters; formation of the Sanitary District of Chicago; Harrison Street (later Cermak), Lake View, and Sixty-eighth Street pumping stations put in operation
1892	Construction of the Sanitary and Ship Canal began; Four-Mile water tunnel and intake crib opened (now on standby for summer service only)
1894	Sixty-eighth Street intake crib opened (no longer in service)
1899	Provisional permit granted the Sanitary District by the secretary of war allowing the diversion of 5,000 c.f.s.
1900	Sanitary and Ship Canal opened; state of Missouri filed suit against the operation of the canal; Carter H. Harrison intake crib opened (no longer in service); Northeast water tunnel completed (no longer in service); Central Park Avenue Pumping Station opened
1901	Springfield Avenue Pumping Station opened
1903	Sanitary District annexed North Shore and Calumet regions; state legislature authorized water power development by the Sanitary District
1904	Thirty-ninth Street Sewage Pumping Station in service; Chicago Avenue Pumping Station Land water tunnel in operation
1906	Hering and Fuller Report to the International Waterways Commission
1907	Sanitary and Ship Canal extension completed; construction of North Shore Channel begun; first electric current delivered to Chicago from the Lockport Power House; Hering's Report to the Sanitary District; Polk Street Land water tunnel completed (now on standby)
1908	Federal government injunction suit against construction of Calumet-Sag Channel
1909	Sanitary District constructed Sewage Testing Station at the Thirty-ninth Street Pumping Station; Blue Island Avenue Land water tunnel opened (no longer in service)
1910	Sanitary District assumed operation of the Thirty-ninth

	Street and Lawrence Avenue Sewage pumping stations; water turned into the North Shore Channel; secretary of war issued permit to construct Calumet-Sag Channel
1911	Construction of Calumet-Sag Channel began; Edward F. Dunne intake crib completed; Southwest Lake and Land water tunnel opened; Roseland Pumping Station opened
1912	Sanitary District began enlargement of the north end of the Sanitary and Ship Canal; Stockyards Sewage Testing Plant opened; Sanitary District petitioned secretary of war for increase in diversion to 10,000 c.f.s.
1913	A second blanket injunction suit instituted by the federal government designed to answer all questions relating to the Sanitary District's diversion
1914	Morton Grove Sewage Treatment Works opened (no longer in service)
1918	Wilson Avenue intake crib opened (now on standby); Wilson Avenue water tunnel and Mayfair Pumping Station opened; Stockyards Testing Station dismantled
1919	Tannery Testing Station opened
1921	Evanston Sewage Pumping Station completed; Corn Products Testing Station put in operation; Calumet Sewage Pumping Station completed; Sanitary District assumed operations of the Ninty-fifth Street Sewage Pumping Station
1922	Wisconsin filed suit in the U.S. Supreme Court against the Sanitary District's diversion; Des Plaines Sewage Treatment Works opened; Calumet-Sag Channel opened; Calumet Sewage Treatment Works began operations (enlarged in 1935 and 1938–1939)
1924	Glenview Sewage Treatment Works began operations (no longer in service)
1925	Permit issued by secretary of war for 8,500 c.f.s. diversion; Minnesota, Ohio, and Pennsylvania joined Wisconsin suit; Northbrook Sewage Treatment Works began operations (no longer in service)
1926	Corn Products Testing Station closed down; Michigan and New York filed similar actions against the Sanitary District; Charles Evans Hughes, acting as special master, began taking depositions in Wisconsin suit
1927	Hughes reported to Supreme Court recommending dismissal of charges, but this was reversed by the full court; Western Avenue water tunnel and Western Avenue Pumping Station opened
1928	North Side Sewage Treatment Works placed in operation (enlarged in 1937); Thomas Jefferson Pumping Station opened
1929	North Branch Sewage Pumping Station opened (replaced Lawrence Avenue Sewage Pumping Station)
1930	U.S. Supreme Court decreed a phased reduction in the Sanitary District's diversion to 1,500 c.f.s.

1931	West Side Sewage Treatment Works placed in operation
1932	Harrison Street cross-connection water tunnel completed
1935	William E. Dever intake crib opened; Chicago Avenue Lake and Land water tunnel completed
1936	Anton W. Cermak Pumping Station opened
1939	Southwest Sewage Treatment Works placed in operation
1940	Des Plaines Street water tunnel opened
1943	Stewart Avenue water tunnel opened
1945	Connection to South District Filtration Plant water tunnel completed
1947	South District Water Filtration Plant opened
1958	Suit brought by six Great Lakes states in U.S. Supreme Court, reopening the 1930 decree
1959	Seventy-ninth Street water tunnel opened
1962	North Lake Shore water tunnel (connection between Central District Filtration Plant and Lake View Pumping Station) completed
1963	Columbus Avenue water tunnel and Southwest Pumping Station completed
1964	Central District Water Filtration Plant opened
1966	Report of special master, Albert B. Maris, in favor of Sanitary District—Chicago restricted to total diversion of 3,200 c.f.s. diversion daily for water supply and sewage disposal

BIBLIOGRAPHY

Books and Pamphlets

Andreas, A. T. *History of Chicago from the Earliest Period to the Present Time.* 3 vols. Chicago: A. T. Andreas, 1884–1886.

Armstrong, Ellis L., ed. *History of Public Works in the United States 1776–1976.* Chicago: American Public Works Association, 1976.

Atwood, Jane Kellog. *Development of the Commerce of the Great Lakes.* Master's thesis, University of Chicago, 1915.

Barrett, George F. *The Waterway from the Great Lakes to the Gulf of Mexico.* Sanitary District of Chicago, 1926.

Belcher, Wyatt Winston. *The Economic Rivalry between St. Louis and Chicago 1850–80.* New York: Columbia University Press, 1947.

Blanchard, Rufus. *Discovery and Conquests of the Northwest with the History of Chicago.* 2 vols. Chicago, 1898–1900.

Boggess, Arthur Clinton. *The Settlement of Illinois, 1778–1830.* Chicago Historical Society, 1908.

Bross, William. *History of Chicago.* Chicago: Jansen, McClurg and Co., 1876.

Brown, G. P. *Drainage Channel and Waterway.* Chicago: R. R. Donnelley & Sons, Co., 1884.

Chamberlain, Everett. *Chicago and its Suburbs.* Chicago: T. A. Hungerford and Co., 1873.

City of Chicago. *Annual Reports—Board of Public Works; Board of Sewerage Commissioners; Board of Water Commissioners; Department of Public Works.*

Civic Federation. *A Report on the Water Supply and Sewerage System of the City of Chicago with a Comparative Study of Certain Other American Cities.* Chicago, 1950–1952.

Colbert, Elias. *Chicago: Historical and Statistical Sketch of the Garden City.* Chicago: P. T. Sherlock, 1868.

Condit, Carl W. *Chicago, 1910–29, Building, Planning and Urban Technology.* Chicago: University of Chicago Press, 1973.

———. *Chicago, 1930–70, Building, Planning and Urban Technology.* Chicago: University of Chicago Press, 1974.

Cooley, Lyman E. *The Diversion of the Great Lakes by way of the Sanitary and Ship Canal of Chicago.* Sanitary District of Chicago, February 1913.

———. *The Illinois River.* Sanitary District of Chicago, 1914.

———. *Supplement to the Brief—The Calumet District.* Sanitary District of Chicago, June 1913.

Currey, J. Seymour. *The Story of Old Fort Dearborn.* Chicago: A. C. McClurg and Co., 1912.

———. *Chicago: Its History and Its Builders, A Century of Marvelous Growth.* 5 vols. Chicago: S. J. Clarke Publishing Co., 1912.

Dean, William H., Jr. "The Theory of the Geographic Location of Economic Activities." Ph.D. diss., Harvard University, 1938.

Dedmon, Emmett. *Fabulous Chicago.* New York: Random House, 1924.

Downing, Paul B. *The Economics of Urban Sewage Disposal.* New York: Praeger Publishers, 1969.

Eckstein, Otto. *Water Resource Development, the Economics of Project Evaluation.* Cambridge: Harvard University Press, 1968.

Egan, James A. *Pollution of the Illinois River as Affected by the Drainage of Chicago and Other Cities.* Springfield, Ill.: Phillips Bros., 1901.

Ericson, John. *The Water Supply System of Chicago.* Sanitary District of Chicago, April 1924.

Espenshade, Esther Elizabeth. "The Economic Development and History of Chicago, 1860–65." Master's thesis, University of Chicago, 1931.

Fergus, Robert, comp. *Chicago River and Harbor Convention.* Fergus Historical Series, no. 18. Chicago: Fergus Printing Company, 1882.

Ford, Thomas. *Ford's History of Illinois from its Commencement as a State in 1818 to 1847.* Edited by M. M. Quaife. 2 vols. Chicago: Lakeside Press, 1945, p. 46.

Fryxell, F. M. *The Physiography of the Region of Chicago.* Chicago: University of Chicago Press, 1927.

Gale, Edwin O. *Reminiscences of Early Chicago.* Chicago: F. H. Revell, 1902.

Gates, Paul W. *The Illinois Central Railroad and its Colonization Work.* Cambridge: Harvard University Press, 1934.

Goodrich, Carter; Rubin, Julius H.; Cramner, Jerome; and Segal, Harvey H. *Canals and American Economic Development.* New York: Columbia University Press, 1961.

Hering, Rudolph. *Notes on the Disposal of Sewage with Reference to Chicago.* Sanitary District of Chicago, 18 November 1907.

———, and Fuller, George W. *Report made to the Illinois Waterways Commission on the Disposal of the Sewage of Chicago and the Calumet Region.* New York, 18 December 1906.

Hirshleifer, J.; DeHaven, J. C.; and Milliman, J. *Water Supply: Economics, Technology and Policy.* Chicago: University of Chicago Press, 1960.

Hough, Jack L. *Geology of the Great Lakes.* Urbana: University of Illinois Press, 1958.

Hoyt, Homer. *One Hundred Years of Land Values in Chicago.* Chicago: University of Chicago Press, 1933.

[InterOcean]. *A History of the City of Chicago, its Men and Institutions.* Chicago: InterOcean, 1905.

———. *Centennial History of the City of Chicago, its Men and Institutions.* Chicago: InterOcean, 1905.

Kirby, Richard S., and Laurson, Philip G. *The Early Years of Modern Civil Engineering.* New Haven: Yale University Press, 1932.

Kirkland, Joseph. *Story of Chicago.* Chicago: Dibble Publishing Co., 1892.

Kneese, A. V., and Bower, B. T. *Managing Water Quality: Economics, Technology, Institution.* Baltimore: Johns Hopkins University Press, 1968.

Knight, Robert, and Zeuch, Lucius H. *The Location of the Chicago Portage Route of the Seventeenth Century.* Chicago Historical Society, 1928.

Lewis, Lloyd, and Smith, Henry Justin. *Chicago: The History of its Reputation.* New York: Harcourt, Brace and Co., 1929.

Lipsey, R. G., and Steiner, P. O. *Economics.* 3d ed. New York: Harper and Row, 1972.

MacGill, Caroline. *History of Transportation in the United States Before 1860.* Washington, D.C.: Carnegie Institution of Washington, 1917.

McKean, Roland. *Efficiency in Government with Emphasis on Water Resources Development.* New York: John Wiley and Sons, 1958.

Maass, Arthur; Hufschmidt, Maynard M.; Dorfman, Robert; Thomas, Harold A., Jr.; Marglin, Stephen A.; and Fair, Gordon Maskew. *Design of Water Resource Systems.* Cambridge: Harvard University Press, 1962.

Mason, Edward G., ed. *Early Chicago and Illinois.* Chicago: Fergus Printing Co., 1890.

Mason, William P. *Water Supply: Considered Principally from a Sanitary Standpoint.* 3d ed. New York: John Wiley and Sons, 1909.

Mayer, Harold M., and Wade, Richard C. *Chicago: Growth of a Metropolis.* Chicago: University of Chicago Press, 1969.

Moses, John. *Illinois Historical and Statistical comprising the Essential Facts of its Planting and Growth as a Province, County, Territory, and State.* 2 vols. Chicago: Fergus Printing Co., 1895.

————, and Kirkland, Joseph. *History of Chicago.* 2 vols. Chicago and New York: Munsell and Co., 1895.

Pearse, Langdon. *The Sanitary Situation of Chicago, Water Supply and Sewage Disposal.* Sanitary District of Chicago, 29 January 1914.

Pierce, Bessie Louise. *A History of Chicago.* 3 vols. New York: Alfred A. Knopf, 1937, 1940, and 1957.

Poor, Henry V. *History of Railroads and Canals of the United States.* New York: Henry Schultz and Co., 1860.

Putnam, James William. *The Illinois and Michigan Canal: A Study in Economic History.* Chicago: University of Chicago Press, 1918.

Quaife, Milo M. *Chicago and the Old Northwest.* Chicago: University of Chicago Press, 1913.

————. *Chicago's Highways—Old and New.* Chicago: D. F. Keller and Co., 1923.

Rafter, George W., and Baker, M. N. *Sewage Disposal in the United States.* New York and London: D. Von Nostrand Co., 1894.

Randolph, R. Isham. *The Sanitary District of Chicago, and the Chicago Drainage Canal.* Sanitary District of Chicago, 22 July 1909.

Riley, Elmer A. "The Development of Chicago and Vicinity as a Manufacturing Centre Prior to 1860." Ph.D. diss., University of Chicago, 1911.

Rea, James David. "Great Lakes Commodity Trade: 1850 to 1900." Ph.D. diss., Purdue University, 1967.

Ringwalt, J. L. *Development of Transportation Systems in the United States.* Printed by author, Railway World Office, Philadelphia, 1888.

Sanitary District of Chicago. *Proceedings of the Board of Trustees.*

————. *Sewage Disposal of the Calumet District* (Report of the Commission on Calumet Sewerage), 8 February 1909.

————. *Calumet-Sag Channel—A Vital Necessity,* 25 May 1910.

————. *The Water Power Development of the Sanitary District of Chicago,* 12 November 1914.

————. *Summary Report on Industrial Wastes from the Stockyards and Packingtown in Chicago,* vol. 2, 1921.

————. *Summary of Packingtown Treatment Situation.* Prepared, 1919, Issued, November 1923.

————. *Copy of the International Waterways Commission Report,* March 1924.

————. *Report of the Engineering Board of Review of the Sanitary District of Chicago on the Lake Lowering Controversy and a Program of Remedial Measures,* part 3, Sewage Disposal, 21 February 1925.

————. *The Quality Problem in Relation to Chicago's Water Supply,* May 1925.

————. *Hydrology of The Great Lakes,* 1927.

————. *Engineering Works,* August 1928.

————. *Formal Opening Program: The North Side Sewage Treatment Project,* 3 October 1928.

————. *Report of Commission Appointed by Federal Emergency Administration of Public Works Reviewing Plans of West-Southwest Sewage Treat-

ment Project of Sanitary District of Chicago, May 1934.

Solomon, Ezra, and Bibija, Zarko G. *Metropolitan Chicago: An Economic Analysis.* Glencoe: Free Press of Glencoe, Illinois, 1959.

Soper, George A.; Watson, John D.; and Martin, Arthur J. *A Report to the Chicago Real Estate Board on the Disposal of the Sewage and Protection of the Water Supply of Chicago, Illinois,* 1915.

Stead, William T. *If Christ Came to Chicago.* Chicago: Laird and Lee, 1894.

Steck, France Borgia. *The Jolliet-Marquette Expedition, 1673.* Washington, D.C.: Catholic University of America, 1927.

Tarr, Joel A. *A Study in Boss Politics: William Lorimer of Chicago.* Urbana: University of Illinois Press, 1971.

Taylor, Charles H., ed. *History of the Board of Trade of the City of Chicago.* 3 vols. Chicago, 1917.

Thompson, Wilbur R. *A Preface to Urban Economics.* Baltimore: Johns Hopkins University Press, 1965.

Vidal de la Blanche, Paul Marie Joseph. *Principles of Human Geography.* Edited by Emmanuel de Martonne. Translated by Millicent Todd Bingham. New York: Henry Holt and Co., 1926.

Walsh, W. H. *An Introduction to Philosophy of History.* London: Hutchinson's University Library, 1951.

Wendt, Lloyd, and Kogan, Herman. *Chicago: A Pictorial History.* New York: Bonanza Books, 1958.

_____. *Give the Lady What She Wants: The Story of Marshall Field and Company.* Chicago: Rand McNally, 1952.

Wentworth, John. *Early Chicago: Fort Dearborn,* Fergus Historical Series, no. 16. Chicago: Fergus Printing Co., 1881.

White, Max R. *Water Supply Organization in the Chicago Region.* Chicago: University of Chicago Press, 1934.

Williams, C. Arch. *The Sanitary District of Chicago.* Sanitary District of Chicago, 1919.

Wing, J. M. *The Tunnels and Water System of Chicago.* Chicago: J. M. Wing and Co., 1874.

Wisner, George M., *Sewage Disposal of the Calumet District.* Sanitary District of Chicago, 9 June 1909.

_____. *Report on Sewage Disposal.* Sanitary District of Chicago, 12 October 1911.

_____. *Report on the Advisability of Building Calumet-Sag Channel.* Sanitary District of Chicago, 1915.

Writer's Program. *Up from the Mud: An Account of how Chicago's Streets and Buildings were Raised.* Compiled by Workers of the Writer's Program, W.P.A. in Illinois for Board of Education, 1941.

Articles

Barce, Elmore. "The Old Chicago Trail, and the Old Chicago Road." *Indiana Magazine of History,* March 1919.

Benton, E. J. "The Wabash Trade Route in the Development of the Old Northwest." *Johns Hopkins Studies in History and Political Science,* 1903.

Cain, Louis P. "Ellis Sylvester Chesbrough and Chicago's First Sanitation System." *Technology and Culture,* July 1972, pp. 353–72.

_____. "Unfouling the Public's Nest: Chicago's Sanitary Diversion of Lake Michigan Water." *Technology and Culture,* October 1974, pp. 594–613.

_____. "The Economic History of Urban Location and Sanitation." *Research in Economic History,* vol. 2 (1977), pp. 337–89.

_____. "Annexation, A Panacea for the Urban Crisis? The Case of Chicago."

Department of Economics, University of British Columbia. Discussion paper no. 76–09.

———. "The Search for an Optimal Environmental Jurisdiction: Sanitation Districts in Illinois, 1889." Department of Economics, University of British Columbia. Discussion paper no. 76–08.

Cole, Ernest E. "From Swamp to City." *Greater Chicago,* Official Bulletin of the Chicago Booster's Publicity Club, October 1920.

Cooley, Charles H. "The Theory of Transportation." *Publications of the American Economic Association* 9, no. 3, May 1894.

DeBerard, W. W. "Expansion of the Chicago, Ill., Water Supply." Paper 2612, *Centennial Transactions,* vol. CT, 1903.

Downing, Paul B. "Extension of Sewer Service at the Urban-Rural Fringe." *Land Economics,* February 1969.

Fuller, George W. "The Sewage Disposal Problem of Chicago." Western Society of Engineers, paper read at the Mid-winter Convocation at Chicago, 19 February 1925.

Healy, Kent T. "Transportation as a Factor in Economic Growth." *Journal of Economic History* 7, December 1947.

Hill, C. D. "The Sewerage System of Chicago." *Journal of the Western Society of Engineers,* September 1911.

Hughes, Jonathan R. T. "Fact and Theory in Economic History." *Explorations in Entrepreneurial History* 3, no. 2, 1966.

Jones, Alexander J. "The Chicago Drainage Canal and Its Forebear, The Illinois and Michigan Canal." Illinois State Historical Society, *Transactions,* 1906.

Kelly, Edward J. "The Sanitary District of Chicago, Its Past, Present, and Future." Progress on Sewage Treatment Program, a symposium, Technical Papers, *Journal of the Western Society of Engineers* 31, no. 7, July 1926.

Lee, Judson Fiske. "Transportation—A Factor in the Development of Northern Illinois Previous to 1860." Illinois State Historical Society, *Journal* 10, no. 1, April 1917.

Leverett, Frank. "The Water Resources of Illinois." *Seventeenth Annual Report,* U.S. Geological Survey, 1896.

McMath, Robert E. "The Waterway between Lake Michigan and the Mississippi River, by Way of the Illinois River." Paper read, 30 May 1888.

Mathews, Louis Kimball. "The Erie Canal and the Settlement of the West." Buffalo Historical Society, *Publications* 14 (1910).

O'Connell, James C. "Chicago's Quest for Pure Water." Public Works Historical Society. Essay no. 1. June 1976.

Paxon, Fred Logan. "The Gateways of the Old Northwest." Michigan Historical Society, *Collections* 38 (1912).

Pearse, Langdon. "Chicago's Quest for Potable Water." *Water and Sewage Works,* May 1955.

Randolph, R. Isham. "The History of Sanitation in Chicago." *Journal of the Western Society of Engineers* 44, no. 5, October 1939.

Ransom, Roger L. "Canals and Development: A Discussion of the Issues." *American Economic Review* 54, no. 3, May 1964.

Sanitary District of Chicago. "Memorandum for use of Sanitary District Representatives at the Pageant of Progress," August 1923.

———. "Memorandum concerning the Drainage and Sewerage Conditions in Chicago," December 1923.

Thompson, William H. "Chicago—World's City Health Standard." *Greater Chicago,* Official Bulletin of the Chicago Booster's Publicity Club 1, no. 3, October 1920.

Usher, Abbott Payson. "A Dynamic Analysis of the Location of Economic Activity." Unpublished paper.

Windes, Frank A. "A Paper on North Shore Drainage." 22 January 1912.

Wood, Charles P. "Factors Controlling the Location of Various Types of Industry." American Society of Chemical Engineers, *Transactions,* 112 (1947).

INDEX